'This groundbreaking book challenges the prevailing disciplinary way of thinking, adopting a transversal perspective by integrating diverse voices of experts in gestalt therapy, relational psychoanalysis, and neo-Bionian psychoanalysis. The dialogue between them focuses on the complex and frequently misunderstood concept of field, widening the lens through which we understand it by presenting and debating clinical cases, theoretical issues, and historical aspects. Simultaneously theoretical and conversational, *Field Perspectives in Clinical Practice* is a towering accomplishment and essential reading for clinicians and researchers in psychotherapy and psychoanalysis.'

Mônica Botelho Alvim, *Ph.D. professor, Federal University of Rio de Janeiro, Brazil; past president of the Brazilian Association of Gestalt Therapy*

'The contributing authors, each with their distinct orientations, demonstrate a remarkable willingness to transcend individual perspectives and engage in a collective chorus that fosters unprecedented development. This collaboration has yielded insights previously unimaginable. Each author's contributions are so substantial that they merit individual volumes or entries in an encyclopedia dedicated to interpretative methods and the understanding of characters that emerge and evolve during sessions. A must-read for anyone interested in the cutting edge of psychoanalytic thought and practice, this volume is a testament to the power of interdisciplinary collaboration and innovative thinking.'

Antonino Ferro, *M.D., past president of the Italian Psychoanalytic Society (SPI), SPI training & supervising analyst, APsaA and IPA member, recipient of the Sigourney Award, 2007*

'This book needs to be read by everyone concerned with the evolution of contemporary psychology and psychotherapy. Like physics, which went from exploring individual bodies to exploring energy fields, cutting-edge psychotherapy concentrates less on individual internal wiring and plumbing and more on the fields that we create in our relationships. Gianni Francesetti and his colleagues have led the way, expanding field theory from Gestalt therapy in important new directions. This book is unique: It brings Gestalt therapy into dialogue with two modern psychoanalytic movements now turning toward field theory.'

Michael Vincent Miller, *Ph.D. former president of the New York Institute of Gestalt Therapy, author of* Intimate Terrorism

Field Perspectives in Clinical Practice

This book is the outcome of fruitful engagement between relational psychoanalysis, neo-Bionian psychoanalysis, and Gestalt therapy on a contemporary growing edge of clinical practice: field theory.

What is happening in contemporary clinical practice that seems to be pushing theories towards a field perspective? Clinical issues are complex phenomena—they cannot be separated from social and cultural changes. Suffering, clients, and therapists change over time, and with them so do the needs and theoretical approaches of clinical professionals, so as to be able to update and adjust care practices.

This book is an independent, yet common study, which through the field concept explores what complexity theories and dynamic systems theories have described as "emerging phenomena," or what phenomenological philosophy categorized as phenomenal field, pathic aesthetics, and atmospherology, or, more generally, our understanding of the relationship between clinical practice and critical thinking and of the centrality of the individual, as developed by postmodern thinkers.

With multiple professional perspectives and essential clinical material, this is key reading for psychoanalysts and psychotherapists.

Gianni Francesetti, M.D., is a psychiatrist, Gestalt psychotherapist, Adjunct Professor at the Department of Psychology, University of Turin (Italy), international trainer and supervisor, co-director of IPSIG and of the Turin School of Psychopathology, and co-founder of IG-FEST.

Michela Gecele, M.D., is a psychiatrist and Gestalt psychotherapist. She formerly coordinated, in Turin, a psychological and psychiatric service for immigrants. She is international trainer and supervisor, co-director of IPSIG and of the Turin School of Psychopathology, and co-founder of IG-FEST.

Paolo Migone, M.D., is editor of the Italian journal *Psicoterapia e Scienze Umane* (Psychotherapy and the Human Sciences), co-chair of the Rapaport-Klein Study Group, and member of the Editorial Board of the *Journal of the American Psychoanalytic Association* and of *Psychological Issues*. He founded the Italian chapters of the Society for Psychotherapy Research (SPR) and the Society for the Exploration of Psychotherapy Integration (SEPI).

PSYCHOANALYSIS IN A NEW KEY

When music is played in a new key, the melody does not change, but the notes that make up the composition do: change in the context of continuity, continuity that perseveres through change. Psychoanalysis in a New Key publishes books that share the aims psychoanalysts have always had, but that approach them differently. The books in the series are not expected to advance any particular theoretical agenda, although to this date most have been written by analysts from the Interpersonal and Relational orientations.

The most important contribution of a psychoanalytic book is the communication of something that nudges the reader's grasp of clinical theory and practice in an unexpected direction. Psychoanalysis in a New Key creates a deliberate focus on innovative and unsettling clinical thinking. Because that kind of thinking is encouraged by exploration of the sometimes surprising contributions to psychoanalysis of ideas and findings from other fields, Psychoanalysis in a New Key particularly encourages interdisciplinary studies. Books in the series have married psychoanalysis with dissociation, trauma theory, sociology, and criminology. The series is open to the consideration of studies examining the relationship between psychoanalysis and any other field—for instance, biology, literary and art criticism, philosophy, systems theory, anthropology, and political theory.

But innovation also takes place within the boundaries of psychoanalysis, and Psychoanalysis in a New Key therefore also presents work that reformulates thought and practice without leaving the precincts of the field. Books in the series focus, for example, on the significance of personal values in psychoanalytic practice, on the complex interrelationship between the analyst's clinical work and personal life, on the consequences for the clinical situation when patient and analyst are from different cultures, and on the need for psychoanalysts to accept the degree to which they knowingly satisfy their own wishes during treatment hours, often to the patient's detriment.

A full list of all titles in this series is available at:
https://www.routledge.com/Psychoanalysis-in-a-New-Key-Book-Series/book-series/LEAPNKBS

Field Perspectives in Clinical Practice

A Dialogue between Relational Psychoanalysis, Post-Bionian Psychoanalysis, and Gestalt Therapy

Edited by Gianni Francesetti, Michela Gecele, and Paolo Migone

Routledge
Taylor & Francis Group
LONDON AND NEW YORK

Designed cover image: © Getty Images

First published 2025
by Routledge
4 Park Square, Milton Park, Abingdon, Oxon OX14 4RN

and by Routledge
605 Third Avenue, New York, NY 10158

Routledge is an imprint of the Taylor & Francis Group, an informa business

British Library Cataloguing-in-Publication Data
A catalogue record for this book is available from the British Library

ISBN: 978-1-032-98145-1 (hbk)
ISBN: 978-1-032-97597-9 (pbk)
ISBN: 978-1-003-59730-8 (ebk)

DOI: 10.4324/9781003597308

Typeset in Times New Roman
by SPi Technologies India Pvt Ltd (Straive)

Contents

Contributors

Annibale Bertola, born in Civitavecchia (Italy) on December 14, 1946, graduated in Philosophy (1971) and Psychology (1978). He worked as a voluntary worker in Brazil from 1974 to 1977 in the educational field as a school counselor and cultural animator. In Italy he worked on applied psychology in hospital settings and on chronic diseases. He is adjunct professor at the University of Tor Vergata (Rome) and guest professor at the Department of Education Sciences "Auxilium," and past president of the Federation of Italian Associations of Psychotherapy (FIAP)

Dan Bloom, J.D., L.C.S.W. (www.danbloomnyc.com) is a psychotherapist, supervisor, clinical trainer, and writer in New York City. He studied with Laura Perls, Isadore From, and Richard Kitzler. He teaches as guest and adjunct faculty at Gestalt therapy institutes worldwide. He leads webinars in gestalt therapy and phenomenology. He is president and fellow of the New York Institute for Gestalt Therapy (NYIGT) and past president of the International Association for the Advancement of Gestalt Therapy (IAAGT). He is a member of the European Association for Gestalt Therapy (EAGT) and an accredited supervisor and co-founder of the International Study Group on Field-Emergent Self and Therapy (www.Ig-fest.com). He is an associate editor of the *Gestalt Review*, member of the scientific board of *Quaderni di Gestalt* and of the Gestalt Therapy Book Series (Routledge). Dan is widely published.

Bernd Bocian, Ph.D., is a Gestalt therapist and psychotherapist (PtG), who also trained in psychoanalytic therapy and Reichian body work. Formerly on the editorial board of the German journal *Gestalttherapie*

(DVG), he is currently a member of the scientific boards of *Quaderni di Gestalt* and the Gestalt Therapy Book Series (Routledge). He is author of various publications on the historical and contemporary relationship between Gestalt therapy and psychoanalysis. Among them, *Fritz Perls in Berlin 1893–1933: Expressionism-Psychoanalysis-Judaism* (2010) and *Gestalt Therapy and Psychoanalysis* (2000), edited with Frank Staemmler.

Giuseppe Civitarese, M.D., Ph.D., is a psychiatrist, training and supervising analyst of the Italian Psychoanalytic Society (SPI), member of the American Psychoanalytic Association (APsaA) and of the International Psychoanalytic Association (IPA). He is a past editor-in-chief of the *Rivista di Psicoanalisi*. He lives and practices privately in Pavia, Italy. In 2022, he was a recipient of the Sigourney Award.

Susanna Federici, Ph.D., is past president of the International Association for Relational Psychoanalysis and Psychotherapy (IARPP), founding member, faculty, and supervising analyst of the Institute for Self Psychology and Relational Psychoanalysis (ISIPSÉ), Italy, and past member of the International Board of the International Association Psychoanalytic Self Psychology (IAPSP). She has presented her work at IARPP conferences, IAPSP conferences, and at many international institutes. She was co-chair of the Fourth European Conference on Self Psychology, held in Rome in 2006, and was guest speaker at the 6th Reunion Anual de IARPP Espana (Valencia 2015). She was co-chair of the IARPP 13th Annual Conference "The Arts of Time: Relational Psychoanalysis and Forms of Vitality in Clinical Process" held in Rome, June 9–12, 2016. She has been published in *Psychoanalytic Dialogues, Psychoanalytic Inquiry*, and other international journals.

Gianni Francesetti, M.D., is a psychiatrist, Gestalt therapist, and Adjunct Professor at the Department of Psychology, University of Turin (Italy). He is co-director of the International Institute for Gestalt Therapy and Psychopathology (IPsiG) in Turin, president of Poiesis (Gestalt Therapy Clinical Centre), past president of the FIAP (Italian Federation of Psychotherapy Associations) and of the EAGT (European Association for Gestalt Therapy), a co-founder of the International Gestalt Therapy Study Group on Field Perspective and Emergent Self, and a member of the NYIGT.

Michela Gecele, psychiatrist and Gestalt therapist, is an international trainer and supervisor who has written widely on psychotherapy, psychopathology, and intercultural issues from a phenomenological and Gestalt therapy perspective. With lengthy experience in community and immigrant mental health services, she is co-director of the International Institute for Gestalt Therapy and Psychopathology (IPsiG) in Turin. Michela is also a published fiction writer.

Paolo Migone, M.D., is editor of the Italian journal *Psicoterapia e Scienze Umane* (Psychotherapy and the Human Sciences), co-chair of the Rapaport-Klein Study Group, and member of the Editorial Board of the *Journal of the American Psychoanalytic Association* and of *Psychological Issues*. He founded the Italian chapters of the Society for Psychotherapy Research (SPR) and the Society for the Exploration of Psychotherapy Integration (SEPI).

Gianni Nebbiosi, Ph.D., is president, founding member, faculty, and supervising analyst of the Institute for Self Psychology and Relational Psychoanalysis (ISIPSÉ), Italy; founding and board member of the International Association for Relational Psychoanalysis and Psychotherapy (IARPP); member of the International Council of the International Association for Psychoanalytic Self Psychology (IAPSP); member of the Editorial Board of the journal *Psychoanalytic Dialogues*; member of the editorial board of *Psychoanalytic Inquiry*; and corresponding editor of the journal *Contemporary Psychoanalysis*. He was co-chair of the IARPP 13th Annual Conference "The Arts of Time: Relational Psychoanalysis and Forms of Vitality in Clinical Process" held in Rome, June 9–12, 2016. He has been published in *Psychoanalytic Dialogues, Psychoanalytic Inquiry*, and other international journals.

Donna Orange, Ph.D., Psy.D. (1944–2024), received an education in the areas of philosophy, clinical psychology, and psychoanalysis. She taught at New York University Postdoc; Institute for the Psychoanalytic Study of Subjectivity (IPSS), New York; and in private study groups. She also provided clinical consultation/supervision in these institutes and beyond. Recent books are *Thinking for Clinicians: Philosophical Resources for Contemporary Psychoanalysis and the Humanistic Psychotherapies* (2010), *The Suffering Stranger: Hermeneutics for Everyday Clinical Practice* (2011), *Nourishing the*

Inner Life of Clinicians and Humanitarians: The Ethical Turn in Psychoanalysis, and Climate Crisis, Psychoanalysis, and Radical Ethics (2016), and *Psychoanalysis, History, and Radical Ethics: Learning to Hear* (2020). In 2021, she was Visiting Professor of Phenomenology, Duquesne University (Pittsburgh, U.S.A.).

Fabio Rivara is a psychologist and psychotherapist with a psychoanalytic orientation. He is psychologist in charge of a public Mental Health Center in Turin, Italy, and adjunct lecturer at the Psychology of Health Postgraduate School (SSPS) at the University of Turin. His previous teaching positions include the School for Professional Nurses and the Specialization Course in Medical Oncology of the Molinette Hospital in Turin. He has conducted courses in Rorschach Psychodiagnostics according to the Exner method. He has thirty years of experience as a psycho-diagnostic assistant in forensic settings.

Jean-Marie Robine, Psy.D., has been practicing psychology and psycho-therapy since 1967 and, more specifically, Gestalt therapy since the mid-1970s. He founded the Institut Français de Gestalt-thérapie in 1980. Though retired, he continues to teach this approach in many countries. He has written or edited a dozen Gestalt therapy books, in particular *On the Occasion of an Other* (The Gestalt Journal Press), *Social Change Begins with Two* (Istituto di Gestalt Press), and *Self, a Polyphony of Contemporary Gestalt Therapists* (L'exprimerie). He has also created a collection of books in France dedicated to Gestalt therapy (www.exprimerie.fr) and has edited and published about sixty books, originals or translations. He lives in the countryside near Bordeaux.

Jan Roubal, M.D., Ph.D., is associate professor at Masaryk University in Brno, Czech Republic, where he also works at the Center for Psychotherapy Research. He is a psychotherapist and psychiatrist. He founded the Training School in Psychotherapy Integration and the training institute Gestalt Studia in the Czech Republic. He also works as a psychotherapy trainer and supervisor internationally. He has co-edited the books *Current Psychotherapy, Gestalt Therapy in Clinical Practice. From Psychopathology to the Aesthetics of Contact* (2014) and *Towards a Research Tradition in Gestalt Therapy* (2016). He most recently authored *Don't Get in the Way of Hope. A Therapist's Guide through the Depressive Field.*

Donnel B. Stern, Ph.D., is Training and Supervising Analyst at the William Alanson White Institute in New York City, and Adjunct Clinical Professor of Psychology, New York University Postdoctoral Program in Psychotherapy and Psychoanalysis, New York City. His most recent book is the forthcoming *On Coming into Possession of Oneself: Transformations of the Interpersonal Field*.

Beatrix Wimmer, psychologist and Gestalt therapist, is supervisor in Vienna, Austria, since 1997. She is a past president of the European Association for Gestalt Therapy (EAGT) and president of the Austrian Association for Gestalt Therapy (OEVG). She has been recently setting up the working group on Climate Change & Biodiversity in the EAGT. She also teaches Gestalt therapy in Nepal and Switzerland.

Paola Zarini is a psychologist, Gestalt therapist, international trainer and supervisor. She is a member of the International Institute for Gestalt Therapy and Psychopathology (IPsiG) in Turin. Within her clinical practice, she mainly works with adults, teenagers, and transgender people. She writes and publishes on the topic of psychopathology and psychotherapy.

Introduction

Gianni Francesetti, Michela Gecele,
and Paolo Migone

The book you are about to read is the outcome of fruitful engagement between relational psychoanalysis, neo-Bionian psychoanalysis, and Gestalt therapy. Engagement that unfolded *live* in an online conference organized on November 4–5, 2022, by the *International Institute of Psychopathology and Gestalt Psychotherapy* and the *Turin School of Psychopathology* on field perspective in the clinical practice of psychotherapy and psychoanalysis. Thus, two fundamental elements characterize this book: the topic it addresses and the dialogical process underpinning it.

The topic

The theoretical construct of *field* was first introduced into psychology by Kurt Lewin, before emigrating to the United States in 1933. His development of the concept built on his observations on the front line during the First World War and the early research of Gestalt psychologists in Berlin. The term itself was borrowed from physics, which by the mid-19th century had formalized the concept of "electromagnetic field" and then "gravitational field" in the early 20th century. From the end of the First World War (1918) until Hitler's rise to power (1933), German culture flowered greatly, driven by an extraordinary vitality in the artistic, scientific, and political fields. It was the age of the expressionist artistic avant-gardes, the Bauhaus, the revolutions of Gestalt psychology and quantum mechanics, new studies in biology by Jakob von Uexküll and in the neurosciences by Kurt Goldstein, and the emergence of the Frankfurt School of Critical Theory in sociology. And it was also, of course, a dynamic time for psychoanalysis, with developments driven from the inside by new, heretical insights, and from the outside

DOI: 10.4324/9781003597308-1

by a political and social environment progressively moving towards the rise of Hitler, which would lead to a diaspora of psychoanalysts fleeing Germany to escape Nazi persecution.

In such a context, the idea that human beings could not be understood by studying the individual separately from the environment was a cultural foundation widespread across many fields of study. They all agreed on the need to consider how humans emerge from something much broader, from a natural, social, historical, and cultural field. The Gestalt principle that the whole cannot be reduced to the sum of its parts was another consolidated concept, bringing profound consequences for many disciplines, including psychology and psychoanalysis. The complex historical variables impacting psychoanalysis, covered in part by some of the chapters of this book, led the theoretical construct of field to be developed differently in the different currents.

Gestalt therapy was established by a group of founders that included two dissident psychoanalysts, Laura and Friedrich Perls, as well as educators, physicians, philosophers, scholars, and social critics, in particular, Paul Goodman. The concept of the organism/environment field was central to Gestalt therapy right from the start, both in Frederick Perls's first book, from 1942, *Ego, Hunger and Aggression. A Revision of Freud's Theory and Method*, and in the foundational work marking the beginning of Gestalt therapy proper in 1951: Frederick S. Perls, Ralph Hefferline and Paul Goodman's *Gestalt Therapy. Excitement and Growth in the Human Personality*. Starting from the concept of self as an emerging phenomenon, nothing in Gestalt therapy theory excludes a field perspective, although in practice the concept is used in different ways by different authors and currents.

The field concept, as developed by Lewin, was also of inspiration for Wilfred Bion, as he himself states in a 1943 letter to John Rickman and as emerges from an article on basic assumptions in groups published by the two in *Lancet* that same year. Later, in the early 1960s, the concept of analytic field was developed by the two Franco-Argentine psychoanalysts Madeleine and Willy Baranger. Bion and the Barangers' work was then developed further by the Italian psychoanalytical school of Pavia, in particular by Antonino Ferro, and by North American thinkers such as Thomas Odgen into a systematic theory of the analytic field, creating one of the major schools today in contemporary psychoanalysis.

Another current within psychoanalysis in which we find a field perspective is relational psychoanalysis. Here, the concept of field can be traced back to Harry Stack Sullivan in the 1920s–1940s. Sullivan's work was influenced by Kurt Lewin and by the American Pragmatist philosophy that held sway at the Chicago School of Sociology, where Paul Goodman, one of the founders of Gestalt therapy, worked. Interpersonal, and then relational and intersubjective psychoanalysis made use of a field perspective mostly in an implicit way, without developing a systematic theory of the concept, but in doing so it supported a development of psychoanalysis which sees the client as not being removable from his/her relational matrix, and the psychoanalyst progressively more involved in the analytic relationship.

The dialogical process

This brief historical introduction can help make sense of the decision to organize a conference—and then this book—on the topic, involving leading contemporary thinkers in relational psychoanalysis, neo-Bionian psychoanalysis, and Gestalt therapy. The field concept found in all three of the models shares, in a certain way, the same roots, which lie in psychoanalysis and Gestalt psychology, in particular as developed by Kurt Lewin. Each of the models has developed field theory in its own different way, drawing on other sources over the years and producing theoretical constructs and clinical practices that are different—but all concerned with that something extra that makes humans irreducible to the individual, as well as with how the perspective can be applied in therapy and how it can support therapeutic techniques and presence that more effectively and appropriately address contemporary clinical issues.

It is an independent, yet common study, which through the field concept explores what complexity theories and dynamic systems theories in recent years have described as "emerging phenomena," or what phenomenological philosophy has had to say over the years in terms of the phenomenal field, pathic aesthetics, and atmospherology, or, more generally, our understanding of the relationship between clinical practice and critical thinking and of the centrality of the individual, as developed by postmodern thinkers.

Here, our topic and the dialogical process intersect with contemporary trends. It is interesting to note how the literature produced by the three models increasingly makes use of a field perspective. It seems there is a progressively growing interest in the theory and its approach to clinical work, which in turn is interesting because, as readers will grasp from the contributions to this book, the field perspective is innovative not only for clinical practice, but for modern Western culture itself.

This was one of the elements that motivated us to organize a conference to explore the topic in depth. What is happening in contemporary clinical practice that seems to be pushing theories towards a field perspective? Clinical issues are complex phenomena—phenomena that cannot be separated from social and cultural changes, for which suffering, clients, and therapists also change over time. And with them, obviously, so do the needs and theoretical approaches of clinical workers, so as to be able to adjust care practices.

All this aroused our curiosity and opened up many questions. This book gathers them together and explores them through the original sensibilities and insights of the various authors. We imagine them like a passage, or a crossroads in a greater story, of which this book, each of us, and you yourselves are emerging phenomena.

The book keeps to the organizational structure of the conference. The chapters from each author representing a model are followed by the critical remarks of authors from a different approach. Then a clinical case study is presented and discussed from the point of view of the three models, followed by commentary from more of a "meta" position by a psychoanalytic author and by a Gestalt therapy author. Finally, we have included a historical overview that was not presented at the conference, but which we felt would be useful to incorporate into this book. The author, in tracing out a brief historical digression on the ties between Gestalt therapy and psychoanalysis, offers readers an insight into the historical relationship between the two clinical trends, thus providing a background to the dialogue and the book itself.

To conclude, we hope this book will be of inspiration for further developments in a therapeutic perspective that is progressively moving towards a field-based approach in clinical practice.

Chapter 1

Working in the interpersonal field

Two clinical narratives[*]

Donnel B. Stern

1.1 "In the cellar"

I remember feeling, even as a graduate student seeing my first patients in the early 1970s, that the clinical process took place *between* the patient and me, and that my experience and that of the patient were not only our own, but also parts of a larger whole. In my first book (Stern, 1997), *Unformulated Experience: From Dissociation to Imagination in Psychoanalysis*, I recently reread a description of the interpersonal field. It brought back to me those first experiences of that sense of the clinical situation and reminded me of how long the interpersonal field has been central in my mind—longer, even, than I have known it by its name. Here is the passage:

> A fully interpersonal conception of treatment is a field theory. The psychoanalytic relationship, like any relationship, takes place in a field that is defined and ceaselessly redefined by its participants. It is not only the intrapsychic dynamics patient and analyst bring to their relationship that determine their experience with one another. The field is a unique creation, not a simple additive combination of individual dynamics; it is ultimately the field that determines which experiences the people who are in the process of co-creating that field can have in one another's presence. It is the field that determines what will be dissociated and what will be articulated, when

[*] I am grateful to Taylor and Francis for permission to publish parts of two articles in this presentation: Part I is a version of material that first appeared in Chapter 1 of *Relational Freedom: Emergent Properties of the Interpersonal Field*, published by Routledge in 2015. An earlier version of Part II appeared in Stern, D.B. (2023). Distance and relation: Emerging from embeddedness in the other. *Journal of the American Psychoanalytic Association, 71*(4), 641–668.

DOI: 10.4324/9781003597308-2

imagination will be possible and when the participants will be locked into stereotypic descriptions of their mutual experience. Each time one participant changes the nature of his or her involvement in the field, the possibilities for the other person's experience change as well. (...) The field is the only relevant context.

(Stern, 1997, p. 110)

One characteristic of the field has always held a particular fascination for me: its emergent properties. The field comes into being between two or more people in a way that cannot be predicted or controlled. It can only be accepted or rejected. To the extent that we can accept it, we sense and understand (and these are not necessarily the same thing at all) something of how this emergent quality informs and shapes the clinical process. The way I generally find emergence to be most compelling in my daily clinical work is not as a reference to attributes of things that feel as if they exist apart from me, but as a way of representing certain parts of my first-person experience, and the patient's, in the consulting room.

"Emergence" in this frame of reference describes a certain affective state of things. It is the felt sense of moments that portend the unexpected, or are themselves unexpected. In moments of emergence I am connected to unseen things that feel, despite their invisibility, greatly important to matters at hand. There is a sense of nascence, of budding, of coming-to-be. When Foehl (2014) describes the felt, or phenomenological, aspect of psychic depth, I hear in what he says a description of what emergence means, as well:

> [It is] a sense of the boundless reaches of what we do not yet know...played out in the immediacy of embodied sensual living, where what we see, hear, feel, and touch swim seamlessly into what we think, imagine, dream, and back again.

(Foehl, 2014, p. 295)

The unseen things I feel connected to in my office, whatever else they may be, are always part of the context of my relationship with the particular person who is with me. That much I can tell, even though I cannot necessarily make out what those things are. It is a feeling of opening-into, of possibility, and so it is generally welcome even when whatever will come next does not itself necessarily feel pleasant or fulfilling.

1.1.1 In the cellar: A clinical illustration

I turn now to a clinical illustration of what I mean by the felt sense of emergence. Let me begin with a word of caution. To select a moment, or a case, that describes the quality of emergence is liable to suggest that the material selected is worthy of special note, thereby drawing attention away from the fact that the state of affairs it describes is actually part of everyday analytic work. That is a risk I will have to take to make my point. I have chosen to write about a portion of one clinical session, but in order to underline the ordinariness of the phenomenon I will also say something about the many other moments of this kind that took place in that treatment.

The illustration comes from the treatment of George, a married man in his 70s with grown children, an artist who continues to spend most of his time in the studio creating art. George is capable and intelligent, and obviously creative. He comes to treatment three times per week. On the day in question, about four years into the treatment, he walked into my consulting room and, as usual, sat down in the reclining chair, leaned all the way back, and closed his eyes. It has never seemed necessary to discuss using the couch with George, because he evolved this posture naturally, and it has always seemed to me to serve the same purpose: It allows him a more intimate kind of contact with his internal world.

On this day, George began telling me about Ted Hughes's English translation of Ovid's *Metamorphoses*, which he was reading at the time. (George is an avid reader, especially of poetry.) In particular, he was taken with a tale about a nymph who, raped by a river god, turned into water and flowed into her attacker, becoming part of him. George thought there was something both intriguing and sexy about this. By "sexy," he said, he meant that turning into water and flowing into the attacker was sensually appealing and would feel good. He said that he also felt that the feeling of becoming part of someone else was similar to something he sometimes experiences with me, as if I were the river god and he were the nymph.

At the time, I was already familiar with the theme in the transference to which George was referring—the characterization of me as powerful and arbitrary, sometimes sadistic, sometimes loving, and him as smaller, weaker, always loving, and deeply attached to me, resulting in his vulnerability to feeling rejected and hurt. Today he was adding the element of sensual pleasure and outright eroticism, not to mention rape, themes that continued to be developed in many of the sessions that were to come.

I had been through many, many sessions with George in which most or all of the content concerned "the cellar," our shorthand for the sexual abuse of George by a faceless older man, events that may have taken place in the basement of George's parents' house when George was very young, perhaps four or five years old. George had been in analysis once before, thirty years earlier, but the events of the cellar, whatever they were, had barely come up then, and had not been explored. Despite his introspective proclivity, George himself had never really thought about these memories or fantasies—a fact that, at this point, given our immersion in these matters, was startling to him. But despite his present-day interest, there was really nothing in George's mind at this point that he felt he could count on to be a literal memory of such events, and so the scenarios of the abuse that George recounted in great detail could not be taken as factual. They were creations, or re-creations. But that did not stop them from being highly significant to George, and therefore to me. Nor did that stop those scenarios from feeling to George as if he were not their author. During those many sessions, what he was telling me about was arriving in his mind unbidden.

George and I were "in the cellar" over and over and over again. Sometimes I was a misty kind of observer or witness, barely there at all; sometimes I was simply absent. But my presence, as significant as it was (I will have more to say about that), was not the main event. In the cellar, the focus was on George, who was vivid, and the faceless man, who was shadowy. As the nature of the relationship between these two changed during a session, George's self-states shifted. I could feel it. No doubt I responded with my own self-state shifts. Sometimes George was a helpless, frightened boy being abused; sometimes there was pleasure and perhaps something like love between him and the faceless man; and sometimes he was ferocious, a big, dangerous cat, a predator with long, sharp claws. When he was in the cat-state, George might feel rage, and he often imagined himself at those moments on the threshold of a mysterious, darkened room within which, he thought, there might be a lot of blood. While the atmosphere at such times could be chilling, I was never particularly uncomfortable. George certainly could be angry with me, sometimes very angry, and there were times, sometimes weeks at a time, when this was the focus of our sessions; but George was never angry at me in the cellar. His cellar rage was not directed at me. Instead, I was a facilitating witness to events that generally seemed to me to be self-affirming on George's part, even the rageful ones. George's fantasies gave shape to affect states—states of self—that I think he needed to be able to experience more explicitly than he had in the past. And to do that, he needed me to be there to know these things with him. My witnessing presence, I believe, contributed to George's capacity to formulate what he told me, and then, eventually, to step back and think about these things for the first time in his life.

The actual physical events that took place in the cellar were seldom clearly discernible to George, although they were sexual in nature. George's visual images of these events were vague. What I can say about George's feelings and fantasied bodily experience was that he could be terrified, sexually aroused, in physical pain, loved and loving, and worried and sad about the possibility of losing the faceless man's interest. Unsurprisingly, there was a good deal of fantasy about penises and long, penis-like objects in his mouth, throat, and anus. George identifies as heterosexual. The idea of sex with men used to intrigue him, but when he tried it he did not feel aroused. Perhaps George would have been interested in both men and women with or without whatever took place in the cellar—or perhaps he was drawn to sex with men because of what took place in the cellar. Or perhaps both alternatives are true. It does not really matter, to me or to him, which, if either, of these things is more true.

Consider all of this as background for what happened on the day George told me the story about the nymph and the river god. I listened to George's thoughts after he told me about the tale, and after he had related the story to his feelings about me. After a while, I said something very simple to him, more or less spontaneously, and from deep within my involvement in the moment and with him. I said, "It reminds me of the cellar." I imagined we were both probably thinking the same thing. Despite that feeling of mystery that comes with the sense of emergence, which I did feel, what I said seemed to me to be uncontroversial.

George was silent for maybe ten or fifteen seconds, and then he said in a low voice, "I'm stunned."

Apparently, we had not been thinking the same thing at all. But George's response conveyed to me that, in response to my remark, an emergent experience had come about in his mind, too. I may have offered him the idea, but his intense affective reaction was the shock of recognition. You experience that only when you are faced suddenly with something that summons an answering, involuntary, emergent, and immediate sense in your own mind that this thing belongs to you.

My remark, and the experience that gave rise to it, were the outcome of a jointly created interactive and affective process that had formative properties. I did not *figure out* my way into the connection between the cellar and Ovid's tale, I *felt* my way into it. Even that way of putting it, though, makes what I did sound more consciously volitional than it was. What I said to George grew from living under the spell he and I, without conscious intention, had cast together around our mutual history, the story of the nymph and the river god, and ourselves in this room, in this moment. My experience was the manifestation of the interpersonal field, in other words, not just of my individual capacity to think, know, or understand. Or put it this way: We should *always* understand the analyst's capacity to think, know and understand in the clinical situation as a phenomenon of the field, not as the creation of the analyst's solitary mind. The analyst does not stand back and observe. She does her best work when living under the kind of spell George and I cast. My thought grew from what was happening between us. It would have been impossible without it.

When George and I are in the cellar, the outside world retreats. It is quiet, the office is dim, and I have noticed that colors tend to darken. There is the illusion that I am there, right there in that cellar. I know something about how it looks, because George has told me the details, and I find that I imagine a version of those details for myself, and I inhabit them. (I am an onlooker to this process of imagining.) The ends of our sessions can be startling. It can be wrenching to return ourselves to the everyday world. That shock testifies to the depth of our involvement, our mutual absorption in the matters at hand. We are thoroughly immersed in a joint fantasy. What comes to exist between us is woven from the strands of George's inner life, from my fantasy of his fantasy life, from George's fantasy of my fantasy, and on and on. *Someone* is weaving this experience between us, but it does not feel to George or me that it is either one of *us*.

I hope that it comes across to you that the process of emergence in this case is not unique, despite the fact that the events between George and me have been particularly dramatic and moving. I could probably use as an example of emergence any treatment of real depth. In fact, the quality of emergence has always been so central to me that I suspect that any one of the many case examples I have published in articles and books, including those in the chapters to follow, could serve as an illustration. Any collaborative treatment contains myriad emergent moments, usually (but not always) during the periods of collaboration themselves.

It is impossible to know whether George's apparent sexual abuse actually took place. There were various reasons, gleaned from George's history and symptoms, for me to suspect strongly that some kind of traumatic sexual contact did occur. I believe that that sexual contact, the betrayal it represented, and especially the terrible rejection that seems to have brought it to an end (I have not explained that part of the material)—or rather, the ways George has devised to live with these things—has shaped George's life in various damaging and distressing ways. The images, fantasies, quasi-memories, and bodily sensations that George described almost continuously during many sessions, over years, came to him without his volition. Their flow, that is, was itself emergent, and it felt that way to him.

I am convinced that all these things came to George when they did, in the forms they did, and in the order that they did, because he was *telling them to me*. It was the field we shaped between us, not just George's intention to free associate (although George did indeed intend to free associate) that was responsible for the emergence of this material. Just as the analyst's capacity to think, know, and understand is rooted in the field, so is the patient's freedom (or lack of it) to formulate his experience.

More often than not, rather than trying to interpret George's cellar experiences by converting them into some other frame of reference, I accepted them at face value. If I imagined they had symbolic import, I usually kept that thought to myself; and if the cellar experiences were vague and hard to understand, I usually did not try to get George to clarify them. George knew perfectly well that I was wondering about what all this might mean, beyond what it signified literally; and of course he wondered, too. But despite sharing that attitude, we usually allowed the material to take us wherever it was going. We were leaves on the stream. It seemed important for the meanings in George's experience to have a chance to emerge by themselves. It usually felt to me that offering interpretations of our time in that awful cellar would have been heavy-handed, risking intellectualization.

I hope that I have communicated in this illustration the quality of felt emergence that frequently characterized this treatment. I hope that this material conveys that the field is woven by the interpenetration of the conscious and unconscious minds of analyst and patient; and that the outcome is really more about a new vibrancy and spontaneity than it is about revelation. Edgar Levenson (1982), in a favorite passage of mine, writes that patient and analyst feel that,

> (...) *some* process is going on which they have not initiated or energized. There is the remarkable experience of being carried along by something larger than both therapist and patient: A true sense of an interpersonal field results. *The therapist learns to ride the process rather than to carry the patient.*
>
> (Levenson, 1982, pp. 11–12; italics from the original)

1.2 An enactment

Now, in the second part of my presentation, as promised, I offer another, more detailed clinical report that I hope contributes to your understanding of how I work and conveys my reasons for what I do. The presentation is intended to convey what it is like to work within the field—within a clinical context that is recognized by the analyst to be continuously, jointly created by the analyst and the patient, especially by their conscious and unconscious affective exchange. What I would like you to see is how the treatment, as I understand it, is an ongoing process of mutual influence, much of it occurring outside the awareness of either participant. For the analyst, the work is the continuous effort to grasp the way they are embedded in unseen aspects of the relationship with the patient, and the equally ceaseless attempt to free themself from these relational strictures and reawaken the spontaneity of the field. I use concepts in this material that may not be immediately familiar: witnessing and embeddedness in the other. I hope and trust that the meaning of these terms will be clear enough from the context within which they are used.

Emma is a very bright and talented, single, white, corporate executive in her late 30s who meets with me four times per week. She wants a family more than anything, but is worried that she just cannot manage a relationship, with its ceaseless opportunities to disappoint the other person and fall into a pit of shame. She is extraordinarily, and more or less continuously, self-critical, not infrequently to the point of self-hatred. But she is just as continuously honest, courageous, and articulate in trying her level best to tell me what is going on in her mind. I am not going to explain here the roots of all these matters in her early life, although Emma and I know a great deal about that. Along with our examination of present-day life and the events that transpire between us, we speak about it in most sessions. For purposes of this presentation, I describe only a week or so of our relatedness, an episode in the continuous sequence of embeddedness in one another and emergence from it. During these sessions we discovered yet another way to set one another at a distance, transcend the enactment that bound us, and think anew about our relationship, and Emma's life and mind. The sessions took place online during COVID-19.

1.2.1 Friday

On a recent Friday, Emma was especially troubled. I know how distressed she can be about the end of sessions, and this was the last session until Tuesday, and so a few minutes prior to the session's end, I offered to meet with her the next day, a Saturday. (I do not work on Saturdays, which Emma knew.) I knew that it would be hard for her to say yes to this offer, because she would have to contend with the worry of burdening me (no matter what I said), which she felt she already did too much just by being with me in sessions.

But Emma surprised me this time. She assented, with gratitude, and we parted.

1.2.2 Saturday

The next day's session was unusually productive, and ended on an up-note. We learned a good deal, and Emma felt much better about what had troubled her on Friday. In fact, that issue between us (which I will forgo describing for reasons of brevity) was resolved enough to have vanished.

1.2.3 Tuesday

Our next hour was on Tuesday. When Emma came in, she began talking in a highly self-critical vein, eventually concluding that the validity of the positive feelings she had had on Saturday was now in doubt. Listening to Emma build to this conclusion, I felt helpless and stymied. It was clear to me that something was demanded of me in this moment, but I could not imagine a helpful way to intervene. Eventually I said, in regard to the return of Emma's self-hating feelings, "That's too bad," with what I thought was a sympathetic attitude. But I was also vaguely aware, too little aware to formulate for myself at that moment, of a certain annoyance on my part. Looking back at this moment from later on, during the email exchange I will discuss below, I saw that I was annoyed that we were right back in the soup. I felt, perhaps unreasonably, that there was a certain recalcitrance to Emma's misery: Did she really *have* to do this again?

In retrospect, I see that both Emma and I were single-minded at that moment; we were caught in a kind of fusion, each of us stuck in a single, rigid role relative to the other. I was not able to deal with Emma as a separate person in this moment, but only as the reciprocal part of my own feelings. This is the world of projection and introjection, in which the other must play the part required by one's own internal drama. My reaction to her therefore had more to do with whatever her refusal to feel good meant to me than it did with the meaning the situation had for her. I did not understand what was happening, but was enough aware that something was the matter to feel vaguely guilty about not being more generous. I could not articulate any of this to myself at the time. (This vague discomfort is what I [Stern, 2004] have elsewhere described as "affective snags and chafing," which are mildly uncomfortable emotional alerts that one's unconscious involvement with the patient needs attention.)

Unsurprisingly, Emma reacted to the unmentalized part of my reaction. She became even more unhappy, but she was no more able than I to say why. She, too, was locked into the enactment and could not think. The session ended on that note. I did not understand what had happened. Neither did she. Neither of us was happy about the situation.

Emma often emails me, and I respond. Later that day, she sent me this message:

Sorry for being so negative.
   I don't know how/if I can keep doing this, I mean meeting and talking, because it's so painful in an unpredictable way. I mean, my emotional states are too unpredictable.

I feel in that electrified grip-trapped kind of way—I want to stop meeting and I can't bear to not meet.

I know I always say this—and I don't really want you to agree—but maybe I should stop seeing you for 3 weeks or so, till maybe January? I can tell it's a little frustrating for you, and that's the part I can't bear the most. Because I feel too ashamed that I can't question better or do it the way you say, so I could feel better. And I don't have enough internal energy to bear quite so much pain, from when I talk about stuff and feel worse and it's my own fault.

I am so sorry.

This message broke through something in me, and I immediately grasped, and could name to myself, the subtle annoyed quality and the impatience with which I had treated Emma during the session earlier in the day. I began to emerge from our mutual embeddedness in one another. In an attempt to offer her a witnessing presence, I wrote back to her:

I'm sorry myself, Emma. The last thing I want to do is contribute to your suffering, and I know that sometimes I do. We should talk about what's best for you going forward. I will keep an open mind about it. Clearly, though, whatever we do about the future, as long as we're meeting we need to talk consistently about what's going on in the room—in a way that's helpful to you, not hurtful. It's really no good for you to go home after a session feeling this bad. We have to prevent that, and I think whatever chance we have of doing that has to do with talking openly with one another.

Was Emma angry with me at some level? Perhaps. One day we will need to be able to imagine and discuss such possibilities, but not now—not yet. For now, the important thing for me to attend to was that my attitude, expressed most clearly in my annoyed and slightly sullen "That's too bad," had hurt her, and she had been ashamed. There had been a break in our connection. This was not a transference distortion to be analyzed, but a retraumatization to be recognized and acknowledged. What was required from me, however I could manage it, was the recognition of what had happened, from each of our points of view. It did not at the moment require that I connect the incident with her history (although we did get there later—I will tell you about this later on).

Whatever bits of therapeutic action may have been set into motion in this email exchange depended less on insight than on a kind of straightforward and affirmative relatedness that requires separateness, and cannot take place from within a merger. In setting my own experience at enough of a distance that I could see and accept that I had been willing to be impatient and exasperated, and had thereby hurt Emma, and that I regretted that outcome but could tolerate knowing this about myself, I began to disembed myself from this particular episode with Emma. It seems that, just as I had apparently done within my own mind when I reawakened my capacity to observe myself, I now set Emma at a distance that made it possible for me to think about her, and about her and me.

Emma answered me as follows:

> That makes complete sense about talking openly, I will try my absolute best. Sometimes I start getting confused, and I don't think I even really understand what's happening (I mean, in the room) or what I'm feeling, except confused and then more and more distanced from you. But we can talk about it more tomorrow, I can do that.

When I read this message, I felt that, reciprocally, in response to my attempt to make contact with her, Emma had begun to observe herself and then to breach the enactment from her end of it, thereby at least partially disembedding from me. I felt in her words (and later events confirmed it) that these emotional events had allowed Emma both an explicit awareness of the shame she had felt before, and the beginning of an alternative to it (i.e., maybe her feelings had something to do with my participation and not simply with her own inadequacy).

In response to Emma's email, and prior to the following session, I responded:

> Yes, I did mean that you need to talk to me. But I also need to try to tell you what my experience of you is. This isn't always easy. But it would make you feel better if I can do it—at least if I can do it in the way I imagine doing it, with an exploratory and curious attitude and without any blaming.

Emma wrote in response:

> Yes, I can imagine it isn't always easy to do that (that's an under-statement). And I always want to know your thoughts and reac-tions. But I know it's hard because sometimes I unpredictably end up feeling worse in some way when I know intellectually that it's never your intention to do that, in fact your intentions are the oppo-site, I know that rationally. I get off track when my emotions start to take me in all different directions.

Here we see that Emma is no longer overwhelmed by bad feeling, but she does not yet see that my intentions are not necessarily simply and uniformly good. She does not yet seem to grasp that I can be impatient with her for my own reasons, reasons that have to do with what I want from life and not with something "wrong" that she has done. She does not yet accept that I am complicated, as she is herself. She sees me, in part, as she needs to see me: she idealizes me, and in that sense she remains embedded in me.

1.2.4 Wednesday

During this session, in a continuation of the email exchange, and as a further step in our emergence from our embeddedness in one another, I told Emma that I knew that I needed to do my best to tell her the truth as I saw it, whether it was pretty or not—and not just about her life, but about the relatedness between us and my reactions to her. I told her that I know that in her family this kind of attitude is in short supply, because her parents, in different ways, in order to satisfy the images of them-selves they each need to preserve above all else, routinely avoid the rec-ognition or acknowledgment of the self-referential nature of their feelings and their relatedness. Their children were, and are, continuously put in the position of having to acknowledge that their parents' feelings arise, without exception, in the service of the parents' intention to serve the children's interests. I told Emma that I had been exasperated and impatient with what seemed to me her insistence on ruining the good feelings of the Saturday session. I told her that I know that it would have helped if I could have found my way to a recognition and acknowl-edgment of those feelings, but that I was apparently guilty enough to be "stuck," unable to find my way through my feelings at that moment. I explained that her email had helped me in that respect, awakening me to what I had felt. I had the impression that telling her the role of her email made her feel better. She does not often understand her own contribution to our small successes.

I thought about why I was stuck at this particular juncture. What was going on with me? I thought it was likely that I had been unconsciously sulking, wanting to be able to see our work as good and productive, and to feel that I was a good and helpful analyst. Like Emma's mother and father, regardless of how Emma felt, I apparently wanted her to cooperate in making me feel like a good analyst. I wanted this outcome badly enough to make me impatient and somewhat intolerant of her expression of unhappiness.

Eventually, in this Wednesday session, I told Emma these speculations. She said that she knows she does do her best to make me feel fulfilled as an analyst—an irony that reveals, despite the fact that Emma granted me permission to use our work as an illustration, that presenting this clinical material is itself likely to be an enactment between us, as most clinical presentations probably are in one way or another. Emma said she remembers that when I said, "That's too bad," she felt I was distancing myself from her. When her parents distance themselves, she said, she feels it is her fault and she searches herself for what she could have done "wrong" to provoke their disappointment in her.

1.3 Coda

I have written this vignette largely from the analyst's perspective, because my subject has been the means by which analysts find their way to the freedom that is necessary for them to locate if they are to "enter into relation" with the patient. But I could just as well have written about the same process from the point of view of the patient, with the analyst as the other—and in fact that is the typical perspective in the psychoanalytic literature. I hope I have made clear that Emma had to go through the process of disembedding herself from me, just as, if I were to help her, I had to emerge from my embeddedness in her. I hope it is clear that this disembedding is a collaborative, dialogic process: Neither Emma nor I could have changed the nature of our participation without the contribution of the other.

Emma sent the last email I will present several hours after the Wednesday session. I read it as confirmation of the value of analysts (and patients) doing whatever they can to set the other at a distance and then emerge from embeddedness in the other:

> I appreciate it so much. All of it, and especially what you said about it being helpful when I feel I'm being told the truth. I'm always anxious and hypervigilant about what the truth is, and whether someone is telling it to me or not. So you hit the nail on the head—it's very comforting when I can tell that you're telling me the truth. And, also as you observed, it's very comforting when you get something right, whether it's "good" or "bad," or whatever it is. When you get it right and it feels true, I always feel a lot calmer and better.
>
> *[Author's note: I understand Emma to mean here that being told the truth about my impatient reaction to her helped her set me at a distance, to emerge from her embeddedness in me, and to accept being witnessed.]*
>
> And when that doesn't happen—and I understand it's just part of life—then sometimes I have meltdowns. And my behavior, or what I say, when that happens is still a little (or maybe a lot) beyond my control. I can't control the freak outs very well at all. I get ashamed, I freak out, and then I get ashamed about freaking out, and it's a full-on meltdown.
>
> I feel a lot comforted now, pretty much over the meltdown of yesterday. And the meltdown was I think a lot related to my having felt unusually better on Saturday, as we discussed. But it IS progress, I think, that I can get through/past meltdowns sooner now. I can reconstitute more quickly, so to speak. I'm kind of surprised about that, in a good way.

A week later, Emma reported an astute observation she made over the weekend. I was delighted with what she said, because her observation involved a creative and frank acknowledgment of her parents' roles in her unhappiness, something it has often been hard for Emma to accept. Emma had come to see, she explained, that the only time her parents, and particularly her mother, said anything sympathetic to her (to Emma) was when Emma expressed self-hatred. When she did that, her mother would question the perception—not because she wanted her daughter to feel better, Emma now observed, but because having a self-hating daughter contradicted her image of the perfect mother she needed to be. She just could not bear it. On the other hand, said Emma, if she felt good or accomplished, and let her parents know about it, they would immediately question her facts or her perception of the situation, making her feel ashamed. Emma had realized over the weekend that these sequences of events were entirely dependable. They happened this way virtually every time. And therefore, for Emma, feeling miserable and self-hateful came to feel safe, and feeling good or accomplished became dangerous, because it would inevitably be ruined, and she would be devastated. Better, and safer, to do it to herself first. Then, at least, she did not have to live with the suspense and the shattered hopes. She added that when she became so self-critical on that Tuesday, about the previous session on Saturday, she might have been unwittingly provoking me to reassure her, as she had learned to do with her parents. She said: "So me enacting a relatedness from my childhood in the Tuesday session might also have been a precipitant for you to feel impatient with me." She meant that she had ruined the good feelings, disappointing me, in order to encourage me to try to reassure her. I saw her point immediately, of course.

I believe this last piece of work—Emma's grasp of an aspect of her relationship with her parents and her extrapolation to her relationship with me—was a direct consequence of a new bit of freedom to think that resulted from our negotiation of the enactment that I have described taking place during the previous week. There have been, and will be, many more such episodes.

References

Foehl, J. C. (2014). A phenomenology of depth. *Psychoanalytic Dialogues*, *24*(3), 289–303.

Levenson, E. A. (1982). Follow the fox: An inquiry into the vicissitudes of psychoanalytic supervision. *Contemporary Psychoanalysis*, *18*(1), 1–15. Reprinted in *The purloined self: Interpersonal perspectives in psychoanalysis*, pp. 117–131, by A. Slomowitz, Ed., 2017, Routledge.

Stern, D. B. (1997). *Unformulated experience: From dissociation to imagination in psychoanalysis*. Analytic Press. (Reprinted in 2003 by Routledge).

Stern, D. B. (2004). The eye sees itself: Dissociation, enactment, and the achievement of conflict. *Contemporary Psychoanalysis*, *40*(2), 197–237.

Chapter 2

Field perspective in relational psychoanalysis

Response to Donnel Stern

Dan Bloom

I am pleased to be leading off this discussion by responding to your presentation.

As a gestalt therapist who has been around a long time, reading and then listening to your ideas intrigued me because I found a commonality across what I once thought divided our modalities. At one time in the history of gestalt therapy and psychoanalysis, this divide might have seemed unbridgeable. Clearly, bridges needed to be built. My conversation with you, however, is more in the nature of our crossing bridges already built and exploring whatever boundaries mark our differences and similarities.

Gestalt therapy and interpersonal psychoanalysis speak different languages with different vocabularies and grammar. When we listen more closely it sometimes seems we are speaking dialects of a parent language. These might be dialects that reflect regional differences, practices, customs, and traditions—of a language whose meanings are common enough for us to have useful conversations.

I see how you are continuing to enlarge the theory and practice of relational psychoanalysis with your and your colleagues' notions of emergence and the interpersonal field. And so are we gestalt therapists who are developing the field-emergent approach within our modality.

I like to think that we field-emergent gestalt therapists are pushing at the walls that have surrounded and perhaps even isolated gestalt therapy into its own world and expanding gestalt therapy beyond its familiar—even comfortable—territory. The world of our patients has changed. What calls us to be therapists has changed—and is changing. I state the self-evident. Not to be responsive and malleable to these changes of our world would condemn us to become artifacts of the past.

DOI: 10.4324/9781003597308-3

Both of our approaches have many things in common. One broad thing is that we are part of a reaction to the monopersonal Cartesian approach to personhood and psychotherapy. I can say that for gestalt therapy, the push against an implied individualistic model has taken us a few decades of effort. And it has succeeded—or is continuing to succeed. More or less, here and there.

The individualistic paradigm in gestalt therapy more or less faded into the relational approach, to the dialogical approach—and now to this more radical, more experiential (at least to me), and more phenomenological field-emergent approach. So you can see how pleased I am to be able to join you here as colleagues across modalities, colleagues who are engaged in similar discussions within and across our own modalities.

In this response to you, I want to describe how gestalt therapy accounts for a field-emergent approach in ways that are relevant to your own. I will offer you some of my reflections on your speech.

Perhaps the similarities and differences in our approaches can stimulate a synergism—generating some further insights, which at this moment neither of us can predict. A central tenet in gestalt therapy is that growth comes from being in touch with the unfamiliar, so long as it is supported by openness and trust. We refer to this as the contacting process. In pursuing this goal, I am going to push on some of our differences and perhaps even magnify them for the purposes of differentiating our approaches. Or perhaps I will push on these differences only to discover commonality. This conference is the foundation that enables us to meet in this way and to touch on the unfamiliar, supported by openness and trust.

It has not been simple to describe the field-emergent perspective of gestalt therapy even to gestalt therapists. Maurice Merleau-Ponty (1908–1961) wrote that the "problem of the world"—he did say "problem" in the translation I have—"is that it is *all there*" (Merleau-Ponty, 2006, p. 230). I modify this: The problem with discussing a field-emergent approach is that to discuss it one must step outside it—and that is impossible. That would be like stepping outside the Cartesian perspective, since common sense and ordinary experience tell us that there is a mind, there is a body, there is an outside, there is an inside, and it is self-evident that you and I are independent agents in the world who are "finding and making" (Perls et al., 1951, pp. 234–235) our separate ways as we go about our separate lives. Emergence? This is by no means obvious. Of course, "emergence" entails a clear notion of a "field."

I will start with field in gestalt therapy. The field is intrinsic in gestalt therapy. The field approach is central and has always been so. It has *always* been explicit from our original theory and practice onward. You have presented an interpersonal field as the basis for your psychoanalytic approach. The field in gestalt therapy and the field in psychoanalysis have common roots, yet the concepts developed in different soils and drew on different sources.

For our part, field concepts of the Gestalt psychology of the Berlin School of Max Wertheimer (1880–1943) and Köhler (1887–1967) (Harrington, 1996) inspired Fritz Perls to formulate a gestalt therapy organized by a psychophysical gestalt field theory. We are after all *gestalt therapy* and gestalten, or forms, are processes of a field. Fritz Perls and Paul Goodman (1911–1972) elaborated this into the "organism/ environment field" in the seminal 1951 text, *Gestalt Therapy, Excitement and Growth in the Human Personality*, which is still studied in the core curriculums at training institutes worldwide (Perls, Hefferline, & Goodman, 1951).

There are different approaches to field in contemporary gestalt therapy, usually depending on whose field theory is being used. Is it the early Kurt Lewin (1890–1947) of the Berlin School, or the later Kurt Lewin of the United States, for example, where the later Lewin had a theory of vectors and systems? Additionally, gestalt therapy was also substantially influenced by the holistic field theory of neurologist Kurt Goldstein (1878–1965) and the holism of the South African philosopher and statesman Jan Smuts. (1870–1950). Smuts's concept of holism (Smuts, 1936) and Goldstein's organism (Goldstein, 1995) are as if watermarks barely visible, yet present in the theory of field-emergent gestalt therapy. The Gestalt psychologist Adhemar Gelb (1887–1936) influenced Laura Perls (1905–1990), an often-undercredited founder and developer of gestalt therapy. Arguably, Paul Goodman (1911–1972), another one of the founders of gestalt therapy, added the pragmatism of John Dewey (1859–1952), William James (1841–1910), and George Herbert Mead (1863–1931) to the mix and this is reflected in the nuances of field processes of gestalt therapy (Kitzler, 2007, 2009). The many different possible versions of "field" among gestalt therapists has led one gestalt therapist to refer to a "Babylonian confusion" among us (Staemmler, 2006).

Given psychoanalysis' structural commitment to the unconscious, conscious, and preconscious mental states, field theory in psychoanalysis and in gestalt therapy necessarily developed along different tracks. The gestalt therapy principles of holism, gestalt forming, awareness, and figure/ground, for example, were nevertheless unstressed, yet might have been present in various ways in the psychoanalytic model. Or perhaps I should say that those concepts took time to find their way increasingly into a Freudian model.

Yet what can this mean in terms of our similarities and differences? At what level or on what basis are what is essential or core to the psychoanalytic and gestalt models incomparable? Or even incompatible? Surely there are fundamental differences.

I know, Don, you and so many of your colleagues in interpersonal and relational psychoanalysis have deconstructed and reconstructed the beams and rafters of psychoanalysis so that my reference to core theories borders on absurdity. And so have I and many of my colleagues reconstituted some of what others considered settled dogma in gestalt therapy. Maybe it is closer for me to put it this way: Our gestalt concepts are less inconsistent with core notions of contemporary psychoanalysis than they used to be. As I said earlier, we may be speaking dialects of the same language. Yet it is a mistake to prematurely conclude that our differences are simply a matter of translation.

Of this I am more confident: The field theories of gestalt therapy and psychoanalysis developed along different tracks. Of this I am less confident: Can anyone confuse a psychoanalytic field with a gestalt field?

Psychoanalysis has been able to integrate field theory within a recognizably psychoanalytic approach that includes the unconscious among many other concepts. Yes, indeed, the unconscious, transference, resistance, and other earmarks of traditional analytic theory may have disappeared from contemporary analytic epistemology or clinical discourse, but their trace is unmistakable.

There is no unconscious in gestalt therapy. There is no transference, countertransference, and so on. What you see is what you get. More or less. That is, even the invisible is visible, the unsaid, said, and so on. This has been so since gestalt therapy was born, so to speak. We never had to discover our way to this. And here is where things get interesting.

Both of your case illustrations show the more or less presence of the conscious/preconscious/unconscious structural model. At the center—at the clinical climax or epiphany of the therapies you present—there is the trace of the unconscious in the "a-ha" moments of each clinical example. Yet, interestingly, what shows itself to me in those instances is pretty much what would appear in a field-emergent gestalt therapy approach—yet differently. For gestalt therapy, the gestalt therapy figure/ground process out of which the figure is emergent of the field can actually account for something roughly similar to, yet *different* from unconscious and conscious processes. Our approaches, though grounded on different structural or epistemological understandings of persons, are *almost* versions of one another in different domains of understanding organized by field theory. Since field-emergent gestalt therapy attends to what emerges of the field, it attends to what comes to awareness out of a less aware or even unaware background. This certainly resonates with the structural model of psychoanalysis. See what I mean by this getting interesting?

Both approaches privilege the kind of insights that emerge of the field, which re-configure and re-organize a person's sense of his or herself in the world. When emergent interpersonal field theory refers to figure/ground emergence—and it does—it still preserves its structural model of the conscious and unconscious with all that entails, even when the dividing line between conscious and unconscious processes is softened. There are still repression, resistance, and defenses, while in gestalt therapy the pole star of our clinical work is the autonomous criterion of the aesthetic felt and sensed qualities of contacting—the figure/ground process itself (Bloom, 2003).

Gestalt field-emergence theory does not use the unconscious, but it might—yet without what it would entail in psychoanalysis. What would be lost if gestalt therapy imported that structural model? What would be gained? Some of us might propose—I propose—that insight emerges from the depths of the ground, from the shadows that may or may not obscure the brightness of the figure. That is the ground as if "behind" the figure. There is no "barrier" that separates figure from the ground, surface from the depth. No "barrier" at all. The figure/ground of contacting is the cohering of the elements of the field—of the past and future in the present: our version of Husserl's primal impression. As William Faulkner put it, "The past is not dead, it is not even past" (Faulkner, 2011, p. 73). It adheres to the present as the ground adheres to the figure. "All of us labor in webs spun long before we were born, webs of heredity and environment, of desire and consequence, of history and eternity" (Faulkner, 2011, p. 73). This coherence is the adhesion of figure to ground. Trauma, for example, threatens this adhesion and the fluidity of figure/ground emergence. I am quite aware that some of the language I am using more than subtly echoes language used by contemporary psychoanalysis that more and more is shedding the structural model. Dialects of the same language? Or different languages?

In each of your case examples, Don, the pivotal moments of clinical surprise—of transformative emergence—would be strikingly similar to, different from, and yet understandable in different ways from those in a gestalt therapy session.

Gestalt therapy's process of discovery is an embodied process of bringing into awareness what is not merely unaware but what is being hidden. Our work seeks to clarify embodied experience from amid an unfocused, unnoticed, unattended to average everydayness, in which sources of personal distress might be hidden. I underscore "embodied" because, too often and historically, the lived-bodily aspects of emergent experience have gone unattended to in psychotherapy.

Taking this further, it is not merely a matter of unaware to aware, but a matter of bringing to the foreground what is obscured and in the background. What is obscured is nevertheless present in the qualities of the felt sense of the ground. Felt sense. That is, the hidden and unaware are just out of sight, yet at the fringes of awareness. They are out of sight, perhaps unseen, but not unseeable. This is very much like your description of the felt sense of the unexpected despite their invisibility. What is important here for us field-emergent gestalt therapists is that what is obscured remains present, not behind a barrier that needs to be lifted. We never have.

Perhaps we could think in terms of Merleau-Ponty's intertwining of the visible with the invisible (Merleau-Ponty, 1968). The sensed and felt qualities of the emerging figure embody the process of the invisible becoming visible. Or mundanely, right now, each of us could experience this directly by shifting our weight in our seat and finding the soles of our feet on the ground. We have made figure what had been ground. Now take a moment and now notice what is different.

Doesn't all this attention to what is hidden and so on sound like we gestalt therapists do have the unconscious in our model? What is all this fuss about, then?

To many of us, aware/unaware is not a binary but rather part of a fluid unfolding gestalt process, while the conscious and the unconscious seems to be binary. Aware/unaware and figure/ground are phenomeno-logically equivalent—or, arguably, they have so close an experiential resemblance that they usefully can be brought together. A therapy based on gestalt process, variously referred to as the awareness continuum, as gestalt forming, or as the sequence of contacting, has no dividing lines and no categories for experiences. It is based on whole phenomena as they emerge, unfold, and develop in the interpersonal field of the therapy session.

In our gestalt therapy process, we as if listen for the unsayable: We then give it voice—an utterance; we find the undoable and give it agency and action. This is a process of unfolding a person into his or her world-with-others, the interpersonal field. We. Therapist and patient. Each and both of us.

Put another way, field-emergence in gestalt therapy is the appearance of what had always already been there, to borrow a phrase from Heidegger (Heidegger, 1962). That is, it is the appearance—again, in the phenomenological sense—of what had not yet been seen, yet whose effects were in some way present. The ground of the figure becomes the figure of the ground. What had been in the dark, so to speak, is now central, in the light.

Am I paraphrasing you, Don, in another language or dialect? Isn't this also how you now consider and work with the unconscious?

Take your case example of George. You describe how it is when you work with him: The outside world retreats and "the office dims and the colors tend to darken."

"What comes to exist between us is woven from the strands of George's inner life, from my fantasy of his fantasy life, from George's fantasy of my fantasy, and on and on."

From a gestalt-emergent perspective, we could say that is the ground out of which the clinical insight emerges.

"*Someone* is weaving this experience between us, but it does not feel to George or me that it is either one of *us*."

"It" is not either one of you. The weaver is a background process affecting each one of you as figures. That is, it is an undifferentiated background out of which the figures you then identify as your own experiences are emergent.

This is the interpersonal field that is undifferentiated in the sense of pre-differentiated. It is undifferentiated in the sense of not-yet differentiated, identified—or personified. In the simplest of terms, the figure/ground emergence process in gestalt therapy moves from the pre-aware/aware to the sensed and felt to the clear, identified, and known. From a gestalt field-emergent perspective, you and George's experience is emergent of the same ground. It is of the same figure/ground process in which therapist or patient can be overcome by an awareness from the depths neither expected—the background that is now foreground experience.

You refer to the end of sessions sometimes as a wrenching return to the everyday world and that the shock "testifies to the depth of your involvement—mutual absorption [...] immersed in a joint fantasy." I want to comment about "depth" since it describes the phenomenal relationship of figure to ground—of perspective. When you speak of the "depth" of experience, we would speak of background or ground in the figure/ground process. In your perspective, emergence of the depth refers to an unconscious-to-conscious process; our emergence is of the foreground/background, figure/ground process. There is substantial overlapping here—and not surprisingly. Gestalt psychologists did most of their work on perception. Merleau-Ponty drew a great deal from their work.

In many ways, we can think of our gestalt therapy clinical work as transforming a two-dimensional way of seeing into a three-dimensional perspective—or better, of turning a photograph into a hologram. Indeed, a person's original way of seeing is multidimensional. As so many phenomenologists discovered, original sight is non-Cartesian. The more restrictive the grid we place on the world, the narrower our perspective, the flatter our vista and the duller our felt sense of the field. I know this sounds familiar to you and other contemporary psychoanalysts. Once again, this had been baked into gestalt therapy's original non-Cartesian holism from the beginning. Perhaps they were also there in Freud's insights on hysteria. Yet the emphasis was embedded and intrinsic in gestalt therapy, woven into our fabric, and has never left our sight.

Those extra dimensions of the hologram are not created in clinical work; they were there, yet just out of sight. In contacting, the familiar is re-configured so that figure/ground flips to ground/figure. What has been unaware background—in the shadows—becomes aware in the clarity of insight. This clarity is reflected in the qualities of the forming figures of contacting, now free to fulfill the limitless dimensions of the lived-world. Those shadows are the haunting shadows you refer to in The Cellar.

This uncanny is nothing more nor less than the unexpected, which you mention—the unexpected as if hiding just behind the expected. It is constituted by the field that organizes us and is organized by us, outside and in awareness. These are the mysteries that come from nowhere and from everywhere, which constitute emergent therapeutic insight—perhaps the very miracles of both of our emergent approaches.

In gestalt therapy's clinical phenomenology, then, we take an open welcoming position and allow ourselves to be surprised by what emerges (Bloom, 2021). Some of us refer to undergoing the clinical situation (Francesetti, 2015), to joining the dance of the situation of emerging figure and re-configuring figure/ground relationship (Spagnuolo Lobb, 2017). This, of course, is the interpersonal field—of therapist, of patient, and whoever else is summoned up in the special world created in the psychotherapeutic magic.

I and my client feel the same light on our faces in my office, albeit in different locations. We are embedded in a kinesthetic web of the field (Frank, 2023), for example, or an aesthetic network of sensations and relational intentionalities (Bloom, 2020) as background.

This is our—that is, gestalt therapy's—interpersonal field.

2.1 Emma and George

I want to end by turning to Emma and George.

There is an elephant in this room. I want to conclude my remarks by talking about it in terms of the emergence of the interpersonal and organism/environment fields. A part of the elephant in the room is the green dot at the top of my screen. It is familiar to me and many of us as the portal to our patient in an online session—as well to us during this conference.

I know that I have been able to do effective gestalt therapy under these techno-phenomenological circumstances overall, due to the fact that experience is unstoppable. That is, even though we are constrained by the limits of technology, I and my patient are able to engage in such ways that, as I just described, the background could become illuminated and both of us could be surprised by the figures that emerged.

Yet how is this different from the clinical work that is directly face-to-face? This topic deserves more elaboration—for another place and time.

Let me turn to the clinical examples you gave and consider them from a techno-phenomenological perspective.

I had a very different experience listening to the two case reports. The obvious reasons, of course, involve the nature of the persons, relationships, and developing therapy.

In gestalt terms, the qualities of the emerging dynamics as you, Don, described them were different in material ways. The atmosphere—the air pressure, temperature, weather, light—was different. Again, there is no reason to be surprised at that since the atmosphere—the affective felt and sensed qualities—of the field must be as changeable as the weather on any day. Yet there were other differences and other ways to account for them.

There was the cellar with George on his recliner with the interpersonal field as if woven by threads of fantasy creating a special world. In gestalt therapy terms, experience is emergent of the boundary of the organism/environment field. You were in the same room as George. You described yourself as sometimes a misty kind of observer or witness and, actually spontaneously, made a comment that you referred to as something that grew from living a spell—a comment that came as if from elsewhere, neither yours nor his: "It was the field we shaped between us, not just George's intention to free associate (although George did indeed intend to free associate) that was responsible for the emergence of this material."

And there was Emma—on the other side of the computer monitor for an online session. Your interpersonal field—the clinical relationship—was woven by the conversations, images, and texts at a distance. It makes sense to me that what is emergent of the online field bears imprints of this field. Much of this interpersonal field was mediated through words—therapeutic conversations and texts. The crisis in the therapy involved mutual embeddedness and enactment, both of which got played out, so to speak, through verbal interactions. The therapy work importantly included the exchanged text messages as well as the actual sessions. And it was clear that the interactions that were not flesh-to-flesh were nevertheless profoundly moving. Or, rather, they were not unmediated flesh-to-flesh. They were mediated by all the flickers, flashes, and hisses that characterize the particular emergent event of a techno-phenomenological relationship.

This brings me to us at this conference. And to ask us to question the qualities of this specific field created by our hybrid conversation.

I appreciated this opportunity to share my thoughts with you. And in my thinking and considering, I found myself interweaving my sense of field-emergent gestalt therapy with my understanding of your interpersonal field psychoanalysis. Our similarities and differences seemed to be playing a game of hide and seek with one another as differences dissolved in similarities and then became clearer from our similarities.

I am left with no conclusion, but with eagerness to continue this discussion.

References

Bloom, D. (2003). "Tiger! Tiger! Burning bright." Aesthetic values as clinical values in gestalt therapy. In M. Spagnuolo Lobb & N. Amendt-Lyon (Eds.), *Creative license: The art of Gestalt therapy* (pp. 63–78). Springer-Verlag.

Bloom, D. (2020). Intentionality: The fabric of relationality. *The Humanistic Psychologist, 48*(4), 389–396.

Bloom, D. (2021). From the night before being: Contacting the other. *Gestalt Review, 15*(25), 116–141.

Faulkner, W. (2011). *Requiem for a nun*. Vintage Books.

Francesetti, G. (2015). From individual symptoms to psychopathological fields. Towards a field perspective on clinical suffering. *British Gestalt Journal, 24*(1), 5–19.

Frank, R. (2023). *The bodily roots of experience in psychotherapy*. Routledge.

Goldstein, K. (1995). *The organism: A holistic approach to biology derived from pathological data in man*. Zone Books.

Harrington, A. (1996). *Reenchanted science. Holism in German culture from Wilhelm II to Hitler*. Princeton University Press.

Heidegger, M. (1962). *Being and time* (J. Macquarrie & E. Robinson, Trans.). Harper & Row.

Kitzler, R. (2007). The ambiguities of origins: Pragmatism, the University of Chicago, and Paul Goodman's self. *Studies in Gestalt Therapy, 1*, 141–163.

Kitzler, R. (2009). *Eccentric genius: An anthology of the writings of Richard Kitzler, Master Gestalt Therapist* (2nd ed.). Gestalt Institute Press.

Merleau-Ponty, M. (1968). *The visible and the invisible*. Northwestern University Press.

Merleau-Ponty, M. (2006). *Phenomenology of perception: An introduction*. Routledge.

Perls, F. S., Hefferline R., & Goodman P. (1951). *Gestalt therapy: Excitement and growth in the human personality*. Julian Press.

Smuts, J. (1936). *Holism and evolution* (3rd ed.). Macmillan and Co.

Spagnuolo Lobb, M. (2017). From losses of ego functions to the dance steps between psychotherapist and client. Phenomenology and aesthetics of contact in the psychotherapeutic field. *British Gestalt Journal, 26*(1), 28–37.

Staemmler, F.-M. (2006). A Babylonian confusion? On the uses and meanings of the term 'field' [Festschrift for Malcolm Parlett]. *British Gestalt Journal, 15*(2), 64–83.

Chapter 3

Post-Bionian field theory and the ethical refounding of psychoanalysis
Giuseppe Civitarese

3.1 My definition of "field"

Authoritatively, Kernberg (2011), Elliott & Prager (2015), and Seligman (2017) have listed the post-Bionian analytic field theory (FT) among the main trends in contemporary psychoanalysis. Kernberg states that:

> The most significant overall developments within the contemporary spectrum of psychoanalytic theory, it seems to me, involve the neo-Bionian approach, on the one hand, and the relational approach, on the other. (…) the neo-Bionian approach has expanded its sphere of influence throughout Europe, particularly in Italy, and, to some extent, also in Latin America, under the influence of Ferro's (…) work.
>
> (Kernberg, 2011, p. 634)

Seligman (2017) has elaborated a fascinating map in which he identifies five main psychoanalytic orientations: contemporary Kleinian psychoanalysis, Freudian psychoanalysis, relational psychoanalysis, Lacanian psychoanalysis, and FT. Given that the main authors who developed FT live in Pavia, we can legitimately speak of the Pavia School of Psychoanalysis. The influence of this school has grown over time.

FT represents the most original evolution of Bion's thought. By incorporating elements from other traditions, it translates Bion's principles into simple, versatile, and easily applicable therapeutic tools. Bion's psychoanalysis can be seen as a conscious or unconscious attempt to reconceptualize individual (Kleinian) therapy through the lens of group theory, which Bion introduced in 1943 with a brilliant essay published in *The Lancet* (Bion & Rickman, 1943; Civitarese, 2021a). Klein revolutionized

DOI: 10.4324/9781003597308-4

Freud's thinking, just as Bion did with Melanie Klein, who had been his analyst. The vocabulary undergoes significant changes, and even where it remains the same (for example, "projective identification"), the concept's meaning is transformed.

With Freud, we have essentially a unipersonal psychoanalysis based on biological concepts of psychic energy, which have no place in Melanie Klein's thought (Abram & Hinshelwood, 2018). Klein introduced a transition from a one-person psychology to a bipersonal psychology. Bion, on the other hand, developed the relational aspect of Klein's work (e.g., inventing concepts like linking, content/container, O, etc.), but gradually began to curve it in a hyper- or "anti-relational" direction, which allows us to glimpse the radically intersubjective model of FT.

In my opinion, this is where FT emerges. Ferro gathers the work of many Italian authors influenced by Bion's seminars held in Rome during the final phase of his life and creates a brilliant synthesis. In this synthesis, he combines Bion's thought with the concept of the field from the Barangers (Baranger & Baranger, 1961–62/2008), themes derived from Umberto Eco's narratology, and ideas from Robert Langs, Meltzer, and others. The lexicon undergoes further changes: Field, field disease, affective hologram, characters of the session, unsaturated interpretations, and transformations in dreams are not found as such in Bion. I have also contributed by introducing concepts such as interpretive metalepsis, immersion vs. interactivity, and transformations into hallucinosis. I have highlighted the role that the romantic aesthetic of the sublime plays in this thought and, in recent works, I have attempted to give FT a more solid metapsychological basis by discussing the concept of intersubjectivity in opposition to authors who, in my opinion, betray its original meaning as elaborated by Hegel (who does not use this term but develops a true theory of intersubjectivity) and Husserl, reducing it to a mere synonym of "interaction" (and not of "transindividual").[1]

Moreover, I have laid the foundations for a new psychoanalytic critique of the aesthetic experience (Civitarese, 2012, 2020a). From this premise, it is clear how I define the "field" in the theory of psychoanalysis. It is a theory that incorporates all these influences and places Bionian and post-Bionian concepts at its core. As I mentioned earlier, Bion anticipates a field theory based on the study of groups. A group possesses a psychic life that surpasses the sum of its individual elements. Understanding the group requires considering this dynamic entity and its emergent properties. For instance, the group may be permeated by violent unconscious emotions known as "basic assumptions" (Bion, 1961), which can disrupt and distort its intended purposes.

From a broad perspective, field theorization, in my view, most radically symmetrizes the figures of the patient and the analyst at an unconscious level. It continues the tradition of psychoanalysis from Freud onwards, which increasingly recognizes how the analyst's unconscious contributions shape the so-called facts of analysis. Bion already emphasizes:

- The importance of focusing on the formation or destruction of psychic bonds in analysis;
- The necessity of emotionally engaging with the patient to facilitate their psychic development;
- The essential role of shared truth as a key nurturing factor;
- The understanding that emotion is not merely a discharge of psychic energy but a space where meaning is co-created (Meltzer, 1984);
- The analyst's practice of intuitively "seeing" what is truly happening in the present moment;
- The acknowledgement that the past cannot be changed;
- The need for the analyst to employ a phenomenological method, similar to Husserl's *epoché* and *eidetic intuition*, to set aside anything that may hinder his or her capacity for intuition (such as memories, conscious desires, and intellectual understanding).

All these ideas would be incomprehensible without considering some fundamental postulates of the theory. To simplify, Bion rejects the dichotomy of primary/secondary processes. He overturns Freud's and Melanie Klein's notions of the unconscious, respectively as a place of evil and the internal bad object,[2] instead viewing it as a psychoanalytic function of the personality. In *Transformations* (Bion, 1965), he suggests speaking of *finite* and *infinite* instead of conscious and unconscious, which is a brilliant insight. It is evident that the subject (self-consciousness), arising from the dialectic of identity and difference, subjectivity and intersubjectivity, is both finite and infinite. If the unconscious is the function of the personality that generates human meaning, as studied in psychoanalysis, it is inherently connected to language. Language is not an individual phenomenon, even though individuals contribute to its creation. Rather, it is a social phenomenon. As philosophers teach us, "Language is the house of Being" (Heidegger, 1949/1977, p. 147).

The reconceptualization of the unconscious in this framework draws heavily on Klein's notion of the mind as a theater populated by internal objects. From this, another fundamental aspect of Bion's thinking and Field Theory emerges. We dream not only at night but also during the day. Dreaming represents our most profound and undivided way of attributing meaning to proto-emotional experiences, continually generating multiple viewpoints on the same object, thus rendering it true and real. As Ogden (2005) writes, those who suffer psychologically are either unable to dream or are temporarily trapped in a nightmare. Bion's concept of transformation and creation of meaning replaces Freud's concept of distortion, concealment, and destruction of meaning in dream work.

Field Theory adheres to these postulates and emphasizes the group or field dimension of the analytic relationship. At an unconscious level, it becomes impossible to determine whose responsibility it is to generate the emotions reflected in the images through which the analytic couple self-interprets and comes into being in real-time. The analyst's task is to continually anticipate the situation, attempting to discern whether the emotional atmosphere of the session (which describes the changes in the set of bonds constituting the analytic field at any given moment) is "progressive" or "regressive" (Civitarese, 2020b). The analyst consciously tries to steer it in the desired direction, often igniting another unconscious emotional wave in the process.

One specific definition of the field, as we previously saw, casts it as a product of the intersection of the projective identifications of the patient and analyst. The Barangers describe it as a shared unconscious fantasy that would not exist without the participation of both members of the analytic couple. It is noteworthy that the Barangers acknowledge their influence from Bion and Merleau-Ponty. Merleau-Ponty's philosophy opposes the Cartesian notion of subjectivity and owes its development to his study of Husserl's unpublished manuscripts. In those manuscripts, Husserl theorizes the ontological realm of co-belonging and mutual implication, which exists both transcendently and beyond conscious awareness. Thus, the circle is completed.

The essential question for me is: Can we gain new insights by examining my specific field of observation through an FT lens? Naturally, this question is rhetorical in nature.

3.2 Difficulties in applying the field perspective in therapy

Regarding the limitations and difficulties in applying the field perspective in therapy, I personally do not perceive them, although others may. Some concerns raised involve the role of the individual as a separate entity and the patient's current historical and concrete reality outside the realm of analysis. From my perspective, if one believes that psychic growth occurs when connections with others infinitely expand and internal "groupality" expands accordingly, it becomes self-evident that when one grows, the other grows as well. The crucial distinction, then, is not between the self and the group, which can be seen as subjectivity and intersubjectivity dialectically united within the subject, but between the self and the mass. When the unconscious fear of not being recognized by the object dominates, the subject defends itself by splitting off everything that does not align with a form of adhesive identification with the object. The analyst's strategy is always aimed at reducing this fear, or, in other words, moving from a cruel and tyrannical superego to a democratic superego.

In Bion's view, the emotions experienced within the analytic relationship constitute the real world of psychoanalysis. He emphasizes that the analyst's primary task is to be able to intuit these emotions, considering them as the psychoanalyst's real world. Bion suggests that any focus on cause-and-effect links, particularly of the trauma-transference type, hinders the analyst's ability to perceive the truth of what is happening in the present moment. Staying in the realm of concreteness, the analyst becomes deaf and blind to the underlying dynamics of the analytic relationship.

To illustrate this, let's consider an example. If a patient tells the analyst about a cat that has run away from home, there is a wealth of information about the patient and the cat. However, unless the analyst de-concretizes, fictionalizes, or "dreams" the cat, they cannot perceive it as a co-created character within the session. The cat's presence or absence in the analytic field reveals something about the emotions that emerge within the analytic relationship.

Nevertheless, it is not as simple as it seems, and this presents a real difficulty. The analyst contributes to the analytic narrative by staying immersed in the patient's proposed narrative, without constantly displacing it with their interpretations. Here, Winnicott's insights are relevant: The analyst's interpretations serve to help the patient understand the limits of their own understanding. Thus, while listening to the unfolding dream of the session, the analyst may keep the real traumas and historical aspects[3] in the background. However, the truly challenging task is to intuit the emotional facts of analysis. Bion suggests that emotion is the closest thing we have to a "fact." Achieving this requires an exercise in voluntary blindness, or what Bion terms "negative capability/faith."

If the analyst were to constantly focus on interpreting and, from a field perspective, become hyper-attentive, it would be counterproductive. The direction is different. Similar to a skilled pianist, it is helpful to engage in numerous exercises that eventually allow the intuitive understanding to arise naturally, without conscious effort, *much like in a dream.*

Some people express difficulty in grasping this field perspective, finding it too challenging. Indeed, it can be challenging if one expects to consistently work with a particular model after reading a couple of books and attending a few supervision sessions. However, this expectation is absurd. Working with the field model requires practice, like learning to play music that goes against one's natural intuitions. Sometimes, when illustrating clinical vignettes, it may seem like we are falling back into the I/You split of relational approaches. To address this, I draw on Husserl's intersubjectivity, Hegel's theory of recognition, and Bion's group psychology. I emphasize a shift in perspective from I/You to We, as I believe that the stakes are high and we have the opportunity to lay the foundation for a true ethical re-foundation of psychoanalysis. It is important to note that, in my opinion, the I/You perspective remains active alongside this broader field perspective.

In using the concept of the field in therapy, there are certain pitfalls and challenges that can arise:

(a) Some analysts who incorporate the concept of enactment may still focus on the past, unknowingly getting involved in acting out scenes that point towards the patient's traumatic history. Instead of recognizing the shared and unconscious emotional truth of the present moment, they become engaged in a time machine that directs them towards the past.

(b) Models that reference "recognition," perhaps influenced by Hegel, often emphasize conscious recognition, which is a mistake or only a small part of the overall process. Recognition in the context of the field perspective should encompass a broader understanding that includes unconscious recognition.

(c) Some authors may inconsistently assign certain elements of the analytic conversation to the unconscious field while automatically relegating others to mere reality. This ambiguity can hinder the ability to perceive oscillation between different perspectives. By acknowledging the possibility of oscillation and seeing facts from the perspective of the "vase" (as in Rubin's ambiguous figure), the entire analytic conversation can be seen as part of the ongoing metaphorical tale of the emotional dynamics of the analytic couple.

From my perspective, the concept of the field serves as a metaphor that helps the analyst be more receptive to the discourse of the unconscious. However, to strengthen this metaphor, I find it necessary to ground it in a more robust theorization of intersubjectivity at both the ontological and metapsychological levels. In the framework of FT, there are virtually no facts of analysis that are excluded from the discourse of the unconscious. The common, relational, and group unconscious is *always* speaking. To perceive the field in therapy, the analyst must have a solid grasp of theory and technique. The concept of the field reveals the dimension of co-existence, mutual implication, symmetry, and mutuality, which is typically hidden but constitutes the subject in a dialectical relationship with the individual pole.

Understanding the field dimension of the session requires having the necessary theoretical and technical tools to be open to phenomena within the dream spectrum, such as *reverie*, hallucinosis, dream fragments, and more. It may be beneficial for analysts to revisit the basic concepts of Gestalt theory, as it provides a foundation for understanding the field perspective.

3.3 Some clinical vignettes that exemplify my work in a field perspective

3.3.1 Concreteness

A colleague prepared a written text for supervision. She asked me to skip the first page of the patient's life story and start directly on the second. During the session she reported using practically only indirect speech for what the patient was talking about: a long list of grief and trauma. From the point of view of the field, it is not just about the session itself, but expands to include the supervisory session. In fact, I immediately wondered who/what could be the most important "character" of the session. The answer I gave myself was its *concreteness*, and therefore also not only the tendency of the patient, but (presumably) also of the analyst to stay on the level of concrete and material reality. The session, when read out aloud, usurps the place usually reserved for the anamnesis, which has *not* been read. In this way, however, *becoming the anamnesis* or taking its place itself assumes the same factual character. This suggests that there might be some kind of (temporary?) deafness of the analyst to what is happening in the analytic field in the here and now—the objectifying dimension that fatally inheres in the story pervades the theater of the setting and occludes it as a virtual space, where what is represented is the unconscious fantasy.

What I mean is that this type of *action rêverie* already anticipates and warns of the fact that the analyst (but also now an analyst and supervisor) may tend to read the analytic dialogue without transforming it into a dream; that is, without asking what the unconscious meaning of the analytic dialogue might be. Instead, they read it as a fact, as is normally done, I repeat, with the anamnestic part. The hypothesis is then confirmed by the actual reading of the text of the session. At this point, it would not be absurd to interpret the climate of mourning that pervades the entire session, determined by the story of a long series of traumatic memories, as a metaphor/dream of the loss of contact between analyst and patient.

This is an example of how a completely marginal event (the decision to leave the anamnesis aside) can be made significant to restore a sufficient level of emotional harmony. The underlying theoretical assumption is to see it as what is dreamed of by a *field alpha function*, which comes into play both in the session with the patient and in supervision. Then, note the paradoxical nature of the gesture of skipping the first page of the text. It expresses both a suggestion (on the conscious level) to put aside history and concreteness—Bion would speak of listening without trying to remember anything—and diagnoses with extreme precision that when the place where we normally find the anamnesis is replaced by the text of the analytic conversation, it is precisely something that (on the unconscious level) is *not* happening. In other words, by virtue of its assumption of the characteristics of the anamnesis, the analytical conversation remains factual and concrete in the same way. A sort of split seems to have crept open between theory and practice, a split that the field is unconsciously trying to repair through a *rêverie in action*.

Obviously, I repeat, the last level to consider would be the one concerning the supervision session itself. Even the supervisor should ask themself if they are not sinking into the sea of objectivity.

3.3.2 Laura or Mario?

Laura told her analyst that she was angry that Mario did not invite her to his party. The analyst speculated that Mario may not have invited her because in fact she always tends to decline such invitations. In this way, the analyst justified Mario by making a logical hypothesis, in accordance with Laura's story. In other words, the analyst confronted the patient by highlighting her contradictory behavior. In supervision, I speculated that in the face of such an interpretation, Laura may have felt as though she were being accused or reflected in a mirror which reveals to her that she is sullied—that is, that she does not deserve to be invited, or that there is something wrong with her.

However, in expressing this hypothesis to my colleague, I mistakenly used Laura's name instead of Mario's ("Laura may not have invited her because…"). It is as if I had said, "In reality, you 'justified' not Mario but Laura; you did not accuse her but supported her." Nor does it matter what the explicit meaning was of what the analyst said to Laura, and that indeed could again "justify" my comment. What counts more is my/our profound perception obtained through a hallucinosis that more accurately records what Laura's true experience of feeling recognized might have been, and not the other way around. So I think, to my great surprise, that it is as if it were I (or rather, "I" as a simple character-spokesperson of the unconscious "we") who recognized that, on the whole, the analyst (again, the analyst + Laura reunited into a third mind) had really managed to take Laura's point of view, that is, to contain Laura (or the Laura + analyst group-of-two), and to share her *(their)* fear *(true, real, justified)* that the others had laughed *(laugh)* at her; or rather, that this can occur in the analytic relationship *(from the analyst to the patient and vice versa)*.

As we can see, the reading changes completely. It is no longer a question of showing Laura that she undermines herself (or the colleague that he undermines his own interpretations by mistake), but of realizing that there is actually a sense of fear in the air (for which she does not go to parties); that this feeling blocks the relationship and does not allow it to evolve, and that this is what the analyst must take charge of after having interpreted it.

In fact, attuning to the fear that colors the therapeutic relationship is already a way to reduce it. Perhaps new reciprocal invitations will arrive and perhaps this time they will no longer be declined. My (*our*) unconscious reading, which significantly implies the emotion of surprise, what in the given context signals the integration of a split, somehow corrects my (*our*) conscious reading of a more rational and routine pattern.

A further step would be to think of the same fear of judgment as being also inherent in the meta-level of the supervisory relationship, and therefore in myself and the analyst who brought the case. I mean that, as in a continuous game of mirrors (or in an inexorable infecting each other with the same virus), the red thread of the same affection (here: fear) colors the relationship between Mario and Laura, between Laura and the analyst, and finally between the analyst and the supervisor. The method for deducing one from the other is always to start from the experience undergone in the actuality of the meeting. At the same time, my hallucinosis informs me that we might also be quite capable of containing our fears.

3.3.3 Veterinary medicine

A. begins the session by saying that her cat is not well and she had to take him to the vet. Then, she asks why she cannot hear the dog that the analyst usually keeps in the room: maybe it is not well? Finally, she says she has given up on the idea of studying psychology and is thinking of veterinary medicine instead. She points out that with animals everything is "physiological" and there is no problem of having to interpret things. And that, she adds, makes her think she would be a great vet, without being afraid of failure.

Her reasoning clearly implies that there is too much anxiety in the air. The causes could be an excessive desire to understand things from the point of view of psychoanalytic theories, and an insufficient ability to empathize with the more "animal" aspects of the relationship. All analysts should study veterinary medicine, yet "Everyone wants to be a psychologist," A. comments, "nobody wants to be a veterinarian."

It is easy to grasp the unconscious level of the text if before A.'s story we put "I dreamed that...," or "I'm dreaming that...," or better still "*We* are dreaming that... the cat is not well and we had to take it to the vet," and so on.

3.3.4 A Nutella *diet*

A., a patient, says that when she was a child everyone at home had to follow a very strict diet that left little room for chips, sausages, sweets, *Nutella*, hamburgers, spaghetti bolognaise, or ice cream. You had to be ultra-healthy. Every calorie was counted. In her teens she started having problems with anorexia, and the issue has never completely gone away.

A. is obviously also describing the dietary regimen that the patient and analyst have prescribed for themselves in analysis, and which seems to aim at achieving top performance, which implies giving up tastier things. The analyst emphasizes the patient's hatred of herself. However, in this way, between the lines, the analyst reminds her of her madness. The analyst fails to consider that the whole question of "diets" could be a true representation of the types of truth-dishes (food for the mind, according to Bion, or emotional attunement) that they allow themselves to consume. In other words, both seem to suffer from a psychic diet that does not leave enough room for pleasure and play (for "tastier" things). It is also interesting to note that in the Middle Ages, "diet" as a "space of a day" also stood for a "meeting" or "assembly."

3.4 How a field perspective in therapy provides orientation and support for both the analyst and the patient

In the context of therapeutic action, there exists a profound interplay of mutual recognition, as elucidated by Hegel (1807/2018) in his seminal work, *Phenomenology of the Spirit*. At its core, this perspective establishes a new bond—a bond that transcends any other structural framework and is essentially rooted in love. Meltzer (1986) aptly characterizes this bond as an aesthetic conflict, encompassing the child's anxious questioning of the mother's true intentions. It is vital to recognize that this conflict pertains not only to the patient's yearning for love and acknowledgment from the analyst but also to *the analyst's own desire to be recognized and loved by the patient.*

Within every analytic encounter, the intricate dynamics of the love bond unfold, with both the joys and perils that accompany it. At the deepest and most unconscious level, no asymmetry can exist in this bond. If anything, the asymmetry inherent in the analytical process serves as a foundation for the transformative experiences that can truly be described as the profound sensation of being loved.

Consequently, as succinctly summarized by Ogden (2019), we find ourselves traversing a realm that is less concerned with an epistemological paradigm centered on knowledge and more deeply embedded within an ontological paradigm of being and becoming. This shift in perspective facilitates our understanding of why Bion and FT both emphasize the significance of transformations, such as the dynamic changes in emotional field configurations or the couple's basic assumptions, as opposed to solely relying on the weaving of causal links between past and present based on historical reconstructions.

When we bear in mind that the essence of this process revolves around recognition—interpreted here as "at-one-ment" or reconciliation, following Bion—it becomes easier for us to grasp the fundamental principle of interpreting emotions as co-created phenomena. Viewing emotions through the lens of a session interpreted as a dream, one realizes, for example, that the fear or anger experienced by one party is inevitably intertwined with the fear or anger experienced by the other. In the depths of this intertwining, the patient who feels unrecognized may inadvertently reject the analyst, who, on a narcissistic level, can end up feeling humiliated, and vice versa.

It is crucial to emphasize that the reference to the theorization of therapeutic action in analysis and the concept of recognition-reconciliation, which lies at the heart of love relationships (Civitarese, 2022a), should not be regarded as generic or "romantic." On the contrary, it serves as a poignant reminder of the inherent truth that the inevitable backdrop to love is marked by the presence of hatred (Klein) or the potential for "destruction" (Winnicott, 1969; Civitarese, 2022b).

3.5 Criticism addressed at FT and the ethical refoundation of psychoanalysis

Lastly, I would like to address a recent incident where I encountered severe criticism of FT. This episode highlights the pressing need for an ethical re-foundation of psychoanalysis, one that encompasses both theory and technique. Such a re-foundation should be grounded in a metapsychology based on an ontology of the "We" (in the vein of Jean-Luc Nancy (2000), for instance), and it should save us from both a suspicious attitude in clinical work and the ongoing religious wars among analysts. I firmly believe that this approach will enhance the value of psychoanalysis as a therapeutic modality, as a theory of the psyche, and as a research method.

In much the same way as the Japanese soldiers who continued to fight in the forests after the Second World War, unaware that the war had ended, there are still analysts whose sole mission seems to be to excommunicate any new thought that emerges. This frequently occurs in the case of the FT, with statements such as, "But reality is important!" or "Where is the subject heading?" and "What about child sexuality?" (with the underlying message being: If you do not believe in the immaculate conception or the sacrament of the Eucharist, you are an infidel).

Often, such behavior is driven by a desire for a fleeting moment of fame beyond their immediate circles, which they may struggle to achieve just on the strength of their ideas alone. On the one hand, those who launch anathemas inadvertently validate the originality of what they seek to destroy, so to speak; on the other, they adhere to a criterion expressed long ago by Bion: "Here is something I don't understand—I'll kill it" (1990, p. 28). In this way, they perpetuate the unfortunate image of a community which, despite its denials, sometimes gives the impression of having more in common with a cult, with a bureaucratic and hierarchical power structure, albeit a very small one.

Regrettably, the problem goes all the way back to Freud himself and the establishment of the secret committee of the ring in 1912, along with the expulsion of Jung and other "heretics" (Civitarese, 2022c). Psychoanalysis has never fully freed itself from this kind of original sin and, as a result, it continues to bear the traces of a religious sect, in addition to functioning as a university and a professional order. Those who truly care about our discipline should strive to eradicate this "religious" framework that invariably infiltrates and distorts both the institutional and scientific life of our discipline.

Another subtler reason that contributes to the debasement of psychoanalysis is the "religious" characterization of the unconscious as the dwelling place of evil. Freud's unconscious is often portrayed as the "evil other" (Terman, 2014), a "cauldron full of seething excitations" (Freud, 1933/1950b, p. 73), or "a mob, eager for enjoyment and destruction" (Freud, 1932/1950a, p. 221), from which springs forth the "immorality of dreams" (Freud, 1900/2001, p. 620)—visions that form the basis of what Ricoeur (1970) aptly termed a "hermeneutics of suspicion."

Intervening on the issue of psychoanalytic controversies, Paul Denis (2023) argues that

> It is obvious that the international psychoanalytic movement is not one of those "organized groups" of which Freud speaks in *Group Psychology and the Analysis of the Ego*, and which are the Church and the Army. Furthermore, Freud's work itself is neither the Gospel nor the Torah, and it is also clear that his own itinerary encouraged us to develop psychoanalysis and to innovate. The difficulty, however, is to remain exactly within the field of psychoanalysis. Many innovations have "drifted" towards practices and theories that have lost all psychoanalytic specificity.
>
> (Denis, 2023, pp. 165–166)

In his critique, Denis caricatures theories on a new interpretation of sublimation (Laplanche & Pontalis, 1988, p. 433: "one of the lacunae in psychoanalytic thought"), which I have extensively explored in numerous articles and books published in prestigious peer-reviewed journals (Civitarese, 2014, 2016a, 2018a, 2018b, 2022d). He goes on associating me and the group of "Bionians" with an alleged loss of specificity. Denis also places me and like-minded colleagues in Dante's circle, where the "culprits" of Jungianism, Adlerism, Kohut's self psychology, and later Lacan are found. This characterization lacks fairness and respect, particularly within the frame of an initiative that should have promoted a constructive exchange of ideas. Rather than engaging in a serious debate, such criticism aims to dismiss alternative perspectives, resembling a war of religions.

Interestingly, Denis fails to connect the dots when he recalls Lebovici's account of someone in the British Society referring to Winnicott as a murderer ("Here comes the assassin"). Yet, in his list of innovators turned dissidents, he includes Melanie Klein, Fromm, and even Freud himself for introducing the death drive, contradicting his previous ideas.

This situation reminds me of Machado de Assis's *The Psychiatrist*, a story much loved by Borges, where Dr. Simão Bacamarte, an alienist, admits all the villagers to the asylum one by one. However, I won't spoil the epilogue. Denis acknowledges the absurdity of virtually banning the most significant authors of psychoanalysis, but he fails to see the contradiction in his own actions when he does the same with me and those who share my views.

This is not the first time Paul Denis has engaged in such behavior. In the past, I have already addressed this type of conduct in the *Revue Française de Psychanalyse*:

> The "bit of shame' (*ipse dixit*) does not prevent him [PD] from defining the model I present as "noumenal psychoanalysis and non-psychoanalytic psychology" (*sic*). In my humble opinion, this means arrogating to oneself the right to decide what is psychoanalysis and what is not, effectively excluding most contemporary psychoanalysis and denying the possibility, as should be normal for a scientific discipline, that new paradigms can emerge, which is an ideological attitude, and not even a well-disguised one.
>
> (Civitarese, 2018a, p. 1346)

Unfortunately, it seems that this author continues to exhibit the same pattern. But I am appalled by a psychoanalysis that claims the right to judge and condemn what it perceives as a threat to its established framework. This inherently ideological and violent stance, which seeks to crush the opponent or burn the heretic at the stake, is no longer acceptable in our field, nor any other. Such prevaricating behavior poses a significant threat to the survival of psychoanalysis as a recognized discipline and a serious tool for treating mental illness in society.

However, in the end, as I patiently and resignedly await the next conflict, I must express my gratitude to Denis for providing me with an opportunity to clarify why I have long argued, in numerous articles, that psychoanalysis is in need of an ethical reformation. It is truly ironic, in a sublime sense, that Denis's anathema has subtly found its way into a section of the *IJP* dedicated, as Allison (2023, p. 147) writes, to "foster productive discussions about our scientific differences" (!) and how such discussions can be conducted in a civil and respectful manner.

Curiously, upon reading the various essays, it becomes evident how everything revolves around the notion of truth—a topic that Jay Greenberg kindly asked me to discuss a few years ago in the *Psychoanalytic Quarterly* (Civitarese, 2016b). Perhaps there is no concept more problematic throughout human history than truth itself. The misunderstanding I wish to address is the belief that since identifying an absolute truth is impossible, the only alternative is to completely abandon the pursuit of truth. This misconception often leads to the contemporary understanding of truth as "anything goes." However, this is not the case. The mistake lies in assuming that truth, for us, is synonymous with a positive and expressible truth that can be encapsulated in verbal concepts. Yet, we are aware that a completely abstract truth devoid of body, meaning, or affect does not exist—it is inherently ineffable and inexpressible.

Does this imply that these truths lack a solid foundation? No, it simply means that we can only perceive their foundations up to a certain point before resigning ourselves to the idea that just because they are inaccessible to us does not mean they do not exist (see Braver, 2014 for more on this). They do exist, and significantly so! The sole criterion remaining to us is, in a way, "tautological" (just like with art: What is the definition of art if not what a society deems it to be at a given time?). Despite lacking alternatives, we must make do with this criterion. Upon reflection, even the truths of science lack a basis beyond the consensus achieved within the ideal community of researchers—a consensus that is more or less influenced by these elusive foundations. Needless to say, the degree of consensus can only be the outcome of the diverse practices embraced by the community itself to engage in the pursuit of truth. Consequently, it would be naive to assume that definitive debates can be designed to resolve conflicts within the field of psychoanalysis once and for all. Similarly, I find it oversimplified to bemoan the absence of debate (often accompanied by an animosity that forebodes no good). In a way, debate is always present within psychoanalysis and between psychoanalysis and other disciplines, whether we acknowledge it or not.

The existence of constant debate, even when it appears to be absent, does not imply that it is impossible to enhance the rules of the truth-seeking game, or, rather, the diverse games that compose it. One approach to achieve this is through the publication of a series of papers on the subject in a specialized journal. Permit me to propose a modest suggestion: It would be valuable to introduce the main models acknowledged in the international psychoanalytic community through a systematic comparative method, starting from the first year of courses in psychoanalytic institutions. These models are not numerous, they can be counted on one hand, just as it is easy to adopt a perspective that can account for continuities, discontinuities, and identify what is the driving force behind change. By doing so, upcoming analysts would naturally become familiar with both differences and similarities, just as one naturally breathes. They would acquire the ability to engage in respectful dialogue with others and become more conscious of their approach to patients and the underlying reasons for it. There would no longer be a need to deny the existence of others in order to assert oneself. An ethic of recognition should guide not only analytic treatment but also the proper functioning of the institution.

It also happens sometimes that serious debate is altogether avoided because of the ghost of orthodoxy hovering in the room. In other instances, even legitimate and accurate criticism is wrongly interpreted as excommunication, resulting in the same inhibition of any criticism and the acceptance of anything without question.

I have mentioned here my recent disagreements with D. Orange, Denis, and I could add less recently with Sandler (Civitarese, 2015), to highlight what is really at stake with FT. It is not merely a model that introduces innovations while leaving the mainstream undisturbed. On the contrary, I believe it involves transforming the game itself, hopefully for the better. The shift from an I/You split to a We implies that the analyst trusts in the collective unconscious effort to transform raw emotional experiences into meaningful imagery. In doing so, the analyst also trusts themself and the patient, while consciously assuming responsibility (without taking the "blame," which would be an entirely different matter) for the authenticity of what unfolds.

In my opinion, this attitude is inherently therapeutic. As I have emphasized repeatedly, it presents a golden opportunity to move away from the paranoid climate in treatment, within psychoanalytic institutions, and often within scientific debates. Finally, we can liberate ourselves from a "confessional" psychoanalysis, one based on an official doctrine, and embrace the best aspects of Freud's legacy. These revolve around psychoanalysis as a critical theory, with dreamwork, but reinterpreted as the poetic function of the mind, serving as both the key concept for understanding the psyche and the paradigmatic principle for clinical practice.

Notes

1 In daring to make this argument (Civitarese, 2021b, 2021c), my paper was criticized by D. Orange (2021), who was surprisingly vitriolic in her response, using phrases such as "sneaky charm" and other questionable remarks. In my humble opinion, for someone who claims to be an "intersubjectivist," her comment shows a glaring lack of scholarly rigor. It is reminiscent of Andersen's famous fairy tale, *The Emperor's New Clothes*, in which the king (or queen) becomes enraged when confronted with the truth that he or she is actually naked, despite believing otherwise.
2 Cf. Abram and Hinshelwood (2018, p. 124): "Edward Glover, and Elizabeth Zetzel [...] both referred to Klein's theory of 'evil' as equivalent to the religious belief in 'original sin'.".
3 These critics could be responded to with the same irony as Ernest Jones when he writes

> the Viennese would reproach us with estimating the early phantasy life too highly at the expense of external reality. And we should answer that there is no danger of any analysts neglecting external reality, whereas it is always possible for them to underestimate Freud's doctrine of the importance of psychical reality.
>
> (Jones, 1935, p. 273)

References

Abram, J., & Hinshelwood, R. D. (2018). *The clinical paradigms of Melanie Klein and Donald Winnicott*. Routledge.

Allison, E. (2023). Debating well: Why don't we, and how can we? *International Journal of Psychoanalysis*, *104*, 147–152.

Baranger, W., & Baranger, M. (2008). The analytic situation as a dynamic field. *International Journal of Psycho-Analysis*, *89*, 795–826. (Original work published 1961–62).

Bion, W. R. (1961). *Experiences in groups and other papers*. Tavistock.

Bion, W. R. (1965). *Transformations*. Basic Books.

Bion, W. R. (1990). *Brazilian lectures*. Karnac.

Bion, W. R., & Rickman, J. (1943). Intra-group tensions in therapy—Their study as the task of the group. *The Lancet*, *242*, 678–681.

Braver, L. (2014). *Groundless grounds: A study of Wittgenstein and Heidegger*. MIT Press.

Civitarese, G. (2012). *Losing your head: Abjection, aesthetic conflict and psychoanalytic criticism*. Rowman & Littlefield.

Civitarese, G. (2014). Bion and the sublime: The origins of an aesthetic paradigm. *International Journal of Psychoanalysis*, *95*, 1059–1086.

Civitarese, G. (2015). Styles of criticism: Answering comments by Florence Guignard, Helmut Hinz and Paulo Sandler on "Transformations in hallucinosis and the receptivity of the analyst". *International Journal of Psychoanalysis, 96*, 1683–1690.

Civitarese, G. (2016a). On sublimation. *International Journal of Psychoanalysis, 97*, 1369–1392.

Civitarese, G. (2016b). Truth as immediacy and unison: A new common ground in psychoanalysis? Commentary on essays addressing "Is truth relevant?" *Psychoanalytic Quarterly, 85*, 449–501.

Civitarese, G. (2018a). Traduire l'expérience: le concept de transformation chez Bion et dans la théorie post-bionienne du champ analytique. *Revue française de psychanalyse, 82*, 1327–1386.

Civitarese, G. (2018b). *Sublime subjects: Aesthetic experience and intersubjectivity in psychoanalysis.* Routledge.

Civitarese, G. (2020a). *L'ora della nascita. Psicoanalisi del sublime e arte contemporanea.* Jaca Book.

Civitarese, G. (2020b). Regression in the analytic field. *Revue Roumaine de Psychanalyse, 13*, 17–41.

Civitarese, G. (2021a). Experiences in groups as a key to "late" Bion. *International Journal of Psychoanalysis, 102*, 1071–1096.

Civitarese, G. (2021b). Intersubjectivity and analytic field theory. *Journal of the American Psychoanalytic Association, 69*, 853–893.

Civitarese, G. (2021c). Symmetry and asymmetry in the analytic process: Reply to commentaries. *Journal of the American Psychoanalytic Association, 69*, 921–935.

Civitarese, G. (2022a). *Sull'arroganza. Saggio di psicoanalisi.* Jaca Book.

Civitarese, G. (2022b). Recognition in Winnicott's "The use of an object and relating through identifications" (in press).

Civitarese, G. (2022c). Not a literal translation... In fact, rather performative—A review of *Translation/Transformation: 100 Years of the International Journal of Psychoanalysis* edited by D. Birksted-Breen, London, Routledge, 2021, pp. 337. *International Journal of Psychoanalysis, 103*, 692–702.

Civitarese, G. (2022d). The identity of the terrible and happiness: On the sublime in art and psychoanalysis. *Fort Da, 28*, 7–31.

Denis, P. (2023). Psychoanalysis, model or truth. *International Journal of Psychoanalysis, 104*, 165–167.

Elliott, A., & Prager J. (2015). *The Routledge handbook of psychoanalysis in the social sciences and humanities.* Routledge.

Freud, S. (1950a). My contact with Josef Popper-Lynkeus. In J. Strachey (Ed.), *The standard edition of the complete psychological works of Sigmund Freud Vol. XXII* (pp. 217–224). Hogarth Press. (Original work published 1932).

Freud, S. (1950b). New introductory lectures on psycho-analysis. In J. Strachey (Ed.), *The standard edition of the complete psychological works of Sigmund Freud Vol. XXII* (pp. 1–182). Hogarth Press. (Original work published 1933).

Freud, S. (2001). *The standard edition of the complete psychological works of Sigmund Freud Vol. IV: The interpretation of dreams (first part),* J. Strachey (Ed.). Vintage. (Original work published 1900).

Hegel, G. W. H. (2018). *The phenomenology of spirit.* Cambridge University Press. (Original work published 1807).

Heidegger, M. (1977). Letter on humanism. In D. Farrell Krell (Ed.), *Basic writings*. Harper & Row. http://timothyquigley.net/cont/heidegger-lh.pdf (Original work published 1949).

Jones, E. (1935). Early female sexuality. *International Journal of Psychoanalysis, 16,* 263–273.

Kernberg, O. F. (2011). Divergent contemporary trends in psychoanalytic theory. *The Psychoanalytic Review, 98*(5), 633–666.

Laplanche, J., & Pontalis, J. B. (1988). *The language of psychoanalysis.* Karnac.

Meltzer, D. (1984). *Dream-life: A re-examination of the psycho-analytical theory and technique.* Clunie Press.

Meltzer, D. (1986). *Studies in extended metapsychology: Clinical applications of Bion's ideas.* The Harris Meltzer Trust.

Nancy, J.-L. (2000). *Being singular plural.* Stanford University Press.

Ogden, T. H. (2005). *This art of psychoanalysis: Dreaming undreamt dreams and interrupted cries.* Routledge.

Ogden, T. H. (2019). Ontological psychoanalysis or "What do you want to be when you grow up?". *Psychoanalytic Quarterly, 88,* 661–684.

Orange, D. M. (2021). Commentary on Civitarese. *Journal of the American Psychoanalytic Association, 69,* 895–907.

Ricoeur, P. (1970). *Freud and philosophy: An essay on interpretation.* Yale University Press.

Seligman, S. (2017). *Relationships in development: Infancy, intersubjectivity, and attachment.* Routledge.

Terman, D. M. (2014). Self psychology as a shift away from the paranoid strain in classical analytic theory. *Journal of the American Psychoanalytic Association, 62,* 1005–1024.

Winnicott, D. W. (1969). The use of an object. *International Journal of Psychoanalysis, 50,* 711–716.

Chapter 4

Field perspective in Gestalt therapy

Is a dialogue possible with post-Bionian psychoanalysis?

Jean-Marie Robine

More than 35 years later, I still remember my pleasure when I discovered the translation of the famous article "La situación analítica como campo dinámico," by Madeleine and Willy Baranger, in the *Revue Française de Psychanalyse* (June 1985). Originally published in 1961, the article was republished for wider distribution in 1969.

Why this pleasure? Simply because in 1936, Frederick Perls, the psychoanalyst who would later become the main founder of Gestalt therapy, gave a lecture at the International Congress of Psychoanalysis in Marienbad. The history of psychoanalysis will have remembered Lacan's lecture above all, but Perls was already insisting in his lecture on the need for psychoanalysis to open up to the contributions of Gestalt theory and of the Gestalt psychology of Kohler, Koffka, and Wertheimer, and their field theory. His contribution was badly received by the orthodoxy of the time. It should be added, however, that Lacan, with his paper, which was nevertheless embedded within another paradigm, was hardly better received since history reports that Ernest Jones did not even let him finish his talk.

Perls took up and developed his lecture, giving rise to a book a few years later, *Ego, Hunger and Aggression* (1943), which, in its first edition, was subtitled "*A Revision of Freud's Theory and Method.*" Again, this text received very little resonance in psychoanalytic circles, such that in subsequent editions the subtitle disappeared. Perls's research, however, continued, and in 1951 the founding book of Gestalt therapy appeared: *Gestalt Therapy, Excitement and Growth in The Human Personality.* Here again, we find an invitation to take into account many of the contributions of Gestalt psychology and of field theory. Once again, except

DOI: 10.4324/9781003597308-5

for the American psychoanalysts that gravitated around the William Allison White Institute, with Erich Fromm, Karen Horney and several others, what was and still is so decried by the orthodoxy of old Europe— proposals that I consider as revolutionary—remain ignored.

A few decades later, thanks mostly to the impact of the article by the Barangers, certain currents of psychoanalysis "discovered" the field paradigm to which Gestalt therapy had been trying to open them ten, twenty, even fifty years earlier. Unfortunately, I have never had the opportunity to hear or read about psychoanalysis acknowledging or admitting any kind of debt to Gestalt therapy, which first introduced field theory into the field of psychotherapy. Rather, I have had the dismay to observe its ignorance, or even its disdain or contempt. Today, however, publications referring to a field theory are numerous in psychoanalysis, at least in certain countries such as Italy, Argentina, or the United States. I am delighted by this because, as Gary Yontef (1991), one of the deans of Gestalt therapy, pointed out, even if there are great divergences between different approaches to the field, it would be interesting to compile all that they have in common, as they would give us valuable information for a better understanding of this highly complex concept.

4.1 The field perspective of Gestalt therapy

Since its foundation in 1951, Gestalt therapy has been based on a field perspective, but the founders never speak of any "field" without specifying which field they are talking about. And it is always "the organism/ environment field." This means that the debates I have been able to attend or participate in for years to define the contours of "the field" do not make much sense, since it is not a question of an *entity* but of the singular *experience* of a subject inseparable from what makes up the environment for them.

Husserl had already insisted that "consciousness" is always consciousness OF something, and, therefore, that to speak only of "consciousness" would remain an abstraction. The same principle can be applied to the concept of field: "THE field" does not exist, only "the field of…"—the field of consciousness, the field of vision, the field of psychology, etc.

Gestalt therapy, therefore, speaks of the field constituted by a given organism and situation that constitutes its environment at a given moment:

> The environment of an organism is by no means something definite and static, but is continuously forming commensurably with the development of the organism and its activity. One could say that the environment emerges from the world through the being or actualization of the organism. Stated in a less prejudiced manner, an organism can exist only if it succeeds in finding in the world an adequate environment—in shaping an environment (for which, of course, the world must offer the opportunity).
>
> (Goldstein, 1934/1995, p. 85)

Our authors often come back to something that is much more than a nuance of language: we are OF a field and not IN a field. To say "in" a field is to consider the field as a space, an environment, a context or even a world, and the field becomes an entity. To say that I am "of the field" is to recognize belonging, inseparability, emergence, and even a possible differentiation. To illustrate this idea in a simplified way, it is easy to understand the difference when I say, quoting my own city: "I am OF Bordeaux" and "I am IN Bordeaux." The relationship I will have with my environment and my context will be very different in each case.

This could be an opportunity to also build on the difference, and even the opposition, formulated by Heidegger, between *place* and *site*: "The site is, for Heidegger, an open infinity whereas the place already has internal reference points and already presupposes an organization of space that the open precedes" (Maldiney, 2014, p. 42, my translation). And to speak of "site" cannot be separated from the idea of "*situ*ation"… I will have the opportunity to come back to this.

So, if what has been named by our founders—perhaps clumsily—as "organism/environment" is considered as an indissociable totality, the movements that unfold there are movements that will sometimes aim at indifferentiation, and sometimes at differentiation. These movements of the field are what Gestalt therapy calls "contacting" and the initial indifferentiation—the creative undifferentiation studied by Friedlander and dear to Perls—can be a working hypothesis at the beginning of any encounter.

Some of us prefer today to use another language and to speak, for example, of "person-life-space." I am not opposed to such a formulation because, in either case, we are not talking about a somehow *common* field but about the environment that is experienced by the person.

Some of the difficulties faced by Gestalt therapy today in dealing with the diversity of field perspectives that have gradually shaped the emergence of this epistemology have been noted by Frank Staemmler, a German Gestalt therapist (Staemmler, 2006):

- For Smuts, the founder of holism, "the multiple fields influence each other since they partially overlap";
- For Köhler, one of the fathers of Gestalt psychology and Gestalt theory, "the neurophysiological and psychological levels are linked by isomorphism";
- For Aron Gurwitsch, a philosopher who crosses phenomenology and Gestalt psychology, "we are dealing with the mutuality of the figure (theme) and the background (field)";
- For Lewin, "the phenomenal person and the phenomenal environment form a shared field in which their respective forces influence each other";
- For Perls and Goodman, "Body and environment cannot be separated since they are integral parts of the same unitary field" (Staemmler, 2006).

Given these wide differences in the use of the concept, it is not surprising that Staemmler uses the metaphor of the Tower of Babel, since specific meanings are sometimes denied and the term can be used interchangeably to refer to various experiences, sometimes even within the same text.

It is likely that I, in turn, will not escape certain contradictions in my remarks today: For more than 45 years, I have been agitated by the question of *the field*. With great, almost cyclical regularity, I have my "Eureka!" moment, where I feel I have finally understood what "field" is, only for it all to collapse a few months later, when I embark on a new direction, which again will all collapse after a few months or years. But I find reassurance in the words of the French philosopher Alain (1942, p. 947, my translation), when he wrote: "Ideas, even true ones, become false the moment we are satisfied with them."

If I try to see if there is a common denominator in these collapses in my personal edifice, I can find a constant: an implicit or explicit *spatiality*, a need to assign contours. That is to say, to think of the field as an entity, as an object or a quasi-object, to reify it in order to better define it, even if I would proclaim and teach that we do not approach the field as an entity. Still today, I am not sure I can escape from a representation free of spatiality, even if I approach it as a "point of view."

Even today—and I suspect that Bionians and post-Bionians do not escape it any more than Gestalt therapists do—when some consider, for example, that the field is constructed "between" the patient and the therapist, or that it occurs at the intersection of the projective identifications of the two protagonists, or that this is "in the field" or must be "brought into the field," we treat it as though there must be an "inside" and an "outside." In my theoretical choices, a field is not built "between" (patient and therapist) but the field *of each* is built "by" the presence of the patient and the therapist.

If I was one of the first in the French-speaking Gestalt community to try to deepen the reference to field theory, which was circulating among us more as a slogan than as a real perspective, it is because at that time, at the end of the 1980s, the question of the use of transference and countertransference in practice as well as in theorization was once again being raised. After having been tempted by the easy solution of repainting the surface of these psychoanalytical concepts to give them the fashionable colors required by Gestalt therapy, I quickly realized that I was thus avoiding making the epistemological leap to which the founders of Gestalt therapy were inviting us. And my reading of various psychoanalytical texts that claim a link with field theory confirms my impression. The simple fact of retaining the word "transference" to designate the essence of the therapeutic relationship, however it is defined, places the displacement and repetition of archaic patterns at the center of the therapeutic encounter.

Yet, as Malcolm Parlett, one of the pioneers in integrating Kurt Lewin's contribution into the theorization and practice of Gestalt therapy, points out:

> (...) it is the constellation of influences in the *present* field that "explains" present behavior. No particular special causal status is accorded to events in the past which, in many systems, are thought of as "determinants" of what is happening now.
>
> (Parlett, 1991, p. 71)

One of the most important consequences of field theory on the globality of Gestalt therapy theory is the "theory of self," elaborated by Perls and Goodman. Indeed, in our approach and unlike many others, including psychoanalytical ones, self is above all considered as an emergence of the field, created by the situation and all the more active when the field is difficult and requires creative adjustment capacities. When routines or repetitions are "sufficient" for the current contact, self is little or non-existent. This approach to self is the backbone of Gestalt therapy, whether it is to guide the process of the work, to elaborate an intrinsic diagnosis, to approach a developmental reading and, of course, to construct the meaning of what is happening in each encounter, both in the moment and over time.

4.2 Moreover, two concepts seem precious to me to qualify the choices I use to define the field, while remaining consistent with the essentials of Gestalt therapy theory

The first invites me to approach the theory of field as an *attitude*. On many occasions in our founding work, Gestalt therapy is presented as an attitude, i.e., a disposition of mind, a natural mode of presence marked by spontaneity and freedom. It is important for me to distinguish attitude from *posture*, a term that is unfortunately too often used when referring to the therapist's presence, but which designates a position that is unnatural, unaccustomed, unexpected, borrowed, and which can be close to immobility, or even to a simulacrum, as most dictionaries highlight.

The field—as an attitude—is to be aware, when I meet the other, that what he/she is here is not a monad, but an organism/environment field, an environment in which I find myself momentarily. Thus, my attitude is of uncertainty in terms of what defines him/her and what defines the impact that I can have on him/her. It is, therefore, to be open to exploration and astonishment. It means not knowing how he/she places me in his/her field. And at the same time, it means accepting my approaching him/her with the same uncertainties as to the impact that he/she will have on what I can call "my field." My reading of the works of Eugene Minkowski (1999) has opened me to a clinical interest in the *vague* and the *confused*: even if my patient's initial statement seems clear to me, welcoming it by making the choice of indifferentiation opens up a progressive differentiation that makes room for *epoché* and allows an attitude of openness to the novelty, to the unknown, and gets us both out of an excess of support from our archives. Because the field is an attitude of contemporaneity, there is no other field than of the now.

The second concept I like to use to talk about the field is that of *perspective*. In doing so, I am aware that I am not totally escaping a vocabulary that refers to spatiality, but it is mostly its aesthetic context that is important to me here. Indeed, "perspective" is more or less synonymous with "point of view." Thus, this concept shows how the glance is situated. Certainly, the landscape put in perspective in a painting exists as such only in connection with a given eye, and, for that eye, it is only a representation. Since it is only a representation, this means that it is the result of a certain work, of an aesthetic *act*, and not only of an aesthetic *experience*, which would remain sensitive and perceptual. And this perspective of the world, by modifying the proportions of the pictorial objects, transfers in the visual register what Lewin tried to express by his concept of "valence," the power of impact of such and such object of the field according to the emotional distance that it possesses or that is attributed to it.

What I am trying to express, perhaps clumsily, is that to try to define "field" otherwise than as a point of view, as an experience, risks making it an entity, or a quasi-entity. This means that at every moment what I say, what I feel, what I enact, the other is not only the recipient, but also the co-creator. This perspective reveals the extent to which we are inextricably linked and that my contours, my subjectivity, are stories that I like to tell myself, myths that I like to believe in, whereas what precedes, what comes first is *the situation*. More than one century ago, Bakhtin, the famous Russian theorist of language and literature, highlighted that "the statement is not the business only of the speaker but the result of his interaction with a listener whose reaction he integrates in advance" (quoted in Todorov, 1981, pp. 69–70, my translation). The other is, of course, both the individual being that I meet and the being that George Herbert Mead (1934) called "the Generalized Other." And Bakhtin was already opening up a fundamental way for us to inscribe psychotherapy in a field perspective when he insisted, in this same logic, that "it is not experience that organizes expression but it is, on the contrary, expression that organizes experience, that gives it a form for the first time and determines its direction" (Bakhtin, quoted in Todorov, 1981, my translation). Because what is expressed is what *ex-sists*, what stands outside and is addressed, if not perceived by the other. What Bakhtin exposes from language, I widen willingly to the whole of the activity, whether expressed or not, because, as the poet says magnificently:

> To exist, what does it mean? It means being outside, *sistere ex*. What is outside exists. What is inside does not exist [...]. That which does not exist *in-sists*. Insists on existing. All this small world pushes itself at the door of the big, real world. And it is the other who holds the key.
>
> (Tournier, 1967, pp. 128–129, my translation)

The Bionian and post-Bionian approaches are very interested in the dream, including in a broader sense than what common language calls "dream." Gestalt therapy has also been very interested in working with dreams and, if one of its approaches remains inscribed in an intrapsychic and individualistic paradigm, another one has opened the way to approach it from a field perspective. I am referring to the approach of Isadore From, one of the founding members of Gestalt therapy and my most influential trainer. He proposed listening to the dream *account*—which is obviously different from the dream—and to unfold it as a message addressed to the psychotherapist, allowing him/her to express what he/she had unconsciously retroflected or repressed during the previous session. Using this possibility as a springboard, it was then easy for me to extend it by considering that any dream narrative (whether the dream was from the day before or from twenty years ago or more) could constitute an appropriate container for telling the present moment, the contact with the therapist, the experience of the situation (I am not talking only about transference). Here again, if we are willing to consider that what is primary is the situation, it becomes obvious that the dream *narrative* is an emergence from the field, a creation of the situation.

A provocative expression used by our founders has remained in the shadows for half a century. When they spoke of the "id," this concept forged by Groddeck and taken up by Freud, which is used to speak of desires, needs, drives, and appetites, they spoke of the "id of the situation." The id was no longer defined as the "reservoir of drives" dear to Freudian psychoanalysis, but was approached as a given that emanates from the situation.

Once again, it is the concept of situation that imposes itself as a figure in my eyes. When I read certain parts of the writings of theoreticians of the analytic field, as well as those of some Gestalt therapists, I sometimes have the impression that what they call "field" is what I would more readily call "situation," in the wake of philosophers, sociologists, and essayists such as Dewey, Goffman and the Chicago School, Sartre, Merleau-Ponty, Barwise, Randall Collins, Fonagy, and many others. My choice, as I outlined above, is to try to avoid making the "field" an entity, and the concept of situation can contribute to this.

Even if the conception of the field developed by Gestalt therapy sometimes diverges from the one initiated by Kurt Lewin, he repeatedly insists on the difference between field and situation through various formulations:

> (…) the field exists for the individual in question at that particular time. (…) Since the field is different for every individual, the situation as characterized by physics or sociology, which is the same for everybody, cannot be substituted for it.
>
> (Lewin, 1952, p. 240)

> The therapeutic device, whatever it is, is first and foremost a certain type of situation. To be conscious of how the situation impacts each of the protagonists is also a way to better understand how we may have been impacted by certain situations throughout our history. To be conscious of how we can be creators or co-creators of situations in the here-and-now is also a way to restore or strengthen our abilities for creative adjustment.
>
> (Robine, 2015, p. 242)

To live and to act is to deal with a situation: Each individual does not limit themselves to analyzing the situation in which they find themself, but really constitutes it. They select and cut out the relevant elements to constitute a situation that will form the context of their action. In the field of each individual, they will perceive possibilities as well as constraints, both implicit and explicit.

I call "situation" the perception and synthetic organization of elements of the field of all the protagonists involved, a perception that structures the context of their encounter, gives it meaning, and implicitly defines the modalities of their interaction. It is a space constructed and limited by each of the actors who, simultaneously, are constructed by it and by the definition they give of it.

To articulate the concept of field with that of situation, I would say that the situation is created by the intersection and interaction of the fields of each of the protagonists involved. The immediate and selective perception by each of the actors of the implicit organization of their field organizes the situation. From the field of the protagonists emerge affordances (Gibson) and valences (Lewin) that combine to constitute the situation. As Lewin wrote: "In psychology, we deal with situational units" (Lewin, 1952, p. 52).

It therefore seems to me necessary to associate the concept of situation with the field perspective, but to clearly differentiate their uses (Robine, 2001).

References

Alain (1942). *Vigiles de l'esprit.* Éditions Gallimard.

Goldstein, K. (1995). *The organism.* Zone Books. (Original work published 1934 in German).

Lewin, K. (1952). *Field theory in social science* (edited by D. Cartwright). Tavistock Publications.

Maldiney, H. (2014). Les philosophies de la force. *L'ouvert, 7,* 41–59.

Mead, G.H. (1934). *Mind, self and society,* University of Chicago Press.

Minkowski, E. (1999). *Traité de psychopathologie.* Les Empêcheurs de penser en rond/ Synthélabo. (Original work published 1966).

Parlett, M. (1991). Reflections on field theory. *British Gestalt Journal, 1*(2), 68–91.

Robine, J.-M. (2001). From field to situation. In J.-M. Robine (Ed.), *Contact and relationship in a field perspective* (pp. 95–107). L'Exprimerie. (Reprinted in *On the occasion of another,* by J.-M. Robine, 2011, Gestalt Journal Press).

Robine, J.-M. (2015). The man of the situation. In *Social change begins with two.* Istituto di Gestalt HCC—Gestalt Therapy Book Series. (Original work published 2015 in French).

Staemmler, F. (2006). A Babylonian confusion? On the uses and meanings of the term "field". *The British Gestalt Journal, 15*(2), 64–83.

Todorov, T. (1981). *Mikhaïl Bakhtine, le principe dialogique.* Le seuil.

Tournier, M. (1967). *Vendredi ou les limbes du pacifique.* Gallimard-Folio.

Yontef, G. (1991). Introduction to field theory. In *Awareness, dialogue and process* (pp. 283–323). Gestalt Journal Press.

Chapter 5

"Where everything shivers and speaks"

Precious fragments of experience

Michela Gecele

Why a field perspective in therapy? And why do we find it today in different approaches to psychotherapy?

The field perspective has been around for decades, informing and shaping, to varying degrees, the theorization of therapy models of a psychoanalytic or humanistic matrix. Yet today it is attracting an increasing, and unprecedented, consensus, in both the theory and the practice of therapy. A possible explanation for this can be found in the social issues prevalent today, which make working within a field perspective useful and beneficial. Here I refer to the fragmentation witnessed in the construction of social groups, roles, and personal identity, but also in personal and collective memory, which has become, all too often, parcellated, brief, and elusive (Gecele, 2021).

Let us take a step back in time. In a somewhat approximate and simplified way, two watersheds can be considered to mark the history of psychotherapy theory and practice—the relational turn and the field perspective "revolution."

In the early days of psychotherapy and psychoanalysis, the social task, or common expectation, for every person was to adjust and be inserted into a well-defined context, with similarly well-defined roles. That continued to be the case, in part at least, until the 1950s/1960s, when humanistic therapies emerged and the balance between society and the individual started to shift in favor of the individual and the importance of personal expression and growth.

A fine line which, in just a short space of time, led to what Lasch (1979), two decades later, would label a "culture of narcissism," where the chief issue was no longer that of differentiating, asserting, and being oneself, but of how to create connections, ties, and relationships in a

DOI: 10.4324/9781003597308-6

world broken up into discrete individuals (Salonia, 1999). This set the stage for a relational turn in therapy. A turn that pivoted on the understanding that any possibility for therapy and change primarily came through the construction of a supportive relationship.

The more recent field perspective "revolution" is instead linked to the growing fragmentation of the social fabric and the lack of, and consequent need for, meaning, containment, and memory for the experiences people go through. Many life events and experiences remain cut off from our social and personal narratives, forming a surplus of potential that eludes our grasp and constantly risks becoming a void.

> We live in a complex world. As much as we try to broaden our awareness, too many stimuli bombard us at every instant. Figures do not have the time they need to emerge and take shape, resulting in "a false integration of experience." Creative adjustment today is primarily a matter of selection. It is about not losing the sense of direction that feeling needs and listening to the body give. It is about maintaining the drive of relational intentionality, the ability to perceive distinctions and orient oneself, the support of pathways, roles, and belonging. All this to give order to the disorder of chaos, to the complexity of the environment. A surplus of stimuli can lower the capacity/possibility of being present in relationships and the experience of emotions. Thus everything that can give the necessary support for distinguishing and deciphering those stimuli becomes fundamental for constructing a web of sense, meaning, and connection.
>
> (Gecele, 2021, p. 29)

On the other hand, what we call "field" is present in social and relational life—in life *tout court*—well before it is in therapy. Bearing this in mind gives us the key to seeing how the field actualizes itself in every aspect and in every instant of our lives. A sort of parallel reality almost, which gives depth and complexity, but also meaning and clarity to the simplified, mechanical reality that we call "daily life." It is not a key that comes immediately, nor easily, as it conflicts with and strikes at the very root of a foundational perspective of our contemporary Western world, built on the prevalence and absoluteness of the concept of the individual, where naked subjectivity is the sole seat of experience.

As concerns not the field perspective, but fields themselves as sets of forces, the idea we are working with here is that they are always actually present, whether theorized or not. Fields exist. At all times and in all situations, manifold forces are at work, manifold factors contribute to determining the situation itself—from trivial, inanimate things, like a table, a couch, a bed, or other furnishings in a room, to the mood and hormonal balance of every person present, through to the values of a society, imaginary worlds, events that have occurred, and the people who are absent but nevertheless with us.

Everything has an influence on everything in the surrounds. Even the weather, or the cyclical alternation of day and night, which connects with our biological rhythms and chronobiology. Focusing just on people and bodies, experiments show how the perception of the sweat of somebody who has been exercising causes hormonal and secretional changes in the people nearby, as though they, too, had been exercising (Brennan, 2004; Rubin et al., 2012).

In short, any presence, any experience, perception, or sensation radiates all around, co-determining other experiences. This means that there is always a multitude and complexity of factors at work in any situation, in any life event. Even in "trivial" day-to-day situations, there are so many factors at work that we could not possibly name them all. No element of a setting or of an experience is neutral. In one way or another, they always have an effect—that is what gives the field its forces. In each and every situation, there is a field of forces acting on and connecting people.

We are therefore working on two different levels here. One level is the field, or reality; the other level is the field perspective, or the theorization of the field and the use of the theory in therapy.

> The concept of field has been used in psychotherapy in a variety of ways by different authors, but also in a variety of ways by the same authors at different times, both in Gestalt therapy and in other approaches.
>
> (Francesetti & Roubal, 2020, pp. 114–115)

Some authors are in line with the original understanding of Kurt Lewin (1951) and suggest that everyone has a specific organism/environment field (i.e., Robine, 2015). Other authors are more in line with the original understanding of Jan Smuts (1926) and consider the focus to be placed on the whole that all people engaged in a common situation perceive, and which influences them all.

A central issue in the history of Western philosophy, which was taken up in psychotherapy, is the problematic of contact between individuals, the possibilities for it and the ways it can occur. The constructed and artificial primacy of the individual renders it difficult to explain the connections that make up life.

If there is nothing that connects us *a priori*, how can we communicate and live together? Or if something of such a kind exists, does it come before the individual? Or does it emerge together with the individual? If so, does it survive the individual? Is it the sum of the parts or is it something more? Or something less? Or is it simply something else? And how do we relate to it—we who perceive ourselves as individuals?

Philosophy, and later psychology, has offered a multitude of answers to these questions. We will not retrace them here, however, but simply note how the underlying issues have become central in the field of neuroscience. What I wish to argue here is that the concept of field (with all its manifold facets, derivations, and meanings) gives a possible answer to these questions. Or rather, it could be said to offer an umbrella covering various possible answers.

From this point of view, the field perspective is not an invention as such, but a way of focusing on something that is part of human experience, to then theorize about it. It is a post-modern lens, but also a very ancient one at the same time, a view that has always been with us, especially in other parts of the world, in other cultures.

Remaining focused here on ourselves and our "Western" world, our view of the individual is a historical-philosophical construct whose sturdy roots run deep, anchored to key turning points in history. They take us back, for instance, to the passage from the Middle Ages to the Renaissance and Humanism, a moment of undeniably great import for European (and Italian) culture, but also a period when the human being was first thrust to the center of the cosmos. In differentiating ourselves from the natural world, individuality progressively came to the fore.

With a rather wide margin of historical approximation, and a good dose of poetic license, it could be said that the seed of our narcissistic society was sown in the Renaissance era, with the overriding value it placed on individual contributions to humanity, progressively overshadowing the significance of the bonds and connections that make life possible—including those that today we call the forces of a field.

Let us now come back to the smaller story of our own theoretical approach. The concept of field appeared in Gestalt therapy right from the start, in the foundational text. There the founders spoke specifically of the organism/environment field, in which animal, physical, and socio-cultural factors are at play (Perls et al., 1994). That first approach to understanding the field centered above all on individual experience and was conceived as the field in which each of us is immersed from moment to moment, and which we contribute to constructing. With the relational turn, the focus shifted onto the relationship, onto the co-constructed field experience. Whereas today, experience and theory focus fully on the forces of the field.

As this was happening, therapy in practice progressively shifted its focus from the figure of an event, a symptom, or a key moment of contact with the client to working increasingly on the ground (Salonia, 1999, 2000; Francesetti & Gecele, 2009; Spagnuolo Lobb, 2011; Gecele, 2021). We will look more closely at the figure/ground concept in the next section.

> The maps of field theory depict well the territory of human beings in their contexts, i.e., of people in relationship, in community. The essence of field theory is that a holistic perspective towards the person extends to include environment, the social world, organizations, culture. The more assiduously we can navigate with the various field theory maps, the more we are likely actually to perceive and recognize the indivisibility of people from their surroundings and life situations.
>
> "Field theory can hardly be called a theory in the usual sense" (Lewin, 1951, p. 45). Rather it is a set of principles, an outlook, a method and a whole way of thinking which relates to the intimate interconnectedness between events and the settings or situations in which these events take place. So remember that "theory" in this case has a broad meaning, denoting a general theoretical outlook or way of appreciating reality.
>
> (Parlett, 1991, p. 69)

Since its foundation, Gestalt therapy has been very much involved and interested in the social context, seeing the person as part of a wider fabric of relationships, conditionings, elements of support, limitations, and possibilities. But also in understanding developments, changes, and the very existence of psychotherapy as connected to the social grounds that both produce them and are transformed by them at the same time.

As society evolves, the knowledge required for care-giving changes. The requests, tools, and methods all change. Psychotherapy is still a young discipline and so in continuous search and transformation. As therapists, we need to continuously evolve and improve ourselves, with the support of other disciplines—in keeping with the spirit of the times, but with a critical approach at the same time. The field concept is a door that opens to all of this.

5.1 Grounds

As I mentioned in the previous section, one of the fundamental concepts of Gestalt therapy is the ground. Similar to the idea of field, the ground is visible and comprehensible within what we call the figure/ground process.

The figure/ground process can be considered in both its actuality, like a snapshot of the present moment (where various figures can emerge in the same instant from the same ground), and in its evolution over time. A figure becomes ground when contact and satisfaction reach a peak and the vital situation comes truly to a finish (Perls et al., 1994). The process comes to a close, to then open up again with the assimilation of the experience.

The figure/ground process continuously gives us the possibility to take up a dual perspective. Just like in physics, which sees phenomena as both waves and particles, we can focus on the figure of an experience, but also on its ground. Dwelling in the ground, we can appreciate how phenomena are multiply determined. Whereas, if we let ourselves be dazzled by the figure, we risk overlooking the complexity of a situation.

> The concept of ground, inseparable from that of figure, comes from theories of perception developed in the early twentieth century. Those theories are well exemplified by Gestalt psychology, which treats perception as a superordinate phenomenon, as a whole that transcends the sum of its parts. Perception is an immediate process that is tied to the present situation, but which is also influenced by past experiences, which form the ground of the experience taking

shape. Different sets of elements can emerge from the same ground, connected by a logic of resemblance, or proximity, or continuity.

Just as perception brings together visual elements into a complete figure that stands out and differentiates itself from a ground that remains indistinct, or even fades away completely, the same happens in all our experiences—in a conversation, a lecture or a conference, when making a joke, reading a book, savouring a dish, or having an argument. We talk about one thing, presupposing and taking others for granted. We follow a line of reasoning, silencing the background noise of thousands of other thoughts. We perform an action, and in doing so bar all the other actions possible.

(Gecele, 2021, p. xiii)

We talk about a figure/ground process because no figure remains such forever. Every sight and experience returns to the ground, nourishing it and constituting it (Perls et al., 1994, Gecele, 2021).

The concept of ground lies close to the concept of field. Its stress, however, is less on the collection of forces present in the moment, and more on the continuous movement implicit in all vital processes. Thus, the field is something of a snapshot, albeit not a static one, of a phase in the figure/ground process. A snapshot that, in part at least, encompasses the whole spectrum—the part of the ground nearest and most meaningful to the experience taking shape, along with the potential and actual figures present.

It is important to correct a misconception arising from the one Lewin quote in PHG, which quotes Lewin saying that we should not include everything in the field we consider, and Staemmler repeats this quote. This is surely true, but the misconception is that it is only the things that are close or immediately visible that are to be considered. If an asteroid is a million miles away but on a trajectory heading for Earth, or a friend dies thousands of miles away, that is definitely part of the significant field of our existence while the person next to me might not be. Modern physics speaks of interconnections at a distance that are powerful but non-causal (cause-and-effect can only travel below the speed of light unlike these connections).

(Philippson, 2017)

Being present to the field's forces, by feeling the resonances of the forces at work and the web of intentionalities, meanings, and interconnections that define and form the field itself, is a key to accessing both the ground and the figure in the becoming. It gives us a vivid and present snapshot that emerges from the multitude and complexity of grounds—or their fragments—present in the situation, mapping a greater or lesser manifold of directions and possibilities. While it is always true that it is the total context that determines the meaning of what emerges as figure (Perls et al., 1994), from a field perspective it is often the details, expressed by the various emotions that color the field, that pave the way for the reconstitution of the ground as a whole and the construction of meaning.

That is another reason why working within a field perspective is so important today, when in clinical practice we focus more on the ground than on the figure, precisely because it is so challenging to perceive and dwell in grounds.

> In our time, it is fundamental and vital to take a step back and delve deeper into grounds, into the implicit, into all that is taken for granted. In life, just as in therapy.
>
> (Gecele, 2021, p. xiii)

> We are increasingly inclined to interpret the problematic issues we encounter and the challenges engaging us as concerning the ground more than the figure. Even the psychopathological suffering we encounter is an expression of our social and cultural context and calls for the priority to be focused on the construction of the ground, so as both to reconstruct the meaning of the suffering and to activate therapeutic interventions.
>
> (Gecele, 2021, p. 29)

What is lacking today—in post-modernity, in our societies—is continuity in narratives, the resistant thread connecting events and experiences. The self that emerges from the situation (Perls et al., 1994; Philippson, 2009; Robine, 2016) is increasingly a "post-modern" self that is fractured and fragmented, made up of parts that do not always connect to each other. In therapy, we often encounter pieces of life and pieces of stories that need to be put together, that need a narrative that gives direction and embeds them in time, that need a relationship to contain them and give them meaning (Gecele & Francesetti, 2005; Gecele, 2021, 2022a).

For us and our Western society, taken in a broad sense, it is only in recent decades that we have discovered the sense of dwelling in the field and in grounds—of dwelling in the situation and in processes, going beyond the individual to remain in the between (Arendt, 1998; Gecele & Francesetti, 2005; Gecele, 2021). Whereas, as I mentioned in the first section, there are societies that have preserved this aspect over time, keeping it alive and present.

From a medical and psychiatric point of view, for instance, it is interesting to observe how some African social groups consider pathology—not just psychopathology, therefore, but all suffering, mental and physical, including physical pain that leads to death. The focus is not—or was not—so much on the symptom, on the suffering body, as on the entire social system.

To exemplify what is otherwise a rather generic assertion, let us consider a situation involving the encounter of two different populations (Remotti, 2002). A situation that takes us to the Congo, to the Ituri forest, where we find the Lese farming people at a particular moment of their social life. There has been a death in the community, and hence suffering, and hence an upsetting of the social structure. And so "the others" are called in, people from outside the community; specifically, members of a different people—the Efe (pygmy) foragers. The Efe are endowed with the special ability to feel and see beyond what is visible. And so they begin to investigate, to ask questions. To sniff out a scent. Where is the poison, the toxic source that released the evil? An evil that is often involuntary, springing from the folds of our closest bonds, our most intimate relationships. A form of resentment, perhaps, or envy, a hurt that becomes anger and lies buried in the heart—buried but not securely sealed off, and so able to seep out into the environment and the community. And cause sickness and death. When the poison is discovered and comes to light, there is a catharsis, a public confession. The deceased remains dead, but the community frees itself of the "evil" (a more appropriate translation of what is usually rendered by "witchcraft").

Here we have presented the example like a story, a timeless tale. However, from our point of view, what is described implies an ability, an aptitude for dwelling in the field, in the knowledge that even our bodies are socialized and determined by a social setting that they contribute to shaping. What is more, our bodies are determined, influenced, and subjected to other bodies and other emotions.

We will not look here at other significant examples or cultural contexts. Suffice it to cite the macroscopic example of the East, again in a very generic way, where grounds and settings are still extremely important, despite the more recent importation and growth of individualism.

But let us return to the here and now of our own space-time.

Starting out from the ground gives us the chance to be more actively present and in a more functional way for the situation, allowing us to work with the forms of suffering that emerge from a fractured and fragmented context in need of reconstruction. Even our own view of the world and reality needs to be reconstructed, in all its facets and complexity, when the dominant narrative—the narrative that even us therapists internalize—continues to be the same old story of the self-determining individual, without roots and without community. The work of therapy today often consists of weaving together a ground to support the very relationship that makes it possible.

Let us look at an example.

> Personality disorders are a stronger call to society and to field than an isolated neurotic symptom is or was. They are a way of seeing, an imitation, an amplification, sometimes even a way to solve social issues. They are the ethnic disorder of our time [...]. In these experiences, the social field is particularly strong in shaping themes, problems, solutions, creative adaptations.
>
> We have to focus on the background from which the different degrees of disorder emerge, in a continuum that includes ways of being not considered pathological, but rather functional.
>
> Considering the background and the context gives us support and keys to interpretation, it gives us more tools to work with "personality disorders."
>
> (Gecele, 2019, p. 315)

It is about preserving traces, connecting moments and experiences, and constructing, through the relationship, a narrative that acknowledges the continuity of experience and the forgotten importance of memory.

Unexplored fragments become interconnected reality. In the slow and careful work of therapy aimed at constructing a relational ground, we are also able to support the unfolding of figures roughly sketched out and in the becoming.

When grounds are complex and fragmented, when clear figures struggle to emerge, working within a field perspective enables the support of the relationship to be focused on the potentiality of the emerging fragment of figure, often unforeseen and unforeseeable, thus transforming and redefining the entire experience.

One of the challenges of therapy work today lies in the difficulty of finding a clear figure to work on; another, at the same time, is not feeling we have a supportive ground (Gecele, 2021). If today we approach therapy thinking we can work on figures that have already emerged or will easily emerge from the ground, on something with implicit and spontaneous meaning and direction, the risk we run as therapists is that of feeling disoriented, confused, and inadequate.

Though it might not appear easy to put into practice, the field perspective allows us to find support and direction in clinical contexts that are difficult to decipher. In such clinical contexts, it is becoming increasingly important to recognize social and cultural grounds. Although such grounds can emerge in the field, in a more or less clear or fragmented way, without any prior analytical work, we also need to be consciously aware of them, in our thoughts and senses, throughout the session, to have a framework of reference. This brings us to and problematizes the concept of awareness itself (Bloom, 2019), because being present here and now and remaining with one's theoretical background are not diametrical and conflicting opposites, but two sides of the same coin. Grasping the fragments of field that strike us, and often surprise us (without treating them as absolutes), while at the same time deliberately considering the context (without being blinded by it) is a tricky balancing act, but it is fundamental. If we overbalance on the first side, the risk is that of attributing general issues to a single person—in our case, to the client. And it is a very real risk, one that can even lead to an amplification and reinforcement of a problem, causing harm.

What do we mean by "general issues"? A ready example at hand is that of the COVID-19 pandemic—a situation that was pan-present and generalized across all of society, which contributed greatly to determining, for a significant period of time, behaviors, and moods. In that period, it was important for us to support our clients in connecting fatigue, anxiety, anger, dampened mood, or whatever else with what was happening in the general context of society. Not in an exclusive and unequivocal way, of course, but where biographical and personal elements were not sufficient to make sense of the experience encountered.

In situations of great general malaise, where the emotional forces that strike and pass through us are clearly and boldly colored, even just coping with daily life is demanding in the energy in takes. If as therapists we consider only the individual elements of a phenomenon, we fail both good clinical standards and our clients themselves. Because we leave them to grapple on their own with broader questions, contributing to a vicious cycle of suffering.

5.2 Choices and actions

The field brings grounds to emerge through an awareness that can increasingly be trained and broadened. Work on the ability to listen and to be present to experience, progressively broadening our horizon and vision, is today a fundamental part of lifelong learning for therapists. It is an awareness that concerns not just bodies and feeling, but also fragments of stories and of possible narratives, past, present, and future. The more we work within a field perspective, the more we are able to hear and grasp elements of the ground that lie further afield, but are still relevant to the situation at hand.

We might also go one step further and say that, if the field is made up of all the forces surrounding us; if it is made up of the social, historical, (epi)genetic, developmental, corporeal, and cultural factors that constitute us; if it is also made up of both potential figures and those in the making; then it means that we are, at one and the same time, both the outcome and agents of the field. In a fractal sense, we can say that we are the field itself.

So where, in all that, do we find free will and deliberateness? Who do they belong to? Such questions open up a giddying realm of experience, one that we certainly cannot explore and trace out in full here.

Both within the therapy setting and outside of it, both in life and in our professional role, we choose whether to consider, dwell in, and respond to a field perspective—whether to broaden our sentience to the awareness of a much vaster horizon. We will not look here at how such a choice is expressed in daily life. Remaining within the scope of therapy, it can be said that when we work with other approaches, that is, with a monopersonal or a bipersonal perspective (Roubal & Francesetti, 2021), or a psychoeducational approach, field forces are always present, in the form of active grounds, and can contribute to the fatigue, loss of energy, and burnout of the therapist. So it is always and in any case important to find a way to let the forces at work pass through us, without becoming the final recipient, or an outlet for their release—and without that happening to the client. The real choice, therefore, is always how to dwell in the field.

Admittedly, much of the care directed at our professional role, at ourselves, and at the relationship is linked to the fact that we are continuously immersed in a maelstrom of affects, potentialities, and fragments of life. Being aware of this enables us to give new and clear meaning to the practices and rules we often automatically take for granted—from the setting to the attention to boundaries, to the importance of supervision.

And if we choose a field perspective? If we feel and place ourselves on that level? The options that appear are different. Because field forces are organized and selected also on the basis of which fulcrums of experience (people), which manifold of stories, roles, and relationships make up the field and are a part of it.

This multiplicity of forces can be visualized as belonging to different, interacting, but discernible planes—a more personal and intimate level, a transgenerational level, a social and political level. These planes, or stratifications of forces, are always co-present, even if they are not always evident or determinant at the same time.

In a field perspective, therapy intervention is always, in a certain sense, a search for meaning. Or rather, it is the construction of personal, relational, historical, and cultural meanings. It is a way of constructing reality.

We choose and we are chosen. In a way, the field's forces lead us to dwell on one plane; but in another, we posit ourselves on one of the levels of meaning of the experience at hand.

In Gestalt therapy, awareness is not just feeling, it is also action (Perls et al., 1994). Hence, action is part of the awareness of the forces of the field. Every choice is itself an action, a redirecting of forces, and a contribution to helping possible directions emerge. But it is also—and this is no less important—a creative adjustment so as not to be overwhelmed by the multiplicity of forces and possibilities present. In a certain sense, the act of choosing, in the sense of selecting (Gecele, 2021), is more important than what is actually chosen.

If we stop for a moment and consider actions, we can appreciate how they imply different levels of awareness and decision-making. They are levels on a spectrum running from supreme and thoughtless deliberateness—almost an individual and solitary act of force in no way connected to the meaning of the situations unfolding—at one extreme, to a "middle mode" in which we act by being acted on (Gecele, 2021), with full presence and awareness, at the other.

Can different actions be matched to different degrees of presence? The dense and exemplary words of Bonhoeffer (2015, p. 450), that "every true action is such that nobody else, but only you yourself can do it," imply, on the one hand, a supreme level of choice and responsibility, while on the other they lead to a dimension of inevitability, to a surrendering to destiny in a process that passes over us.

In the "Introduction" to *Gestalt Therapy. Excitement and Growth in the Human Personality* (Miller, 1994), we read that as human beings we take everything that we have experienced, and hence domesticated, to be "us," while the experiences and possibilities we have yet to encounter are the "inexhaustible otherness of the world," a wilderness that is uncontaminated ("by us"). It is like saying that the world reproduces, echoes, mirrors, multiplies, and divides itself into endless parts that lie closer or farther from the fulcrums around which experiences are unfolding. A closeness or distance that is also determined by the actions that are undertaken.

5.3 Psychopathology and psychotherapy today

Looking more closely at the experience of suffering, the field's forces are an expression of both actual experiences gone through without support and possible experiences that are remote or not yet existing (Francesetti et al., 2022). They are real and unpredictable potentialities.

When the field is extremely polarized by a form of suffering, through the transmittance effect of one of the fulcrums of experience present (in our case, the client), the forces themselves are also extremely polarized. The experience, in therapy, is that as psychopathological suffering heightens, the field becomes more unidirectional, and short of breath.

When situations involving more serious or challenging personal problems, often tied to developmental years, present themselves in the therapy setting, it is as though the field shrinks. The suffering brought is so overwhelming that it does not allow us to widen our perspective. Space itself narrows, cutting off and excluding much of the world and reality—even experiences directly at hand struggle to find a place, because everything is loaded with the suffering of one life. Even time changes. No longer open to different potentialities and possible experiences, it becomes repetitive, still, circular, held back by a suffering that imprisons the relationship and hence the authentic flow of instants. A fullness in which there is no space for anything else. Paradoxically, a fullness often built around an emptiness.

The more psychopathological a field is, therefore, the harder it becomes to take the step of broadening awareness to encompass elements of the field lying further afield, as I discussed in the section "Choices and actions." It is difficult not to focus solely on the problems of the specific life story, to open up to broader perspectives.

In our work, we encounter all the different degrees of suffering. From the narrow and suffocating psychopathological fields we have just described, through various combinations and proportions of "personal" and "social" elements, to suffering that is almost exclusively socially determined. Encountering such suffering that is so closely tied to the context draws us into vaster grounds, where the field's forces are multiple and stratified. If we are not aware of the grounds we are moving in, of how societies produce narratives of themselves that leave out many of the possibilities for human construction; if we do not dwell a bit at the margins of those narratives and question the worlds in which we live, we effectively abandon our patients to their own devices, as described in the previous section. We leave them grappling on their own to construct meaning and make sense of the pieces of life—experiences, perceptions, thoughts, memory—that pass through them. The more the field's forces are made up of elements not integrated into narratives, the more those fragments of stories are powerful and dense in irradiating energy, which propagates and is emitted without filter.

As I was saying in the first section, we are always and continuously thrown into experiential fields. We are part of a multitude of grounds and we move with them, both in life and, as interests us here, in our professional role as therapists. What makes the difference is whether we are aware of them or not. Because if we are, our presence is better placed for perceiving possible forms and directions within the complexity of the field and making a contribution to actualizing them.

Human beings feel they are the masters of themselves. Or, in a more modern version of that, they feel guilty or responsible for anything and everything, even the moods, emotions, experiences, and malaises that come from the "outside," from the social climate, the moods of others, their presence or absence, from their own corporeity (Gecele, 2022b). Everyone believes that feeling sad or feeling hurt is something that is intimately personal—in the sense of being tied to our essential character, or in the sense of being connected with our more recent reactions to life events. The risk really is that our little egos, to which we are so attached, become indistinguishable from reality, and so we think we are the only ones who suffer, for instance, while losing the capacity to see whether it is the people around us instead who are transmitting waves of their own suffering.

In our role as therapists, if we take up the dominant narrative that posits the individual at the center of everything, we risk losing touch with a fundamental capacity, that of empathy—the capacity, which is also cognitive, to differentiate and perceive one's own and others' states of mind and reciprocal influences, to grasp how the pathways of personal life combine with social and cultural dynamics in our choices, actions, thoughts, and worldviews. As I mentioned, working within a field perspective is a way of meeting the need, for the therapist, to be in contact with grounds, precisely because suffering today concerns, above all, grounds (Gecele, 2021). And also because, where suffering revolves around emptiness, efforts need to focus on giving value and meaning to what little there is, to the unorderable fragments of experience.

Sometimes, today, the possibilities narrow to such an extent and suffering becomes so dense that the field—not just the psychopathological field in a strict sense, but all socially determined situations—becomes a sort of black hole, a void that draws us and sucks everything in, thoughts, theories, abilities, and sensibilities. To construct some theory around that void, around the black hole, it can be useful to draw on the concept of mode 1 and mode 2 pathologies, as outlined in my chapter in the book *Psicopatologia e Atmosfere, Prima del Soggetto e del Mondo*, where phenomena are described through the filter of the concept of atmospheres. As I explain there, two modes of psychotherapy can be identified:

1. The mode for which atmospheres are so internalized, introjected, individualized and fragmented that they are barely there anymore; they become an absence.

[...]

2. The mode in which we find madness in its classical form, the unconceited form described by Erasmus of Rotterdam (...), as represented by the Shakespearean fool. Here, atmospheres remain on the outside and become words or silences with weight, actions that capture us, tangible emotions. This is a world in which affects are stirring and engaging. Here, life, the in-between, shared and common values, all burst back and find space in a scapegoat of prophetic force.

[...]

Nevertheless, it should not be forgotten that every form of psychopathology, whether mode 1 or 2, is a creative adjustment to the world and life, a signal, a call, a warning addressed to us all—whether it is about ways of living together characteristic of our space-time or about unavoidable and painful elements implicit in life. Mode 2 pathologies are driven more by the latter, shaped by timeless elements, constants of the human condition; mode 1 pathologies are driven more by the former, elements of greater contingency, present in the specific space-time of a society, or a civilization.

(Gecele, 2022b, pp. 292–293, my translation)

Faced today with forms of suffering that are largely mode 1 pathologies, as defined above, it could be said that it is the therapist, and not the client, who is called to dwell in a sort of excess or other dimension, made up of potential, unactualized realities. A dimension of therapy that we might call "shamanic" expands for us to dwell in, or perceive at least, worlds that apparently do not exist. A sort of alchemical dimension, in which the therapeutic process slowly and strenuously attempts to transform emptiness into matter (experience).

Let us conclude with a paradox. The paradox of a field full of forces in which the complexity and multitude of forces risks imploding into nothingness. While the therapist—every therapist, every one of us—engages ceaselessly in a titanic, if Sisyphean, effort to steal pieces of the world away from that void.

References

Arendt, H. (1998). *The human condition*. 2nd ed. Chicago University Press.

Bloom, D. (2019). From sentience to sapience: The awareness-consciousness continuum and the lifeworld. *Gestalt Review, 23*(1), 18–43, Penn State University Press.

Bonhoeffer, D. (2015). Lettera 8 giugno 1944 da Tegel. In *Resistenza e resa. Lettere e scritti dal carcere* (A. Gallas Ed.). Edizioni San Paolo.

Brennan, T. (2004). *Trasmission of affect*. Cornell University Press.

Francesetti, G., & Gecele, M. (2009). A Gestalt therapy perspective on psychopathology and diagnosis. *British Gestalt Journal, 18*(2), 5–20.

Francesetti, G., Gecele, M., & Roubal, J. (2022). Being present to absence: Field theory in psychopathology and clinical practice. In P. Cole (Ed.), *The relational heart of Gestalt therapy. Contemporary perspectives* (Ch. 3). Routledge.

Francesetti, G., & Roubal, J. (2020). Field theory in contemporary Gestalt therapy. Part one: Modulating the therapist's presence in clinical practice. *Gestalt Review, 24*(2), 113–136.

Gecele, M. (2019). Chasing joy in the liquid time of emptiness: Obsessive-compulsive experiences in postmodern era. In G. Francesetti, E. Kerry Reed, & C. Vázquez Bandín (Eds.), *Obsessive compulsive experiences. A Gestalt therapy perspective* (pp. 202–211). Los Libros del CTP.

Gecele, M (2021). *Gli sfondi dell'alterità*. Fioriti.

Gecele, M. (2022a). *Is everyone a narcissist? Even me?* L'Exprimerie.

Gecele, M. (2022b). Atmosfere e psicopatologia: gli sfondi culturali. In G. Francesetti, & T. Griffero (Eds.), *Psicopatologia e atmosphere: Prima, del soggetto e del mondo* (pp. 273–299). Fioriti.

Gecele, M., & Francesetti, G. (2005). La polis come "ground" e orizzonte della terapia. In G. Francesetti (Ed.), *Attacchi di panico e postmodernità, la psicoterapia della Gestalt fra clinica e società* (pp. 142–176). FrancoAngeli.

Lasch, C. (1979). *The culture of narcissism: American life in an age of diminishing expectations*. W.W. Norton & Company.

Lewin, K. (1951). *Field theory in social science: Selected theoretical papers* (D. Cartwright Ed.). Harper & Brothers.

Miller, M. (1994). Introduction. In F. S. Perls, R. F. Hefferline, & P. Goodman (Eds.), *Gestalt therapy. Excitement and growth in the human personality*. The Gestalt Journal Press.

Parlett, M. (1991). Reflections on field theory. *The British Gestalt Journal, 1*(2), 68–91.

Perls, F. S., Hefferline, R. F., & Goodman, P. (1994). *Gestalt therapy. Excitement and growth in the human personality*. The Gestalt Journal Press.

Philippson, P. A. (2009). *The emergent self. An existential-gestalt approach*. Karnac Books.

Philippson, P. A. (2017). *Paper 1: Revisiting the field*. (Topics in Gestalt therapy: Occasional Kindle papers by Peter Philippson). E-book. https://www.amazon.co.uk/gp/product/B01N4WQ484?ie=UTF8&linkCode=as2&camp=1634&creative=6738&tag=&creativeASIN=B01N4WQ484 (last accessed March 1, 2024).

Remotti, F. (2002). *Prima lezione di antropologia*. Edizioni Laterza.

Robine, J.-M. (2015). *Social change begins with two*. Istituto di Gestalt HCC.

Robine, J.-M. (2016). *Self: A polyphony of contemporary Gestalt therapists*. L'Exprimerie.

Roubal, J., & Francesetti, G. (2021). Field theory in contemporary gestalt therapy. Part two: Paradoxical theory of change reconsidered. *Gestalt Review*, *26*(1), 1–33.

Rubin, D., Botanov, Y., Hajcak, J., & Mujica-Parodi, L.R. (2012). Inhalation of stress sweat enhances neural response to neutral faces. *Social Cognitive and Affective Neuroscience*, *7*(2), 208–212.

Salonia, G. (1999). Dialogare nel tempo della frammentazione. In F. Rametta, & M. Naro (Eds.), *Impense adlaboravit* (pp. 571–585). Facoltà Teologica di Sicilia.

Salonia, G. (2000). La criminalità giovanile tra vecchie e nuove regole. Verso l'integrazione dello straniero nella polis. *Quaderni di Gestalt XX*, *30/31*, 100–108.

Smuts, J. (1926). *Holism and evolution*. Macmillan. (Reprinted in 2013 by the Gestalt Journal Press.)

Spagnuolo Lobb, M. (2011). *Il now-for-next in psicoterapia. La psicoterapia della Gestalt raccontata nella società post-moderna*. FrancoAngeli.

Chapter 6

"Necessary light that makes me the chosen host"

Field theories in Gestalt therapy and clinical practice

Gianni Francesetti

6.1 Introduction[1]

The title of this chapter is taken from a poem by Livia Chandra Candiani. A poem which captures several elements that I believe are central to working in a field perspective, offering a good introduction to my thought on the topic:

> So much faith/to do nothing at all./To stand hesitating at the thresh-old/smiling at that emptiness/That emptiness there/that settles itself down/Around me right here./Necessary light/Is this instinct/That keeps me away from everyone/and without any recognition strategy/ Makes me the chosen host [...].
>
> (Candiani, 2014, my translation)

Field theory has been a core concept of Gestalt therapy since the beginning of its development (Robine, 2001; Wollants, 2008; Parlett & Lee, 2005; Staemmler, 2006; Philippson, 2017; Francesetti et al., 2020; Francesetti & Roubal, 2020). However, it has been used with different meanings by different authors, to the point that this theoretical domain—if not based on explicit definitions—can lead to a Babylonian confusion (Staemmler, 2006). This is not just a sign of lack of definition and clarity, but indicates the richness of a concept that can have multiple understandings and applications (Philippson, 2017). Nevertheless, to be able to engage in dialogue, it is our responsibility to define the terms we use, so as to bring out the similarities and differences between the various conceptions. Here, I claim that field theory is not only a bedrock of Gestalt therapy's approach, but one of the possible paradigms informing clinical practice in psychotherapy and in psychiatry.

DOI: 10.4324/9781003597308-7

Other paradigms that we can identify, and that we have discussed elsewhere (Francesetti & Roubal, 2020; Roubal & Francesetti, 2022), are the monopersonal paradigm and the bipersonal paradigm. They are perspectives that came to the fore at different moments in the history of psychotherapy and psychoanalysis, with the monopersonal approach followed by the bipersonal (relational) turn of the 1980s. Today we are instead witnessing a movement towards what we can call a "field-based clinical practice." It is an attempt to focus on the *something more* or the *something before* the monopersonal and bipersonal perspective: It is, rather, a prepersonal perspective. As different as they are, these three perspectives integrate each other, allowing us to grasp different aspects of therapy processes.

In this chapter, I wish to present two conceptualizations of field theory in Gestalt therapy and explore their implications for our understanding of psychopathology and psychotherapy. They are the organism/environment field and the phenomenal field, where the former is explicitly conceptualized in Perls et al. (1951/1994), whereas here I will argue that the latter is found implicitly in the foundational text of the model. I will then conclude with two brief examples, one from a psychotherapy group and another from a supervision session.

6.2 Organism/environment field versus phenomenal field

The field perspective, in its various forms, challenges the deep-rooted split in our culture between the inner world and the outer world. Merleau-Ponty offers a radically different view when he writes, "The interior and the exterior are inseparable. The world is entirely on the inside, and I am entirely outside of myself" (Merleau-Ponty, 1945/2012, p. 430). Through field theory, Gestalt therapy has taken a step in this same direction.

The wide debate on the definition of field in Gestalt therapy gives rise to many questions that often reflect different conceptions found as far back as the cultural and scientific ground from which the model emerged. Putting aside their differences, they all show an attempt to go beyond a conception of the human being as an isolated and isolable individual (Francesetti, 2015). Among the many contours shaping this discourse, I believe one of the central questions for determining the definition of field we implicitly or explicitly use is this: Is the field different for each person or is it a common dimension in a given situation?

There can be no answer to this question if we do not clarify first what is meant by "field." My argument is that the field is an individual attribute under one definition (the organism/environment field), whereas it is a common dimension under another (the phenomenal field). Each definition obviously grasps aspects that the other leaves in the shadows. I consider the two conceptualizations as an expression of the irresolvable tension and oscillation between an individualistic perspective and a prepersonal perspective.

In the incredible cultural ferment of 1920s Germany, the movement to go beyond an individualistic conceptualization of the human being encompassed many currents and fields of inquiry, reaching across philosophy, psychology, sociology, political theory, and psychoanalysis. It was an extraordinarily rich melting pot bubbling with possibilities and insights, a nascent state of new, if sometimes contradictory ideas that sought to go beyond a mechanistic and reductionist vision of the world and the human being. The roots of Gestalt therapy lie deep in that humus. In developing the potentials offered for therapy, it brought with it, however, some theoretical ambiguities, one of which concerns the conceptualization of the field. Circulating at that time were conceptualizations of the field both as a primarily individual attribute (see, for instance, Kurt Lewin, 1951), and as a totality encompassing everybody and constituting the root of life itself (see, for instance, Jan Smuts, 1926/2013).

6.2.1 The organism-environment field: An isolated organism does not exist

In the first part of the book marking the foundation of Gestalt therapy (Perls et al., 1951/1994), the concept of field is fundamental, with the word "field" itself cited 122 times[2]: "Our approach in this book is 'unitary' in the sense that we try in a detailed way to consider every problem as occurring in a social-animal-physical field" (Perls et al., 1951/1994, p. 5). As Jean-Marie Robine has stressed repeatedly (see his chapter in this book), in that work the field is explicitly considered an "organism/ environment field." Max Wertheimer (1944), one of the founders of Gestalt psychology, had been very clear about this: "The notion of a separate ego only 'develops under very special circumstances'" (quoted in Harrington, 1999, p. 121). Indeed, the idea that an organism cannot be studied separately from its environment was not an original one for our founders. The man who introduced into the biological sciences the idea that the organism and its environment form an indivisible and integrated whole was Jacob von Uexkull. He called it "Umwelt" (Harrington, 1999). In this regard, it is essential to cite, although we cannot discuss it further here, the contribution and great influence of Kurt Goldstein[3] and his work on traumatic brain injuries, which for him could only be understood by considering the irreducible unity of the organism and its relationship with the environment (Goldstein, 1939). The concept of field was instead first borrowed from physics by Kurt Lewin. In the mid-1800s, the physicists James Clerk Maxwell and Michael Faraday had described the electromagnetic field in mathematical terms as a region of space where specific forces act: "The region where a particular condition prevails, especially one in which a force or influence is effective regardless of the presence of a material medium" ("field" in *The New Oxford Dictionary of English*, 1998, p. 680). Lewin connected the indissoluble unity of the organism and its environment with the idea of field, saying: "Psychology has to view the life space, including the person and his environment, as one field" (Lewin, 1951, p. 240).

From the end of the 1800s and into the early 1900s, the lively debate sweeping Germany's cultural milieu took aim at the reductionism and mechanism of Newtonian science, promoting instead a holistic dimension of totality to understand phenomena (Harrington, 1999). Although the term *holism* was introduced by Jan Smuts (1926), the concept of the whole, or totality, had been used and emphasized in German Romanticism from as far back as Goethe in opposition to a mechanistic view of the world and humankind, profoundly shaping German culture. The word used by Goethe to indicate this totality that cannot be reduced to a mechanistic worldview was "Gestalt."

For Wertheimer, the choice of the word *Gestalt* for his research was far from predictable and it was a brave and risky move. It meant taking up a cultural and philosophical legacy that at the same time was inspiring vitalistic and mystical developments that would be incorporated into and exploited by Nazi propaganda. It meant seeking out and forging a path that differentiated itself from both mystical and spiritual vitalism and from reductionist and associationist mechanism. It meant affirming that the values of beauty and goodness—aesthetics and ethics—were not merely subjective projections onto external objects, but perceptions of Gestalts—intrinsic qualities in the emerging of phenomena—that resulted "as much from the external world as they did from internal processes" (Köhler, quoted in Harrington, 1999, p. 131).

Friedrich Salomon Perls and Laura Posner (Bocian, 2010 and his chapter in this book) participated directly and actively both in the philosophical and experimental developments of Gestalt psychology and in the psychoanalytic movement, adhering to the left wing of psychoanalysis. They were also actively involved in the artistic avant-garde movements of the 1920s. All these disciplines, studies, and movements converged on the principle that it is impossible to understand human beings if they are abstracted from their environment—an isolated organism does not exist. Friedrich Perls and Laura Posner would take this enormously rich Mitteleuropean culture and bring it into the conceptualization of a new way of conceiving psychotherapy. Their work pivoted on two central and revolutionary aspects of theory: the concept of the organism/environment field and the self as an emergent process.

Both these ideas were current in German intellectual circles in the 1920s, a time full of new and revolutionary ideas of powerful political impact. Yet they did not filter into Freudian psychoanalysis. Those who tried to bring them into psychoanalytic thinking were quickly ostracized as heretics. Among them was Perls, as the story of his address at the Marienbad Congress in 1936 shows.[4] There Perls presented his ideas on the importance of dental aggression in infant development, but his address—as a psychoanalyst in analysis with Wilhelm Reich, a "heretic" and Communist—attracted a negative reception.

In clinical work, the concept of the organism/environment field helps us consider the client through his/her complex and indissoluble connections with the environment, including the therapeutic situation. What happens to the client always implicates his/her relationships and interactions. This conception consider every organism to "have" its own, different field, for which the field is, therefore, an individual attribute—at this moment, we each have our own visual, auditory, or affective field, which is different for each of us.

This conceptualization leaves open a central question, which arises from how the self is conceived in Gestalt therapy as an emerging phenomenon and not as a given structure (Robine, 2016). If the self emerges, if it is a ceaseless process of differentiation between self and world, *from where* and *how* does it emerge? How can there be a *my field* before there is a *me*? The question is clearly a philosophical one, but not only; it is also a crucial clinical concern and a matter of neuroscientific inquiry. In reality, just asking the question is itself of great therapeutic significance as many of the phenomena we encounter in psychopathology and clinical practice pivot on *"from where and how"* the self and the world emerge (Francesetti et al., 2020).

6.2.2 The phenomenal field: The origin of the self and the world

In line with the various phenomenological perspectives, Merleau-Ponty highlights the need, in psychology, to not take the constitution of the subject and the world for granted: "A psychology is always led toward the problem of the constitution of the world" (Merleau-Ponty, 1945/2012, p. 60). Jean-Luc Marion (2002) points out how one of the characteristic and constituent features of our culture is the *forgetting of origin*, of how self and world originate and take shape. They are given and not problematized. Marion stresses how what is *given* is *gifted*. He problematizes the matter by asking: *given how, when, where, by whom*? To be able to use the concept of the individual as the center of the world, as the modern Western world does, it is necessary to "forget" its origin, to treat it as if it had always existed as a separate, independent, even self-sufficient entity: as the center of the world and the measure of all things. Just asking such a question itself is, therefore, somewhat subversive.

If the self is an emerging phenomenon that differentiates itself from the world in the making of experience, to explore its origin we need a theory of experience. Gestalt therapy develops just such a theory, building on Gestalt psychology and American Pragmatism, another major influence on the foundation of the approach.[5] This is not the time and place to go into the complexity of that theory; for an in-depth description of the theory itself, readers can refer to the foundational text of Gestalt therapy (Perls et al., 1951/1994), and to later works (Robine, 2016; Francesetti, 2015, 2020; Francesetti & Roubal, 2020; Roubal & Francesetti, 2022; Francesetti et al., 2022) for a discussion of the clinical and psychopathological implications of the process. Suffice it to say here that experience is a process that emerges from an undifferentiated ground and which progressively gives rise to a contact boundary that separates and unites a self and a world. Subjects and objects emerge from that originary dimension: "Neither the object nor the subject is *posited*" (Merleau-Ponty, 1945/2012, p. 251).

We are grappling here with a phenomenon that is difficult to describe and easy to neglect. In the apparently paradoxical words of Bernhard Waldenfels (2011, p. 84), "we start elsewhere, in a place where we have never been and will never be." We emerge from a ground in which we are not yet constituted as distinct subjective entities in a distinct world. A ground in whose shadows experience dawns. Object and subject are nominal precipitates—they have become "things"—as a result of a historical transformation in their linguistic connotation. Until the Middle Ages, they were considered a process in which a *sub-jectum* was cast under and an *ob-jectum* was cast away (Marková & Berrios, 2012). Their origin is the locus of the vague and confused, of the undifferentiated, of the chiaroscuro, of the indefinite (Minkowski, 1999)—a locus Descartes discarded with his method of inquiry based on clear and distinct ideas and which positivist science then swept away completely, producing as an effect the disenchantment of a world where everything is mechanically knowable and transparent (Max Weber, Munich, 1918, in Harrington, 1999). Hence, there is a dimension that is "neither subjective nor objective" (Francesetti & Griffero, 2019), a dimension that "comes before the subject and the world" (Francesetti & Griffero, 2022), which has largely been forgotten by the modern world. Or rather, such forgetting constitutes the birth itself of the modern world.

I call this nascent dimension the "phenomenal field," from the title of Chapter 4 of the Introduction to *Phenomenology of Perception* (Merleau-Ponty, 1945/2012). It is the undifferentiated field—undifferentiated as it comes before the definition of subject and world—from which phenomena emerge. It is the threshold of the world and of the self. In this field (just like in Maxwell and Faraday's electromagnetic field and in Einstein's gravitational field), there are forces that condition the emergence of phenomena—forces that are *intrinsic tensions* of the field, the intentionalities of the field.[6] They are anonymous (they are not yet mine nor yours) and they are agential (they produce effects) (Merleau-Ponty, 1945/2012).

Experience, therefore, emerges from the undifferentiated, a locus in which the polarity of subject and world has yet to be defined. Evidence for this also comes from infant research (Stern, 1985), neuroscience (Damasio, 2010), phenomenology, and phenomenological psychiatry (Fuchs, 2021; Zahavi, 2017).

In an attempt to provide a working definition that is as clear as possible, I define the phenomenal field as *the horizon of probabilities for the emergence of phenomena in the present situation.*[7] Phenomena (or we can also say figure/ground processes) emerge on the basis of forces that make them more or less likely or unlikely. These forces bend the horizon and warp it, opening up or closing off possibilities. For example, at a party with friends, it is easier for jokes and jests, moments of good cheer, and feelings of lightness to emerge, during which time will tend to flow quickly. At a funeral wake, it is more likely that feelings of heaviness will emerge, along with the slowing or rarefaction of time, gloominess, and immobility. With black holes, the force that bends the event horizon is gravity; with the phenomenal field, it is the intentionalities at play that bend it. In the therapeutic encounter, those forces—embodied intentionalities—move both the client and the therapist, who are functions of them. In this paradigm—in which the self is not a structure but a process that emerges in the situation—the forces in the phenomenal field are in motion before the subjects are differentiated and defined. Therefore, we can say that the therapist and the client emerge, they *are made*, within the situation and are moved by the forces of the field. The phenomenal field is *pathos*: It is *suffered* and not chosen (Waldenfels, 2011; Botelho Alvim, 2021). The phenomenal field is not "a thing"; it is a process and cannot be reified. It is an ever-changing horizon that shifts, sometimes more, sometimes less, from moment to moment.

The phenomenal field acts here and now and, like a gravitational field, I can grasp it by feeling its effects. The gravitational field in the here and now is common to us all, but its effects are different on each of us. Conceptualizing the field as an *organism/environment field* helps to avoid abstracting the organism from its environment, but it remains centered on the individual. Conceptualizing the field as a *phenomenal field* helps to highlight the forces to which we are all subjected in a given situation. The phenomenal field (horizon of probabilities) is thus the set of forces that act in a situation, forces that constitute the limits and potentials for transformation. They are the dynamic forces that activate in a given situation. It should be noted how the phenomenal field is in turn affected by the developments that emerge, which makes it an incessantly changing process. Once again, we can take a gravitational field as an example, where the bodies affected by the gravitational field in turn affect the field itself, in proportion to their mass. In the clinical encounter, client and therapist are affected by the field's forces and at the same time they affect them, in a process of circular complexity that cannot be reduced to the oversimplification of cause-effect relations.

One way of grasping the phenomenal field is to focus attention on the atmosphere of the situation. An atmosphere is the *affective quality permeating a space* (Griffero, 2010). It is a concept we have explored through the interesting aspect of how it resists and challenges Cartesian dichotomies—an atmosphere is neither solely in the environment nor solely in the organism; it is neither solely subjective nor solely objective; it is neither solely agentive nor solely pathic (Francesetti & Griffero 2019, 2022). There is a wide and lively debate on the topic of atmospheres in clinical work (see *Gestalt Review*, 2018, Vol. 22, No. 3; Staemmler, 2023). Here, however, let us go back to a quote by Kurt Lewin:[8]

> To characterize properly the psychological field, one has to take into account such *specific* items as particular goals, stimuli, needs, relations, as well as such more general characteristics of the field as the *atmosphere* (for instance, the friendly, tense, or hostile atmosphere) or the amount of freedom. These characteristics of the *field as a whole* are as important in psychology as, for instance, the field of gravity for the explanation of events in classical physics. Psychological atmospheres are empirical realities and are scientifically describable facts.
>
> (Lewin, 1951, p. 241)

The gravitational field is not just a metaphor for the phenomenal field. It is one of the forces that act on the phenomenal fields from which we emerge and which bend the probabilities for the emergence of phenomena. Suffice it to imagine the field being modified like in a spaceship: Other experiential—sensorial and motorial—phenomena would emerge. The fact that it is common to us does not mean it does not have different effects on each of us. The effects of a gravitational field are different for each of us; all it takes is a set of scales to measure them. Yet we are all subjected to the same force. In turn, we affect the field itself. The effects may be imperceptible when it comes to gravity, but they are potentially significant for other types of acting forces. In a depressive field present in a given situation, we are all subjected to depressive forces, in that they pull downwards, and we might experience time slowing down, or, on the contrary, a manic reaction, or binge eating, or alcohol abuse, or other infinite possibilities. In any case, the forces of a depressive field affect everybody in that situation.

For a description of clinical phenomena, I find it useful to refer to two other concepts connected with the conceptualization of the phenomenal field: the *phenomenological field* and the *psychopathological field*.

6.2.3 *The phenomenological field*

The phenomenal field (*where I am subject-to*) can be transformed into the phenomenological field (*where I am the subject-of*) that is, into a field where it is possible to reflect on what is happening and make choices, where the sphere of possibilities can expand. Such a transformation is enabled by the capacity to be aware of the phenomenal field, to notice the forces at play that move us, to be curious about what is happening. *To reflect* comes from Latin *reflectere*: to flex means to bend; to re-flect means to bend a second time, or to turn back on being bent. The forces of the phenomenal field move us, they bend us a first time; they flex us. If we bend a second time and turn back from being bent, we re-flect. In that passage, there is a space-time gap in which we become aware of being bent, of being differentiated by being bent, and hence there is the conquest, initially at least, of a certain degree of agency. The first degree of freedom and differentiation is being aware of what is happening to us. *Pathos* gives some room to *agens*. *Patient* becomes *agent*. We could say that the phenome*logi*cal field (PhLf) is the phenomenal field (Phf) + '*logos*' (L): Phf + L = PhLf. *Logos*,[9] from the Greek, is the possibility to bring order, meaning, sense; to think, reflect, and to give words. That passage from the phenomenal to the phenomenological field is close to what Fonagy (Fonagy & Target, 1997) describes as the capacity for mentalization.

Nevertheless, from the perspective that we propose, the ability to reflect and verbalize is not only a passage to a cognitive competence, since it is combined with an embodied awareness of the sensorial phenomena in motion. In that passage, the therapist *does* nothing; he/she does not act. Yet the very fact of realizing how the forces affect him/her—and hence the possibility to re-flect—creates a space for differentiation from the phenomenal field, which is a fundamental therapeutic intervention. In this way, an added degree of freedom is introduced, which itself modifies the phenomenal field suffered. The fact that the forces are prepersonal, i.e., they do not belong *in primis* and *in toto* to either the client or the therapist, is a key support for differentiation from experiences. They are how I grasp the forces at work in the field—they are neither "mine" or "the client's" nor "caused" by me or the client. Obviously, the differentiation of the phenomenal field from the phenomenological field is not intended as the differentiation of two fixed entities, but a way of accounting for the ceaseless and circular movement between feeling and making sense of feeling.

6.2.4 The psychopathological field

The psychopathological field is a phenomenal field in which it is not possible to be present one to the other according to the potentialities of the situation. Either because sensations cannot take shape, or affective sensitivity is dulled or restricted, or because people cannot be fully constituted as differentiated and connected subjects belonging to a common world (in which case the experience has a psychotic quality). It is a phenomenal field where an absence is struggling to become present. Unsuccessfully. There are rigidities that hold back the emergence of the novelty expected from the potentials of the present field. Psychopathology can be seen as an expression of the ways in which something is rigidly kept absent in the situation; where there is insufficient freedom to allow the potentials of the field's dynamics to develop. Psychotherapy, then, is a situation in which therapists can be present to those absences. They feel these absences by their aesthetic competence (Francesetti & Gecele, 2009; Francesetti et al., 2017). In a psychopathological field, a potentiality is struggling to exist and there are not the conditions to reach the degree of freedom and support for its actualization. One of the artists who described this process in the clearest and most provocative way was arguably Luigi Pirandello, who won the Nobel prize in 1934. In his preface to *Six Characters in Search of an Author*, Pirandello (1925/1952, p. 363) boldly declares: "I wrote this play to free myself from a nightmare." He writes that one day he came home and found six characters: "I can only say that, without having made any effort to seek them out, I found before me, alive—you could touch them and even hear them breathe—the six characters [...]. Born alive, they wished to live" (Pirandello, 1925/1952, p. 3630). They asked him to tell their story. He refused, because he never wrote a story before making sense of it.[10] But they insisted, and continued to come to Pirandello's home every day.

It was a nightmare for him, until he started to grasp an emerging meaning and decided to write their story.

Psychopathological suffering is not existential pain; it is not discomfort ensuing from the limitations or losses that we all experience in our lives (Salonia, 2013; Francesetti, 2019c). Psychopathology starts when an experiential potentiality is not free to emerge. It can be the result of a difficult situation, for which the experience cannot be processed and assimilated: When the other, needed to afford and to process the sensorial and affective elements, is not there; or when there is an environmental pressure (social, cultural) that does not allow a present possibility to emerge and be met (Gecele, 2021). Or when the other is there but is not differentiated, and so it is present but absent at the same time.

Hence, psychopathology starts when the *other* is missing. The sensorial and affective elements are proto-feelings[11] that cannot be assimilated and which persist as sensorial footprints that are more or less chaotic and disorganized. There are various ways we can protect ourselves from such chaos. We can ignore it, put it aside and render it minimally disturbing, or even irrelevant. We can dissociate it (in the sense of not integrating it) and "pack it up" in patterns of symptoms, syndromes, and blind spots of the personality. The tables of contents of nosographic psychiatric systems present a list of the forms of those packages.

Psychopathological forms are the result of our ability to adjust creatively to what cannot be fully met, experienced, processed, and assimilated. With such transformations, the absent-other becomes the absence in the present contact. A person becomes blind, absent, less existent, and less alive in those not-met or not-processed coordinates of experience. Such absence is the emergent psychopathology that we experience when meeting our clients. In the therapy setting, the absences become present, and so therapy can be seen as a way of allowing the absences to become present. Therapy is an enhancement of freedom and presence— an enhancement of being, as Simone Weil (1952/2002) would have put it.

6.3 Some consequences for clinical practice[12]

From a field perspective, the clinical situation is not considered as being co-created by the therapist and the client. The client and the therapist are seen as processes emerging here-and-now in the flow of the situation (Robine, 2001, 2016; Philippson, 2009; Spagnuolo Lobb, 2013; Vázquez

Bandín, 2014; Roubal, 2019; Francesetti, 2016; Francesetti, 2019b; Francesetti et al., 2020). There is something new that appears in a meeting of people that transcends the individuals involved and even the relationship that they co-create. The whole of the situation is more than the sum of the people who meet each other (Wollants, 2008). Moreover, the situation is forever changing from one moment to the next. This constant change, the flow of the situation, follows its own dynamics and the people involved are constantly transformed by it, since they are functions of the situation in every moment here-and-now. In terms of the theory of complex systems:

> General synchronization implies that whenever two free-energy-minimizing agents, the therapist and the patient, are sensorially coupled, *they begin to share a phenomenal landscape.* Therefore, their experiential possibilities are governed by a common relational field of free-energy gradients.
>
> (Sarasso et al., 2024, my italics)

The therapist and the client are, in a way, used by the field dynamics that come to life in the therapy situation. Here, we abandon any concept of causality, even a circular one. We no longer see the situation as created by the therapist and the client, nor do we see the therapist and client as just created by the situation. Here we use a holistic paradigm of complexity that cannot be reduced to linear causes and predictable effects (Prigogine, 1997; Morin, 2008; Haken, 1977). Even the *active/passive* dichotomy is too limiting to understand the phenomena described here. We prefer to rely upon the concept of "middle mode," a natural spontaneity transcending (and including) both activity and passivity (Perls et al., 1951/1994). The change emerges by itself; in relating it to a specific cause, we reduce the actual complexity. In a certain sense, change is knocking at the door—we need only open it: "A poet does not reject an image that stubbornly but 'accidentally' appears and mars his plan; he respects the intruder and suddenly discovers what 'his plan' is, he discovers and creates himself" (Perls et al., 1951/1994, p. 137).

Both client and therapist are exposed to the field forces that are pushing to become embodied. These forces are perceived as sensations, impressions, or atmospheres[13] (Francesetti & Griffero, 2019) in the form of *proto-feelings.* They call in order to emerge through the embodiment of the client and therapist, opening up an opportunity for a change in the field organization processes.

A healthy situation has a good-enough degree of freedom and follows a natural flow enabling the intentionalities to be expressed and developed. The situation is grounded in the here-and-now and naturally aims for the next moment. The intentionalities give power to the flow; they channel it and give it a direction, which enables the situation to move naturally and smoothly to the next here-and-now. The individuals involved, being functions of such field dynamics, can then be seen by each other, express themselves towards each other, receive responses from each other, and be transformed by the experience of the live contact flow.

In psychopathological situations, the natural flow of the situation is distorted in a specific way, in which both the client and the therapist are functions. Such psychopathological dynamics actualize them into rigid repetitive patterns, squeezing them into rigidly formed processes, like flowing water in a deeply eroded riverbed. The client is unable to experience satisfying contact and this suffering becomes embodied as observable psychopathological symptoms. The therapist also experiences the devitalizing dynamics, because they also emerge as a function of the psychopathological field organization.

During the therapy session, the unformulated and dissociated proto-feelings that cannot be processed circulate in an undifferentiated level of experience as a disturbing "stranger knocking on the door" (Francesetti, 2019a, 2019b; Francesetti & Roubal, 2020). The proto-feelings are seeking an opportunity to emerge, to become feelings that can be processed (felt, recognized, named, expressed, validated, valued) and assimilated (integrated into the personality and so memorized as a past experience). In order to achieve this, the client's body is not enough, just as it was probably not enough in the client's life story. The proto-feelings need another flesh; the body of the therapist in the therapeutic situation must be involved. Therapists lend their flesh (Marion, 2003/2008)[14] to the field's forces in order to allow these change processes to happen. The phenomenal field can sometimes be very difficult to bear and many impasses in therapy are related to the therapist's inability to bear the strong affects present, along with the intentionality's forces. A fundamental element of the ground that supports the therapist in staying present in such difficult situations is the expectation of emerging beauty (Francesetti, 2012; Sarasso et al., 2024).

Adopting the field perspective, we assume that change transcends the individuals involved and presents a process with its own dynamics, a process which is "using" the people involved. Here, the therapeutic approach is based on the therapists' aesthetic experience (Bloom, 2003; Francesetti, 2012) of their embodied presence in the flow of the situation. Therapists lend their flesh to embody the forces of the field. Their way of being in the situation thus presents an opportunity to allow what is striving to emerge to come into existence.[15] "We perceive no *Thou*, but none the less we feel we are addressed and we answer... with our being" (Buber, 1937, p. 6).

Therapists find orientation in the field's forces through a phronetic process (Francesetti, 2019a; Francesetti & Roubal, 2020). According to Aristotle, *phronesis*[16] is an orientation that comes from the wisdom emerging in a situation. We use different orientations in different situations. When driving a car, for instance, we know how the car works and the rules of driving (*epistemological* knowledge), and we know what to do in order to have an effect on the car (*technical* knowledge). But knowing *when* and *how* to accelerate or brake, to turn left or right, depends upon our sensing the very moment of the present situation (*phronetic* knowledge).

For the field-theory perspective on psychotherapy work, the *metaphor* of a river can be used. The client and the therapist are together in a river being moved by forces far exceeding all human power. There is the complex, more or less turbulent flow of the river, and the therapist and the client are carried along by it. Whether the water runs fast, or spins around in whirlpools, or stands still, the movements of both client and therapist are part of the phenomenology of the situation, which the therapist needs to accept and respect in his/her responses.

From this perspective, what we do is less important than how we are with the client. Or, let us say, whatever we actively do as an intervention is important primarily as a way of staying calm and collected enough to listen to the tacit call of the potential, natural, fluid flow of the situation longing to be released from the prison of psychopathological field organizations. By changing our way of being with the client, the situation itself follows a transformation process, the fixed dynamics of the field processes are re-directed, and an opportunity arises to free the natural flow of the situation. The therapist's presence changes the degrees of probabilities of the actual phenomenal field.

As therapists, our main task, therefore, is not to stand as an obstacle in the way of this newly developing movement but to allow it to find its own way in the unique conditions of the here-and-now situation. A way that we cannot plan or arrange, or even foresee. If the change happens, we welcome it, whatever shape it takes. We as therapists do not make the change; we just become a door for it. The dynamics of the situation transform and the client and the therapist as individuals, being functions of the field, are transformed too. Not standing in the way of change does not mean the therapist steps aside from the forces' movements; on the contrary, it means being taken, moved, and transformed by them. As the Paradoxical Theory of Change describes it (Beisser, 1970), when we stop trying to achieve a change, the change arrives on its own.

6.4 Two clinical vignettes

I now present two clinical cases: personal work in a group setting[17] and a supervision.

6.4.1 "Welcome!"

In a first-year psychotherapy training group, Andrea asks to work on an unpleasant feeling in his belly, which first appeared the previous day and which he connects with a sense of isolation he feels in the group.

We sit opposite each other and I immediately find myself in a landscape of great tension. Andrea's body almost doubles up on itself to resist the turmoil inside his tummy and which gives no rise to words. He says he feels a tumultuous knot inside him which refuses to open up, even now. I struggle to stay with the intense sensations rippling through my body. I feel helpless, at a loss for direction and for words. A threshold vibrates intensely, almost irresistibly, between my diaphragm and my tummy. The minutes pass, almost speechlessly; looks become intense and almost undecipherable. I hint at a few questions or formulations of what I am observing, but I realize they are more for myself, to help me cope with the tension. The words, few and far between, with no real communicative intent, are lightning rods that make the unbearable tension there is in the air precipitate, if only slightly and just for an instant. In the looks in our eyes, in our nodding to each other, I feel like we are mutually saying, "Okay, this is it. We're here. We're alive." It takes all the energy I have to bear this tension. I let it all dwell in me and try not to back away, to support myself by breathing, to contain it all.

After a while that seems like an eternity to me, swimming in affective waves of great intensity, unspeakable and senseless, Andrea tells me how his brother suffered serious psychiatric problems at the age of thirteen, when he himself was eleven years old.

Something opens up on the bodily plane. It seems I can now feel in my body tellurian clumps subjected to extreme forces. Forces that could warp and sculpt rock. Forces that are blind to life, but also the premises for life. Something emerges and immediately sinks again. It is like a volcanic eruption that eases the tension, making it easier to breathe.

Andrea looks at me differently. He smiles and it surprises me. He tells me how he first met me years ago, at a course I give at university, and how grateful he is for this encounter and for being able to be a part of the group now.

I feel something precious in that, a soft movement in the midst of those blind forces. Before even thinking it I say, becoming emotional and smiling, "Welcome!"

Something flickers rapidly and freely between us. Even Andrea is moved. After a pause he says, "Can I ask you why you are emotional?"

"Hold on while I try and understand..." I briefly delve into my experience and it seems to me a miracle that he and I are here. I have a picture of us, so tiny in an infinitely vast cosmos, whose forces could sweep us away anywhere. So I reply,

"I think it's because you and I are here, despite the infinitely greater probabilities of us not being here... despite the infinite risks we have run of not being here."

Andrea bursts into tears, weeping, and then sobbing...

A long time passes without words, made up of looks and signs of understanding. A stream of emotions wells up, alternatively held back and left free to flow. Over the course of the session we then touch delicately, almost wordlessly, on the topic of suicide. On how it had run through his life and his brother's.

Later, in the feedback given by the group, someone says, "I saw tears flow from the rock." Another relates, "I felt an incredibly strong tension in my tummy, as though something had to burst but it wouldn't happen..." Feedback enriches our knowledge of the forces in the field and their trajectories in the therapeutic process.

How can we interpret this therapy experience from the monopersonal, bipersonal, and field perspectives?

From a monopersonal perspective, we could say that the therapist intervened with the client to allow him to access and articulate unexpressed and difficult emotional states. But that does not correspond to the therapist's experience at all. He had no knowledge nor any intention to intervene as such. It is a description made in hindsight and that does not grasp the experiential process of the therapist and how he found orientation.

From a bipersonal (co-creative) perspective, we could assume that the therapist tried to co-regulate the client's affective states and his own affective states in the client's presence. But again, that was not the therapist's experience. He was not trying to co-regulate the client's and his own affective states—he was not trying to do anything, except seek to bear the affective forces emerging. He did not seek to change the situation, but instead modulated his way of being and did what was supportive for him (and so, hopefully, for the client), in order to stay there and open the door to the emerging forces and processes.

From a field perspective, we can notice how in bearing the emerging landscape with Andrea, a turning point occurred somehow by itself, when the therapist said the word "Welcome!" Though he did not know where it came from, it proved the key for the transformation of the affects in play. Andrea's question, "Why are you emotional?" opened up a *logos* that the therapist did not know or expect. He discovered the preciousness of being together here and now, after the infinite risks of missing each other. And that—surprisingly—had a profound connection with the topic of suicide, which was so important in Andrea's life. The character in search of an author here could be the immense fragility and preciousness of life, showing how meaningful it is to be here, now, together. The richness of just being together in the same place and time can only be realized if we are aware of the risky journey that brought us here—of the continuous existential risk of dying or missing each other.

Of course, from a field perspective, what we did was not to somehow "repair" Andrea's history. The theme was meaningful and immediately became a fruitful topic for the group, helping all the members to become aware of the profound meaning of being in the same group, though that meaning was different for each person. Another way of looking at this case from a field perspective is to see the theme—so relevant for a group starting on long-term training—finding embodiment in Andrea, in order to emerge and be processed by all the group.

Of course, no perspective is better than another in an abstract way. Each allows us to focus on some aspects and leave others in the background.

6.4.2 A strange and shameful sense of stickiness

In an individual supervision session, Johan wishes to explore the therapeutic process with a young woman, Mary, thirty years old.

Johan: I've been seeing her for about six months and we haven't reached a sense of therapeutic alliance. This creates discomfort for me in our sessions together, but a sense of duty in me tells me I have to try harder to do more.

In our last session she asked if everything was okay with me and I reacted by saying "yes, of course!" but I felt a sense of shame for having lied.

I perceive myself as working on auto-pilot mode, trying to say the "right" things, while I don't recognize in myself a sincere involvement in the process.

Something strange, and again shameful, has also been happening to me more and more. During our sessions, and after them, I feel a sense of stickiness surrounding Mary. If I have to describe it, it is similar to the experience of children's skin after they have been playing outdoors for hours and are sweaty and a bit dirty, or when they have been eating sweets and their hands are all sticky and dirty.

My sensory experience is focused mostly on the sense of touch. I wouldn't ever want to touch Mary, even though she is always well-groomed and she isn't repulsive in an aesthetic sense. I don't even want to touch the couch she was sitting on, when I go to wipe it down to prepare the room for the next session.

Describing this sensory experience of stickiness and exploring it, Johan comes to express an unformulated and unconfessed feeling of disgust. At the same time, Johan is overcome by a wave of shame: "*How can*

I, as a therapist, feel disgust at another human being, not to mention a client that comes for help! It feels so inappropriate." Interestingly, a feeling of nausea starts to circulate in our session, felt by me and by Johan before we are able to recognize it. Or rather, we need time to give it shape and to formulate it. And when we are able to do this, we have an aesthetic signal that informs us that we found a good enough form for our feelings.[18]

I notice and share with Johan how disgust is more immediate than fear; it is an immediate bodily repulsion that protects the organism from being poisoned. As a next step we explore how this process could be meaningful for the client's life. Johan relates how Mary is the youngest child in a family of four (two parents and two children), where the parents are together and have a stable relationship. Her brother is ten years older than her and has been a heavy drug addict since his teenage years and suffers from recurring psychotic episodes. Still today he is in and out of psychiatric facilities and programs. Mary had to take care of herself from a very young age, while emotionally supporting both her parents and her brother.

The family has always been concentrated more on helping, supporting, and dealing with the consequences of her brother's behavior, and less on protecting Mary from what was emotionally dangerous and toxic. It seems that there was never any space to express disgust—just anxiety and fear, and perhaps a bit of anger. Disgust was probably never recognized nor named and a boundary to protect the family members from what was poisonous was never set. Disgust was not recognized and legitimated. "That's enough" was never expressed in the family.

Similarly, Johan 's feeling of disgust was "not allowed" during the therapy process. It was not legitimate. All that was allowed to emerge in his perception was a sense of "dirty stickiness" on the client's skin and his own skin. Johan just wanted to shut out these feelings—they were not appropriate for a "good therapist," who should instead accept the client.

This awareness allowed Johan to feel compassion instead of embarrassment, insecurity, and shame when imagining himself with the client. This shift was accompanied by a wish to explore the issue of disgust in the client's life.

In the supervision session we felt a feeling of vitality, of possibility, grow between us. From an initial sensation of oppressive deadlock, we arrived at an atmosphere of luminous aperture. I think that passage was significant even for us. The legitimation of his experiences and my experiences in our supervisory relationship is progressively growing, acknowledging and legitimating his way of being a therapist and my way of being a supervisor. Mary stepped into the room today, bringing this possibility with her and helping to transform the air that Johan and I both breathe. I can image that the many defeats that Johan, and I myself with him, experienced in his personal and professional life were able to come to existence thanks to the *Mary-form* that we encountered today. And which enabled a transformative passage in our relationship.

Johan sent me an email after the session with Mary following our supervision.

> Today I perceived Mary differently. It was like her face was brighter and her hands cleaner. I was so surprised, I even adjusted my glasses to see better, then I glanced away and when I looked back at her she seemed even more brighter and cleaner. There was no "sticky" sensation today. I almost couldn't believe my senses.
>
> I felt lighter as well and more prepared to just accompany her and not try so much.
>
> We talked about Mary's dance classes, about the child ballerinas she teaches, and a sense of joy, purity, and innocent beauty filled the room today. It was a novelty, also for the client's life.
>
> We explored a bit of the history of the boundaries in her family and in Mary's relationships. A feeling of heavy burden in her chest came and then disappeared. When not ignored the heaviness can be regulated with breathing. It also brought the image of a wound, which for Mary is carrying the responsibility for all the family.
>
> That has to be explored in the next sessions.

The character in search of an author here was disgust, a very basic feeling that informs us something poisonous is too close for comfort. To exist in the supervision session changed the process in therapy, allowing a new way of being together in therapy. Instead of being *forever-outside-time* and *everywhere-outside-space* (Francesetti, 2022), the feeling came to *ec-sist*—to find its place in space and time—enabling the therapeutic process to move on. And, of course, our relationship, too.

6.5 *Become yourself the prey*: Conclusions

A wonderfully poetic description of what I have been seeking to illustrate is found in the words of the poet Mariangela Gualtieri:

> Go slowly. Let your hand/Express the fragile suggestion./Have faith in that nothing/That comes—that nothing that happens. Don't speak a word./Let it come on its own. Become yourself/The prey. Let it capture you.
>
> (Gualtieri, 2019, p. 50, my translation)

In this chapter, I have sought to describe how field theory impacts the conceptualization of therapeutic processes. Psychopathology becomes a quality of absence in the phenomenal field, and therapy a modulation of the therapist's presence. Therapists, from this perspective, are not the agents of change, nor the co-creators of change. They are, rather, at the service of the field's forces; they lend their flesh to these intentionalities in order to let them produce a transformation. Therapy, on this view, can be understood as the "art of doing nothing"—but it is not a passive attitude. On the contrary, it is a very active one, even though it may not be seen as such from the outside. In psychotherapy, we are like artists who are at the service of the therapy process itself. At the service of life's flow. This brings us back to the foundations of Gestalt therapy: "(…) we reiterate that the suggestion is a spectacularly conservative one, for it is nothing but the old advice of the Tao: 'stand out of the way'" (Perls et al., 1951/1994, p. 24). Change can grow from our humble, grateful, and joyful acceptance of what is. From a field theory perspective, the crucial point is that the therapist's acceptance does not only refer to the client, but to whatever emerges in the session, because everything that emerges is a function of the field dynamics. Accepting the client, in fact, means accepting everything that happens to us in the presence of the client. The art of therapy is to be aware of what is happening, without reiterating the rejection of the *stranger knocking on the door* or the neglect of *the one who is always there*. Being present to absence—this is the very simple core of the therapeutic process in a field theory perspective. Simple, however, does not mean easy. To become *the prey* or *the chosen host* requires a long journey of training and of personal therapy. And an openness to accepting what life ceaselessly brings.

Notes

1 This chapter is partly based on papers already published (Francesetti, 2015, 2019a, 2020, 2022; Francesetti & Griffero, 2019; Francesetti & Roubal, 2020; Roubal & Francesetti, 2022; Francesetti et al., 2022; Gecele, 2013, 2021), to which I refer the reader who is interested in more in-depth study. I am particularly grateful to Michela Gecele and Jan Roubal for our ongoing dialogue on these themes, to the point that my thinking and writing are the result of this entangled common exploration. The Turin School of Psychopathology is both the outcome and the ground of this theoretical and clinical development.
2 I thank the trainees at the Centro Clinico Mattia Maggiora run by the cooperative Poiesis in Turin for having counted them all.
3 Friedrich S. Perls was one of Goldstein's assistants in Frankfurt in 1926, together with Siegmund H. Fuchs, who later emigrated to the United States. There he changed his name to Foulkes and developed group analysis. See the chapter by Bocian in this book.
4 See the chapter by Bocian in this book.
5 In particular, it was Paul Goodman, who worked at the University of Chicago Library, who brought the thought of William James, John Dewey, and George Herbert Mead into the foundation of Gestalt therapy.
6 Intentionality can be understood as a force belonging to the individuals, but this is not the meaning I am referring to here. Here I refer to the anonymous intentionality that precedes individuals as it is conceptualized by Merleau-Ponty: "We are just a place of passage" (Merleau-Ponty, 1945/2012, p. 201). As Martin Heidegger (1927/1962, p. 192) put it: "There is always a depersonalisation in the heart of consciousness.".
7 This definition allows us to explore field theory in the light of complex systems theory. See Pietro Sarasso, Wolfgang Tschascher, Felix Schoeller, Gianni Francesetti, Jan Roubal, Michela Gecele, Irene Ronga, Katiuscia Sacco (2024). *Nature heals: An informational entropy account of self-organization and change in field psychotherapy.*
8 Quoted in Staemmler (2023).
9 Logos/'lɒgɒs/noun. L16. [ORIGIN Greek = account, relation, ratio, reason(ing), argument, discourse, saying, speech, word, rel. to legein choose, collect, gather, say]. *Shorter Oxford English Dictionary Sixth Edition (2007).*
10 It is impressive how this moment of waiting for meaning corresponds to our conceptualization of clinical work in a field perspective (Francesetti & Roubal, 2020).
11 According to Damasio's definition of the stage of proto-self (when object and subject are not yet separated and defined in the process of perception), "proto-feelings" are what we call the feelings that are not processed, nor clearly defined, which remain as vague sensorial impressions not clearly belonging to the person (Damasio, 2010; Francesetti & Griffero, 2019; Francesetti & Roubal, 2020).
12 For more on this see Francesetti and Roubal (2020), Roubal and Francesetti (2022), and Francesetti et al. (2022).
13 I am referring to Böhme's (2017) conception of atmospheres as perceptive phenomena that are not independent from the subjects' presence. This understanding is different from that of Schmitz (2011). For the first author, an atmosphere is a perceptive phenomenon in the process of perception itself (that we can place in the phase of fore-contact); for the second, the atmospheres exist in the world independently from the subject.
14 In a personal communication with one of the authors, Jean-Luc Marion recognizes the important role that the phenomenon of lending the flesh (what he calls the "Erotic Phenomenon") can have in therapy, as conceptualized in Francesetti (2019a, 2019b) and in Francesetti and Roubal (2020).

15 To *ec-sist*, from Latin, *to come up*.
16 The concept of *phronesis* is used by intersubjective psychoanalysts (Stolorow et al., 1999; Orange et al., 1997) and by some Gestalt therapists (Sichera, 2001; Francesetti, 2019a).
17 In Gestalt therapy training, one of the experiential possibilities in groups is to do personal work. It is a therapeutic exploration that a participant may wish to do with the trainer, usually starting from something that emerges during the seminar. The group remains in the background (even though it can be involved in the process) and at the end of the personal work, all the participants can give their feedback to the person. The aim is both to process a theme that emerges from a participant but is meaningful for the group process too, and to give rise to a learning experience of therapeutic processes that can be theoretically discussed and commented on.
18 On the aesthetic criterion see Bloom (2003), Francesetti (2012), and Sarasso et al. (2024).

References

Beisser, A. (1970). The paradoxical theory of change. In J. Fagan, & J. Shepherd (Eds.), *Gestalt therapy now*. Harper.
Bloom, D. (2003). "Tiger! Tiger! Burning bright". Aesthetic values as clinical values in gestalt therapy. In M. Spagnuolo Lobb, & N. Amendt-Lyon (Eds.), *Creative license. The art of gestalt therapy* (pp. 63–78). Springer.
Bocian, B. (2010). *Fritz Perls in Berlin 1893–1933. Expressionism, psychoanalysis, Judaism* (P. Schmitz trans.). EHP.
Böhme, G. (2017). *The aesthetics of atmospheres*. Routledge.
Botelho Alvim, M. (2021). Sensing with the other: The pathic-aesthetical dimension of human experience. *Gestalt Review, 25*(1), 31–63.
Buber, M. (1937). *I and Thou*. Touchstone.
Candiani, L. C. (2014). *La bambina pugile ovvero la precisione dell'amore*. Einaudi.
Damasio, A. (2010). *Self comes to mind. Constructing the conscious brain*. Pantheon Books.
Fonagy, P., & Target, M. (1997). Attachment and reflective function: Their role in self-organization. *Development and Psychopathology, 9*(4), 679–700.
Francesetti, G. (2012). Pain and beauty. From psychopathology to the aesthetics of contact. *British Gestalt Journal, 21*(2), 4–18.
Francesetti, G. (2015). From individual symptoms to psychopathological fields. Towards a field perspective on clinical human suffering. *British Gestalt Journal, 24*(1), 5–19.
Francesetti, G. (2016). "You cry, I feel pain". The emerging, co-created self as the foundation of anthropology, psychopathology and treatment in Gestalt therapy. In J.-M. Robine (Ed.), *Self. A polyphony of contemporary Gestalt therapists* (pp. 147–167). L'Exprimerie.
Francesetti, G. (2019a). The field strategy in clinical practice: Towards a theory of therapeutic phronesis. In P. Brownell (Ed.), *Handbook for theory, research and practice in Gestalt therapy* (2nd ed., pp. 268–302). Cambridge Scholars Publishing.
Francesetti, G. (2019b). A clinical exploration of atmospheres. Towards a field-based clinical practice. In G. Francesetti, & T. Griffero (Eds.), *Psychopathology and atmospheres. Neither inside nor outside* (pp. 35–68). Cambridge Scholars Publishing.

Francesetti, G. (2019c). La metamorfosi del dolore. In V. Conte, & A. Sichera (Eds.). *Avere a cuore. Scritti in onore di Giovanni Salonia* (pp. 109–118). Edizioni San Paolo.

Francesetti, G. (2022). Atmospheres as media of transgenerational transmission. "Children and pet dogs understand everything, especially that which is not spoken" (Dolto, 1988). *British Gestalt Journal, 31*(1), 6–20.

Francesetti, G., Alcaro, A., & Settanni, M. (2020). Panic disorder: Attack of fear or acute attack of solitude? Convergences between affective neuroscience and phenomenological-Gestalt perspective. *Research in Psychotherapy: Psychopathology, Process and Outcome, 23*, 77–87.

Francesetti, G., & Gecele, M. (2009). A Gestalt therapy perspective on psychopathology and diagnosis. *British Gestalt Journal, 18*(2), 5–20.

Francesetti, G., Gecele, M., & Roubal, J. (2017). Aesthetic diagnosis in Gestalt therapy. *Behavioral Sciences, 7*(4), 70.

Francesetti, G., Gecele, M., & Roubal, J. (2022). Being present to absence. Field theory in psychopathology and clinical practice In P. Cole (Ed.). *The relational heart of Gestalt therapy. Contemporary perspectives* (pp. 44–56). Routledge.

Francesetti, G., & Griffero, T. (Eds.). (2019). *Psychopathology and atmospheres. Neither inside nor outside*. Cambridge Scholars Publishing.

Francesetti, G., & Griffero, T. (Eds.). (2022). *Psicopatologia e atmosfere. Prima del soggetto e del mondo*. Giovanni Fioriti Editore.

Francesetti, G., & Roubal, J. (2020). Field theory in contemporary Gestalt therapy. Part one: Modulating the therapist's presence in clinical practice. *Gestalt Review, 24*(2), 113–136.

Fuchs, T. (2021). *In defence of the human being. Foundational questions of an embodied anthropology*. Oxford University Press.

Gecele, M. (2013). Introduction to personality disturbances. Diagnostic and social remarks. In G. Francesetti, M. Gecele, & J. Roubal (Eds.). *Gestalt therapy in clinical practice. From psychopathology to the aesthetics of contact* (pp. 601–608). FrancoAngeli.

Gecele, M. (2021). *Gli sfondi dell'alterità. La terapia della Gestalt nell'orizzonte sociale e culturale: tra frammentazione e globalizzazione*. Giovanni Fioriti Editore.

Goldstein, K. (1939). *The organism*. The American Book Company.

Griffero, T. (2010). *Atmospheres: Aesthetics of emotional spaces*. Routledge.

Gualtieri, M. (2019). *Quando non morivo*. Einaudi.

Haken, H. (1977). Synergetics. *Physics Bulletin, 29*(9), 412.

Harrington, A. (1999). *Reenchanted science. Holism in German culture from Wilhelm II to Hitler*. Princeton University Press.

Heidegger, M. (1962). *Being and time*. Harper & Row. (Original work published 1927).

Lewin, K. (1951). *Field theory in social science: Selected theoretical papers* (D. Cartwright Ed.). Harper & Brothers.

Marion, J.-L. (2002). *Being given. Toward a phenomenology of givenness*. Stanford University Press.

Marion, J.-L. (2008). *The erotic phenomenon*. University of Chicago Press. (Original work published 2003).

Marková, I. S., & Berrios, G. E. (2012). The epistemology of psychiatry. *Psychopathology, 45*, 220–227.

Merleau-Ponty, M. (2012). *Phenomenology of perception* (D. A. Landes Trans.). Routledge. (Original work published 1945).

Minkowski, E. (1999). *Vers une cosmologie.* Payot & Rivages.

Morin, E. (2008). *On complexity.* Hampton Press.

Orange, D. M., Atwood, G. E., & Stolorow, R. D. (Eds.). (1997). *Working intersubjectively: Contextualism in psychoanalytic practice.* Analytic Press.

Parlett, M., & Lee, R. G. (2005). Contemporary gestalt therapy: Field theory. In A. L. Woldt, & S. M. Toman (Eds.). *Gestalt therapy. History, theory, and practice* (pp. 41–63). Sage.

Perls, F., Hefferline, R., & Goodman, P. (1994). *Gestalt therapy. Excitement and growth in the human personality.* Gestalt Journal Press. (Original work published 1951).

Philippson, P. (2009). *The emergent self: An existential-Gestalt approach.* Karnac Books.

Philippson, P.A. (2017). *Paper 1: Revisiting the field.* (Topics in Gestalt therapy: Occasional Kindle papers by Peter Philippson). E-book. https://www.amazon.co.uk/gp/product/B01N4WQ484?ie=UTF8&linkCode=as2&camp=1634&creative=6738&tag=&creativeASIN=B01N4WQ484 (last accessed March 1, 2024).

Pirandello, L. (1952). Preface to "Six characters in search of an author". In *Naked masks* (E. Bentley Ed. and Trans., pp. 363–376). E.P. Dutton. (Original work published 1925).

Prigogine, I. (1997). *The end of certainty. Time, chaos, and the new laws of nature.* The Free Press.

Robine, J.-M. (2001). From the field to the situation. In J.-M. Robine (Ed.), *Contact and relationship in a field perspective* (pp. 95–107). L'Exprimerie.

Robine, J.-M. (2016). *Self: Artist of contact.* In J.-M. Robine (Ed.), *Self. A polyphony of contemporary Gestalt therapists* (pp. 213–232). L'Exprimerie.

Roubal, J. (2019). Foreword. In G. Francesetti, E. Kerry-Reed, & C. Vázquez Bandín (Eds.), *Obsessive-compulsive experiences: A Gestalt therapy perspective* (pp. 7–20). Los Libros del CTP.

Roubal, J., & Francesetti, G. (2022). Field theory in contemporary Gestalt therapy. Part two: Paradoxical theory of change reconsidered. *Gestalt Review, 26*(1), 1–33.

Salonia, G. (2013). Social context and psychotherapy. In G. Francesetti, M. Gecele, & J. Roubal (Eds.), *Gestalt therapy in clinical practice. From psychopathology to the aesthetics of contact* (pp. 189–200). FrancoAngeli.

Sarasso, P., Tschascher, W., Schoeller, F., Francesetti, G., Roubal, J., Gecele, M., Ronga I., & Sacco K. (2024). Nature heals. An informational entropy account of self-organization and change in field psychotherapy. *Physics of Life Reviews, 51,* 64–84.

Schmitz, H. (2011). *Nuova fenomenologia. Un'introduzione.* Christian Marinotti.

Sichera, A. (2001). A confronto con Gadamer: per una epistemologia ermeneutica della Gestalt. In M. Spagnuolo Lobb (Ed.), *Psicoterapia della Gestalt. Ermeneutica e clinica* (pp. 17–41). FrancoAngeli.

Smuts, J. (1926). *Holism and evolution.* Macmillan. (Reprinted in 2013 by the Gestalt Journal Press).

Spagnuolo Lobb, M. (2013). *The now-for-next in psychotherapy. Gestalt therapy recounted in post-modern society.* FrancoAngeli.

Staemmler, F.-M. (2006). A Babylonian confusion? On the uses and meanings of the term field. *British Gestalt Journal, 15*(2), 64–83.

Staemmler, F.-M. (2023). In response to Gianni Francesetti's Atmospheres as media of transgenerational phenomena. *British Gestalt Journal, 32*(1), 58–61.

Stern, D. N. (1985). *The interpersonal world of the infant. A view from psychoanalysis and developmental psychology.* Basic Books.

Stolorow, R. D., Brandchaft, B., Atwood, G. E., Fosshage, J., & Lachmann, F. (1999). *Psicopatologia intersoggettiva*. Quattro Venti.

Vázquez Bandín, C. (2014). *Sin tí no puedo ser yo. Pensando según la terapia Gestalt*. Los Libros del CTP.

Waldenfels, B. (2011). *Phenomenology of the alien: Basic concepts*. Northwestern University Press.

Weil, S. (2002). *Gravity and grace* (E. Crawford, & M. von der Ruhr Trans.). Routledge. (Original work published 1952).

Wertheimer, M. (1944). Gestalt theory [conference held in Berlin in 1924]. *Social Research, 11*, 78–99.

Wollants, G. (2008). *Gestalt therapy. Therapy of the situation*. Sage.

Zahavi, D. (2017). Thin, thinner, thinnest: Defining the minimal self. In C. Durt, T. Fuchs, & C. Tewes (Eds.), *Embodiment, enaction, and culture*. The MIT Press.

Chapter 7

Discussion for Gianni Francesetti and Michela Gecele

Donna Orange

It is a tremendous honor to be asked for a brief response to the important contributions of Gianni Francesetti and Michela Gecele, eminent theorists and practitioners in Gestalt therapy. I do hope that the words I have written will meet what they have said to you in some way. Nevertheless, truth-in-advertising requires me to tell you that I have never been trained in Gestalt psychotherapy and that I have never seriously practiced it. Instead, dear friends like Lynne Jacobs, Gary Yontef, and, more recently, Margherita Spagnuolo Lobb, have invited me to teach in their residentials and workshops, perhaps from curiosity to see how a psychoanalyst thinks and works. In these workshops, I have learned far more than I have taught. The purpose was, I think, to enrich Gestalt therapy, but instead their work enriched mine as an independent, theoretically and clinically inclusive psychoanalyst. Clinical work, likewise, hard as it often is, seems to me an unmatched privilege as our patients, those who suffer, place their souls in our hands so that we too are often healed. The invitation to show and tell one's own work to others becomes an honor and an opportunity.

In my early years at the California residentials, you may recall that the request or demand to work in public clinical demonstrations initially terrified me. Nothing in my psychoanalytic world had prepared me for what I encountered. We just don't do that. But I watched and learned, and now I have had dozens of rewarding experiences, both for me and for the patient or volunteer. I have carried this learning with me directly and indirectly into my psychoanalytic work and into supervision workshops.

Now, what has all this to do with my task here to think with you about field and fields? The field concept, of course, comes to us all

DOI: 10.4324/9781003597308-8

from the Gestalt psychologists of the early 20th century. Both Gestalt psychotherapists and the early phenomenologists like Husserl and Merleau-Ponty picked it up and used it, constantly refining both its meaning and its use. In the same years we learned from Wittgenstein that the meaning *is* the use, and that meanings come from their contexts in what he called language games. In my early work with psychoanalytic phenomenologists Robert Stolorow and George Atwood, we spoke and wrote constantly of the intersubjective field, emergent from the interactions between or among two or more subjective worlds of experience. We believed that individual subjective worlds themselves emerged from parent, infant, analyst, patient, and other such meetings, and that only through such intersubjective encounters could personal worlds of experience change for good or for harm. Clearly our intersubjective psychoanalysis relies on many of the same ideas and sources that Michela Gecele has outlined.

In particular, we psychoanalysts suggested that organizing principles, an expression from Stolorow, or emotional convictions, in my words, derived from early relational experience, shaping our worlds of experience for good or ill. These tightly held convictions, or those with an enormous grip on us, last our entire lives. My simplistic but always present example is that as a child, my mother called me "worthless" and "good-for-nothing." She would say, "Hey, worthless. Get those dishes done." Complete this or that task. My name was worthless. Those kinds of early relational experiences become our organizing principles. In other words, my sense of who I am and how I can expect you to perceive me and relate to me, constitute my organizing principles. These tightly held convictions, with the disasters they create in our lives, often brought us into psychotherapy or psychoanalysis. Certainly they did for me, in hopes that there might still be help in the human world. I am thinking about Gianni's case now, the hope that there might still be help in the human world. Both people begin to realize that it is about suicide, as it is for many of us who rarely talk about it. There might still be help in the human world even when we could not understand the relational sources of our suffering. We psychoanalytic phenomenologists intended these ideas to counter, to fight back against what we saw as an excessive emphasis on the individual psyche in traditional psychoanalysis as well as in self psychology.

Over time, our view came to speak more of context than of field and to involve more forms of background. Others, like Michela, have already alluded to this. Today, we might include, for example, systematic racism and sexism, as well as climate destruction, all of which characterize our patients' grounds and ours, too. Making the unconscious conscious, an old psychoanalytic mantra, now means coming to be familiar with features of our fields that we do not want to know, but that have shaped those rigid ways of organizing our experiential worlds. But fields themselves remain a central concern in Gestalt therapy, as Francesetti and Gecele explain theoretically and clinically. They distinguish their view of the total field or situation from one-person and two-person psychologies. Each of the three approaches has a history in Gestalt therapy, in theorizing and practice as they explain, or as they have explained in some of their writings. Treating the suffering individual as one thought to be ill or impaired was the earliest form, as in psychoanalysis. Here in the United States, the family systems theory of Murray Bowen in the 1980s called these assumptions into question, calling the child brought for therapy the designated patient, then treating the whole family system as the patient.

Still, no one back then questioned that the doctor *was* the doctor and not part of the system to be treated. The next big move questioned this assumption, both in Gestalt therapy and in interpersonal, intersubjective, and relational psychoanalysis. You have heard a lot from Don Stern already about this, and I do not have time or space to distinguish all of these properly. Anyway, the next big step originated with Heinrich Racker in South America, who reminded us that the great myth of psychoanalysis was that it concerned an encounter between a healthy person and a sick one. Instead, we are two human persons with our gifts, our warts, and sufferings. We work together in the service of one who has sought the help of the other. Now the field has become a Buberian encounter between one of those who suffer, the patient, and one who bears more responsibility. A dialogic encounter, to be sure, but Buber reminded us of important asymmetries when one is a teacher, therapist, or rabbi. In Gestalt therapy, the relational school has taken this road, also emphasizing Buberian inclusion and confirmation, as well as the paradoxical theory of change, a theoretical and clinical treasure that I need not explain to this audience.

In psychoanalysis, my own work has also followed this path and has probably formed a bridge with the Gestalt people with whom it has been my privilege to work. My phenomenology study group, working on Husserl, Merleau-Ponty, and Waldenfels, among others, is, to my surprise, nearly filled with senior Gestalt trainers. Much of my supervision time also goes to Gestalt people. An odd psychoanalysis, you might say. Or maybe an odd psychoanalyst, a strange one. But now we have a new path in field theory, led by the two authors to whom I have been asked to respond, as well as by Jean-Marie Robine. We might call it a field theory of the total situation in which change in any part or quality of the system or field creates spreading effects as in chaos and quantum theories. Indeed, we do not describe these fields in terms of their parts, but rather by the qualities of the whole. It was a dark and stormy night, to plagiarize from the *Peanuts* cartoon. Not here or there, for you or for me, but the night was dark and stormy as a whole until something in the weather changed for better or for worse.

As a therapeutic theory, this field describes the whole, not the individuals who live in the night or in the disturbance. It perhaps returns to the sensibility of early family systems theories. It also resembles our psychoanalytic work that looks for emergence, noticing the ways in which tiny changes in one part of the field begin to produce larger changes in the whole field or system. Nevertheless, its Gestalt therapy proponents believe it is new. They write: "There is a dimension of the ongoing process of the emergence of self when self and world are not yet differentiated and from where the poles of self or me, other or subject object, or organism environment emerge." "We think," they continue, "that this paradigm is revolutionary for understanding the human suffering and for clinical practice" (Francesetti et al., 2022). Having studied and taught the postwar psychoanalytic and developmental work of Donald W. Winnicott and Hans Loewald, I am less inclined to regard this understanding as new or revolutionary. It has undergirded my thinking and practice for many years. I would agree, however, to the importance of this view. Many clinical experiences make more sense when we begin to think in this way. I think that is a lot of what Gianni was showing us.

Because this field begins in preverbal infancy and remains in great part unformulated and unformulable, we may be less surprised that important changes occur in many psychotherapies without either participant becoming able to say what changed or why it changed. I remember a seriously and chronically ill patient with the most severely painful and disfiguring form of scleroderma thanking me after seven years for having helped her to accept her illness. But neither of us, to my memory, then and now, had ever spoken of accepting her illness or her suffering. There was simply a way we were together, I might call it accompanying or walking alongside, that created this result outside my range of vision. I was astonished. It is therefore no surprise that the teachers of this new field theory love the paradoxical theory of change, a wonderful and useful idea that I have found made explicit only in Gestalt therapy. When I first heard of Arnie Beisser and his theory, I thought of parents and teachers who tell children to do exactly the opposite of what they want them to do, knowing that they may well get the desired result. This theory, though less dramatic, is deceptively simple and resembles, as many have noted, the Daoist injunction to do nothing, not to interfere so that the other side of the Dao can come out.

It actually also relates to the silence that Gianni was talking about, I think. It replaces the expert with one who accompanies, one who provides the quality of space for the other's wisdom to emerge. When I shut down my inner *Besserwisser*, the "know-it-all" person who always knows better, I may be able to tune in to the wisdom or to the emotion of the room and respond to that. Then the patient may not feel crowded by me or by my agenda. Gestalt therapists and theorists have, I think, described pathology as absence and therapy as bringing the absent to presence. Making the unconscious conscious again. My only objection would claim a more central focus on violence and violation. But clearly, we actually agree here. Not only do we agree that incomprehensible and unassimilable violence often underlies the absence, but we agree that our "you should feel" is itself a form of violence. The absence, albeit, of course, not in every instance, creates concerns, an unspoken, unspeakable history of violence now becomes speakable in the presence of the therapeutic witness who non-intrusively accompanies. The trauma and madness work of Françoise Davoine and Jean-Max Gaudilliere teach us to invite the ghosts, including those inhabiting the therapist, into the therapeutic space.

For this reason, I often think of our work as a haunted phenomenology in which the absent presence of the violent and violating past can become explicit and available for shared experience. Germans speak of psychoanalytic *Behandlung*, which translates in English to psychoanalytic treatment, but this does not fully capture what the Germans are saying here. They are saying that treatment consists in a witnessed hands-on encounter with the ghosts of the past and a hands-on encounter with the patient here. Thus, the patient becomes able, in biblical terms, to choose life. These authors seem at times to suggest that we must choose between a monopersonal, a bipersonal, and a field psychology to ground our work. At other times, they seem to say we need access to all three psychologies to keep us flexible enough to respond in any given treatment. My guess is that they would prefer us to adopt their field theory and then explain how focus on the individual or the couple works within that theory. Individuals and couples would then be seen as functions or processes of the field or of the situation. I am not so sure. While this field theory helps to explain paradoxical change and perhaps even the transgenerational transmission of trauma, it seems to me that no field, system, situation, atmosphere, or other totality can eclipse, or take priority over, the singular, irreplaceable individual other.

The individual who emerges from the parent–infant bond grows up to be a person whose face commands me and requires my non-indifferent response. This other may often be the stranger knocking on my door, the one for whom I am always already responsible. They may also be the traveler beaten, robbed, and lying in the ditch. They may look and sound different, but our shared humanity calls out to me. At the same time, the stranger may be the one who is always there, waiting for rescue or response. Therapeutically, the always-there requires attention to features shaping the field, race, religion, language, gender, that is, whatever joins or divides us in the therapeutic work. What characterizes the situation of a black candidate seeking a training analysis in institutes where the senior analysts (or Gestalt trainers) are all white, or most of them are? What characterizes that? How do the cultural, historical, and economic disparities shape the field? How can the white analyst or therapist become aware how her endless sense of privilege downgrades her patient of color?

I particularly value the sketching out of these two aspects of otherness. First, the personal strangerhood or outsiderness, and second, the structural taken-for-granted features of the field. Once again, let me say what an honor and pleasure it is to be invited into your conversation to be the stranger knocking at your door.

Reference

Francesetti, G., Gecele, M., & Roubal J. (2022). Being present to absence. Field theory in psychopathology and clinical practice. In P. Cole (Ed.), *The relational heart of Gestalt therapy* (pp. 44–56). Routledge.

Chapter 8

Anna

A clinical case study

Paola Zarini

8.1 Premise

This case study looks at 20-year-old Anna, a client I have met at three different moments over a period of six years. The first time I met Anna, it was after a few sessions of parent support with her mother. The second time, when Anna was around 17 years old, we began a course of therapy sessions, initially at the request of the mother. However, these sessions were interrupted after just a few months due to the outbreak of the COVID-19 pandemic. Recently, again through the mediation of the mother, I met with Anna again to pick up where we left off, and we have started a new therapeutic relationship.

8.2 First phase

8.2.1 Outline and construction of the anamnestic-existential background

Anna's mother first contacted me for support regarding the relationship with her daughter, which had changed profoundly in recent months. In particular, she wanted and needed support in dealing with the separation process she was going through with Anna, in a phase typical of adolescence. She felt weary and pained by the distance her daughter was taking from their relationship, and by her newfound "opacity." At the same time, she expressed concern about the fact that Anna no longer wanted to see her father.

The mother explained that she had given birth to Anna when she was just over 20 years old, the child of a casual relationship with a man she broke off with a few months after her daughter's birth. A year later she married another man, one able to give her a "sense of security and stability." Anna grew up in that new family setting, seeing her biological

DOI: 10.4324/9781003597308-9

father only occasionally, each month or so. Anna has never had a "good relationship" with her mother's husband; she has always been distant, showing indifference and, at times, even annoyance. Until recently, however, she describes the mother/daughter relationship in very exclusive terms, the two of them being close and completely "open" with each other. A relationship without boundaries, permeated by a "paradisiacal" atmosphere.

The pain the mother conveyed seemed to flow from a wound, gushing from a deep and violent rupture. However, against this background of distressing and lacerating pain, *Anna the adolescent* took shape in her mother's account in all her subjectivity—a subjectivity that was harder to make out in her account of *Anna the child*, where boundaries of differentiation between them did not emerge.

After checking with her, I decided to meet with Anna a few times, both with and without her mother. As Anna entered the therapy room, what immediately struck me was her statuesque beauty and her almost-regal stare, which seemed to reach me from a far-off dimension, from "up on-high." My experience of her in that first encounter was of an indifferent presence, "but also warmth, at some far-off level." She uttered only a few polite, but curt words: that as she did not want to see her father, that she had never understood the point in seeing him, and that for 14 years their encounters had mostly been about meeting his constant stream of new partners and the babysitters. She had no requests of her own to make, but she said she was prepared to meet with me again, if her mother so wished. However, I decided not to push for further meetings with her and preferred to continue working on the maternal front, given the absence of personal motivation and the risk of Anna only formally agreeing to possible future sessions.

For the following three years I saw the mother on a sporadic basis; she would occasionally ask for support in a somewhat haphazard manner, but I came to realize that this was probably the only approach she could take. From her mother's words, I learnt that Anna had "suddenly become all grown up," and often went out with friends and boys.

8.3 Second phase

8.3.1 *The beginning of therapy with Anna*

Not long before Anna turned 18, after almost a year of no contact, her mother contacted me, explaining that her daughter was not well, and that she had withdrawn into a shell and refused to communicate, but had said she was willing to talk to me in a confidential environment. So I met with Anna who, for the first time, was bringing an autonomous request "for help."

Anna was, at first glance, very grown up, but a bit gloomy and seemingly folded in upon herself. She immediately outlined the current scenario of her life as one characterized by compulsive sexual behavior. She would seek out male partners, even men who were much older, whom she would encounter for casual sex, sometimes even seeing more than one partner on the same day. She herself defined these behaviors as uncontrollable, even though they did not bring her any pleasure.

In reconstructing together the story of the sentimental and sexual relationships of her young life, it emerged that her first sexual experience had come about two years earlier, at the age of 15, with a boy she had not known for long. The description of this encounter bore more resemblance to an experience of sexual violence rather than being one of mutual sexual interest. Anna recalled the place where it happened— on the terraces of a stadium—the sharp physical pain she felt, and how after the act itself she was left alone. Just as when it happened, she described the event with no apparent "feeling," using language similar to that in which she described the compulsive behaviors of the present. Regarding these experiences she appeared to me the way she appeared to herself: indifferent, even though "she didn't expect herself to be."

It is only in relation to one very vague and laconic story that Anna told me—that of a sexual experience with more than one partner at the same time—that for the first time her tears threatened to spill. They never did, like a bodily event which can never become feeling. I could also feel, "hung" somewhere within her, a far-away echo of fear. It was only later on—intentionally after she turned 18—that she confirmed that this second episode was actually an account of rape, committed by three boys under the influence of drugs. This was an event that also had a serious impact on Anna's body, but that she had chosen not to report to the police.

In these first encounters, during this second phase, her question and her call for help came to me on two separate levels. The first of these concerned her sexual behavior; this was the level of the "why." This was a logical and rational question that Anna asked me with such a disarming simplicity and lack of emotion that it made me skip a breath as I heard it: "Why is it, do you think, that I have this unstoppable urge to sleep with every man I meet, to the point that it makes me go out to bars to look for them?"

The second level was more implicit or indirect. After the first few sessions, in fact, Anna began to tell me of episodes of anguish that inexplicably happened to her, especially when she was on her own. She talked about this intermittently, almost under her breath. What she called "anguish" in this case was a sudden and inexplicable bursting into tears, which did not seem to have a connection with any clear feeling. These tears reached me as small movements towards a possible opening to dimensions of feeling that in part I was imagining, and in part I could feel vibrating within me. I realized, while she was speaking, that those images were coming to me all on their own, without me forcing them to, and I started feeling a sense of sadness and deep loneliness.

A few months after the beginning of the sessions, I met with Anna's mother at her request. This time I was struck by how she spoke of Anna's sexuality, describing her daughter as having "positively blossomed" and normalizing the number of her sexual partners (which Anna would mention to her in passing) in the name of female sexual freedom—a freedom she endorsed, attributing to Anna's experiences the same meaning as her own. She explained that she herself had always had numerous sexual partners, and so she felt it was a natural behavior for her daughter—"she must take after me," she remarked. What struck me in that context was something that in supervision we would call "a blind spot of the mother," making it very difficult for experiences concerning sexuality to emerge. The hypothesis of a family field marked by dissociation in relation to sexual abuse began to take shape.

During that second phase, which lasted for a few months, the therapeutic intervention took place almost exclusively on the field level. The initial emergence of sadness and loneliness through me, and then of Anna's "disconnected" tears, even within the therapy setting, were all positive signals of a possible movement towards integration. These small and delicate movements in therapy, in the face of these powerful sexual "acting-outs," were, however, brought to an end by the outbreak of the COVID-19 pandemic. The thin ground on which we were moving was not sufficient for us to continue in an online setting, which for Anna was a totally new and unexplored one. After one attempt, the therapy process was put on hold—just like many other things in our lives—at the beginning of March 2020.

8.4 Third phase

8.4.1 The present

After more than two years of silence, Anna's mother contacted me at the beginning of summer 2022, asking to see me urgently in order to help her daughter. She told me that about a year earlier, Anna had decided to move abroad. Initially staying at her father's holiday house, she had soon left and moved in with a man who quickly became her partner and father-to-be of the baby girl she was now carrying, and who was due to be born at the end of the year.

The specific reason for her mother's urgency was that Anna's new partner was a drug user (in particular, he made use of crack cocaine), which led him to become violent and suffer from major psychotic episodes. During one of these, he had beaten her up, and in a delirious bout of jealousy he had threatened her with a knife and kept her locked up for hours at home without access to her phone. When Anna told her mother about what was going on, both her parents flew out to see her and persuade her to "come back home." A few weeks later, she "made up her mind" to leave her partner and return to Italy.

About a week before returning to Italy, Anna contacted me on her own. We met for a session the day immediately after her arrival. Anna's statuesque beauty, which I remembered so well, had only been enhanced by her pregnancy. The moment she walked through the door, what I saw in my mind's eye was a picture of divinity, a sort of young mother-goddess. This picture was so dazzling that I felt almost hypnotized by this aspect of her beauty, and it took me some time to compose myself enough to listen to her. Glowing, she looked at me and smiled. After that, the sound of the words coming out of my mouth seemingly brought us both back to Earth. I informed her of my encounter with her mother and of what she had told me. I laid it all out on the ground and then waited for her to speak.

Anna explained how this man, the father of her unborn daughter, was the only person in her entire existence with whom she had ever felt "something." Drug abuse is a hard habit to break though, and so she gave in and decided to leave him, hoping that he would not ask to be recognized as the father of the child. "It all seemed to be going so well at first, but then when I became pregnant he started smoking crack. It's something that makes you completely lose your mind and there's no way out of it."

I asked her how she was doing, and what she was feeling, and she answered that she could not feel anything and that the "absence of feeling" was actually something that had always characterized her life, even as a child. "I've never felt a thing about anybody or anything, and even now that I should probably feel distraught by everything that has happened, instead I feel fine, as though none of it has actually happened." Even the deaths of her maternal grandmother the year before and her step-father's mother—with whom she had lived almost all her life—had made no apparent impact on her.

I asked Anna what she expected from our encounters this time, and how I could help her. She replied that she wanted help to "distinguish right from wrong," because she seemed to muddle them up. Specifically, she was worried about what was right for her baby. In our second encounter, the "disconnected" tears from two years earlier began to emerge once more, almost like an old red thread that we could pick up again because it was now taut and vibrating anew. What was completely different in our recent encounters, however, was the presence I could feel of the baby growing inside of her. This change in her life was very much a pronounced figure for me—I was worried about her, about how the environment would treat her, and I struggled to focus on Anna alone.

My experience of Anna's pregnancy was two-fold. When in contact with Anna, it was as if her womb carried neither life nor death, suspended instead in a separate dimension of "non-being." To grasp the vital movement of her pregnancy, which her body expressed in all its parts, I found myself needing to shift my thoughts and imagine the baby growing and moving, Anna's delivery and the baby's birth, the image of her breastfeeding. But in trying to keep that vibration of life close at the contact-boundary with Anna, I would lose sight of her. I could not keep hold of them both.

What I would feel in the field, with Anna in front of me, was often a sort of delicate and gentle tenderness, the touch of something that faintly moved and would keep us softly wadded. Sometimes, it was like a sort of lethargy; I could fall asleep without sleeping. Falling into a pleasant lethargy warmed by Anna's "divine" beauty; worrying and being afraid for the baby; feeling vitality and joy for the baby but only if I thought of it or observed it "from the outside"; feeling the baby suspended in an elsewhere between life and death. These were all movements that I felt could not coexist. Even now as I write, I can feel the effort it takes to bring them together into a single sentence on the page, as though they have nothing to do with each other. I also realize that in my own lived experience, I tend to confuse Anna with the baby.

My desire to bring this situation to supervision mainly had to do with my need to rely on a greater, more solid and defined ground. It was a need to have other adults alongside me, and thus to build a network that functions on several levels—that of reflection and of the exploration of experience—a network of containment and resonance to remain whole and grounded. As I write, if I let myself be guided by the images that come to me, I could say that what I needed was an experience "like co-parenting." Does that make sense? Maybe it does.

8.5 Notes on the "after"

Before the birth of her daughter, I met with Anna on a number of other occasions. She was concerned about her former partner, who was insistently trying to contact her in order to resume the relationship. He was now promising her that he would go to rehab, and that he wanted to look for a new job and move to Italy. Anna was hovering between the powerful call of this man and the instinct of protection towards her soon-to-be-born daughter. She was at a crossroads between two paths, and both of them felt impossible to take.

She asked for help in finding a lawyer, and after a final meeting with her ex-partner, she decided not to see him again. In the meantime, she had begun dating a young man, who also happened to be a separated father. He had been introduced to her by her mother, and within a short time she had agreed to move in with him. She did not feel "taken in" by this man, she explained, but she did see that he could offer her safety and serenity, and that was what she needed the most. There is a strong parallel here with the story of Anna's own mother. This drew my attention, but not hers.

Anna's daughter was born shortly before term. The birth took place completely naturally, and Anna did not even ask for an analgesic. The doctors and nurses in the ward complimented her on how well she did, "much better than the average mother." She messaged me on the same day, attaching a photograph of the baby and her together. She came to my office two weeks later, bringing her baby with her. That is, for now, the last time I saw her, and it is the last image I have of her.

Anna moved around and tended to her baby as if she had always been a mother. There was a great ease and spontaneity in their relationship. It was amazing to see how a young woman with such a history of "anesthesia" can take care of a new-born creature with such warmth and gentleness. They are deeply connected on all levels. Anna is entirely with her daughter, and her daughter is entirely with her.

There was something about seeing them that reminded me of the beauty I was so struck by when I first met Anna; the beauty of that first encounter was, right then, vibrant and alive. I found myself in a sort of contemplation in a never-ending present. There was nothing to be added or taken away from the experience of that moment.

Anna did not have any questions for me; she just wanted me to meet her baby. After saying goodbye, however, I was left alone in the therapy room and I immediately felt the need to rely on that broader and more solid ground that first guided my request for supervision. I let myself think back to everything I received from all my colleagues during the conference, and I make it the basis for what is to come.

Chapter 9

Affects and dissociative field

Discussion of the clinical case
by Paola Zarini

Susanna Federici and Gianni Nebbiosi

First of all, we would like to thank the co-chairs of the conference and editors of the book for involving us in this important initiative. We have always been especially interested in comparing theories and models of therapeutic work, believing that no single perspective can exhaust the complexity of the clinical phenomena in which we are immersed in working with our patients. The comparison and dialogue between different approaches broadens the capacity for clinical processing, and sometimes one approach can illuminate blind spots in the other. We believe that the only condition for comparative dialogue to be fruitful is that the basic epistemological assumptions be shared, to avoid that, rather than a mutual exploratory spirit, a confrontation may arise over who is right and who is wrong with respect to a hypothetical clinical "truth." We believe that in the course of the conference, it was possible to engage in a fruitful comparative dialogue thanks to the epistemological compatibility of the approaches and especially thanks to the sensitivity and intelligence of the co-chairs.

As part of the dialogue among theoretical-clinical perspectives, we consider ourselves very fortunate to have received the invitation to comment on the clinical case presented by Paola Zarini, which proved to be of great intensity and truly valuable in getting to the heart of some absolutely topical issues in our work with patients. Paola was able to transmit all her clinical sensitivity, in spite of the fact that presenting in an online mode often makes it difficult to convey to colleagues the intensity and depth of the experience that unfolds in the analysis room.

We will try to comment on the clinical process presented by Paola mainly with the intention of illustrating and comparing possible contributions from the perspective of contemporary psychoanalysis, which

DOI: 10.4324/9781003597308-10

focuses reflection on the relational matrix (Mitchell, 1988), mutual recognition (Benjamin, 1995), and dissociation (Bromberg, 1998), to name just three of the most important authors.

In Anna's case, we see a perspective being put into practice that we can immediately note as commensurate with contemporary relational psychoanalysis: a systemic approach to therapy with adolescents and young adults. The therapist presents us with three different moments of the clinical history with her patient Anna that also represent the effective synergy of three different interventions, all converging in the therapeutic field. Over a period of six years, the therapist has been involved in providing parenting support to the mother; conducting psychotherapy with Anna at the age of 17, when the issue of the relationship with the mother was at the forefront; and the resumption of psychotherapy at Anna's request to deal with the problem of sexual dysregulation.

Anna has had as her only parental reference her mother, with whom she appears to have developed a problematic fusional relationship that, in the subsequent growing-up process, leads to a painful "tear." The therapist notes that this "tear" for Anna is a way of "shaping" her own subjectivity. We would add that Anna was exposed at a very early age to the relationship with her mother's husband, with whom she developed a relationship of "distance, indifference, and at times annoyance." We believe that these two relational modes—fusionality and indifference—constituted a radical polarization that we think profoundly affected Anna's later relationships, both with others and with herself.

Here we can point to a theoretical update that is very important for contemporary psychoanalysis and transforms the developmental view according to which growth and individuation is not necessarily a "tear" but, rather, a complex process of change in ways of being-with (Stern, 1985). Within the framework of the relational perspective, reference is systematically made to the findings of Infant Research, which in fact radically changed the developmental theory of classical psychoanalysis. The separation/individuation model (Mahler et al., 1975) has been deeply challenged based on observations of early infant/caregiver interactions (Sander, 2007; Stern, 1985; Beebe & Lachmann, 2002). Individual subjectivity, it emerges, is the result of relationships in the very process of co-constructing ways of being-with (Stern, 1985). We see that Anna manifests her distress and difficulty in negotiating the self/other relationship and that her mother is likewise struggling. We can assume that this difficulty was most likely there from a very early age; in other words, we can assume that Anna developed a "disorganized attachment style." From research we know that "disorganized" is the relational mode most likely to be linked to psychopathology and a tendency toward dissociation (Solomon & George, 1999).

Very much in tune with the relational approach are the therapist's notes regarding the patient's bodily presence. There are, however, some significant differences in relation to the therapist's subjectivity, and perhaps an interesting dialogue between the compared perspectives can be developed further on this aspect. The therapist dwells on her own emotional experience in the presence of the patient, but does not go on to explore in depth the issue of her own personal subjective contribution to the therapeutic field; this is an area that in recent years has, instead, often been the focus of clinical reflection in relational psychoanalysis (for a concise review see Kuchuck, 2021). For instance, the therapist is struck by Anna's "statuesque beauty" and "regal" gaze; surely these are characteristics belonging to Anna, but we wonder: What is the therapist's personal experience with respect to beauty? Or with respect to regal distance? Or with respect to a woman's perfection? And so on.

The field is something fluid and in constant motion. The relational perspective—but also our Bionian training—leads us to consider the therapeutic field as something that is really broader than the dyad encountered in the therapy room; for instance, it includes the social dimension that forms the backdrop of the clinical encounter. Let us also bear in mind that language itself is something learned relationally and mimetically.

For Anna, the encounter at age 17 with Paola, albeit mediated by her mother, is positive and indeed she decides to go back to therapy. Upon resuming after the COVID-19 pandemic, Anna shows her trust and brings as the foremost reason for her seeking help her compulsive, even risky, sexual behaviors, which she cannot quite explain: "Why do I do it?"

It is no surprise that Anna is dysregulated; in fact, no one has helped her to regulate/negotiate and thus self-regulate her own psychophysiological states. Her fusional relationship with her mother has not allowed her to modulate a sense of security and warmth in the alternation of closeness/remoteness that enables the structuring of a sense of being a subject in relation to other subjects in a relationship of mutual recognition of needs and desires (Benjamin, 1995). Her difficult and dramatic relational history is then marked by her first sexual encounter at the age of 15, which was in fact abuse—or rather rape. As we know from the many in-depth studies on trauma (Van der Kolk, 2014), the freezing of emotions is the extreme defense that is activated in a person who suffers violence. For Anna, the freezing of emotions continues to this day in her promiscuous encounters. We are struck by the phrase "tears that stop behind the eyes and cannot become or accompany emotions," which the therapist senses like an echo of fear. Perhaps Anna puts herself in risky situations because she wants to "feel" something, to "feel herself," something comparable to the state sought by persons who inflict self-harm? Up to the rape by the three boys that Anna decides not to report to the police.

Anna seeks help in order to understand "why" she does all this. She also relates the episodes of "distress" in which she cries without knowing why. As we said, a first likely reading is on the level of affective dysregulation. Anna seeks forms of sexual hyperstimulation in order to feel herself, but in doing so she uses her own body—concretely—to stun more than to "feel" herself. At other times, instead, the overwhelming need for consolation pours forth in unrestrained tears; after all, tears are a way of giving oneself warmth and consolation, but this is a desperate way of going about it because the self-regulating self-object (Stolorow's intersubjective perspective (Stolorow & Atwood, 1992)) or the empathic other (Kohut's (1984) self psychology) is not there. In regard to the disconnected crying that appears in the here-and-now of therapy, we also recall Bromberg (2006), who describes the process of bringing the patient's self-states into the here-and-now of therapy.

The therapist notices a resonance within herself, a "vibration." We would say that a process of affective attunement and recognition toward the patient is activated (Benjamin, 1995). The therapist focuses on her own bodily experience. We, too, regard this attention as very important (Nebbiosi & Federici, 2022) and it shows how the focus on implicit communication is more and more at the forefront of contemporary thinking. As we have mentioned, perhaps here an analyst would delve into her own experience in a more comprehensive way by including not only the patient's past but also her own.

It is striking how completely out of tune the mother is with her daughter's suffering to the point of downplaying Anna's risky behaviors: What we see as signs of strong discomfort, the mother regards as displays of Anna's "happily blossoming" sexuality (!). Anna's sex life is pervaded by violence and annihilation: a blind spot of the mother who proves to be non-empathetic and incapable of affective attunement. A question arises: Perhaps the mother, too, has problems in this sphere, after all, she does say, "She takes after me." We must also keep in mind that Anna is the child of a chance encounter. As rightly noted by the therapist, "the hypothesis of a family field with a dissociation related to sexual abuse comes to the fore." We also wonder to what extent shame—a feeling that *seems* to be hardly present in this patient and her family field—is not instead an important dissociated phenomenon of the field.

Bromberg writes:

> [...] it is my view that *routine* anxiety, the affect that Sullivan (1953) associates with an impending threat to one's "self esteem" differs not only quantitively but qualitatively from what he calls "*severe* anxiety." The latter, I would argue, is better called shame, and differs from routine anxiety both subjectively and in its consequences. Shame signals a traumatic attack upon one's personal identity, and typically calls forth dissociation processes to preserve selfhood. Routine anxiety signals a problem in self-image regulation, and allows learning from experience because dissociation is not needed. [...] for individuals experiencing intense shame, no words can capture the assaultive intensity of the experience. It is only through *reliving* the trauma through enactment with the analyst that its magnitude can be known by an "other" hopefully this time an 'other' who will have the courage to participate in the reliving while simultaneously holding the patient's psychological safety as a matter of prime concern. [...] The process of experiencing the interface between overvalued and disavowed domains of self is the source of any patient's greatest anxiety, dread, and shame, but it is also his only hope for authentic analytic growth.
>
> (Bromberg, 1998, pp. 295–296)

We greatly appreciated Paola Zarini's theoretical and clinical reference to the family field pervaded by dissociation regarding abuse. To better describe this field with an image—a practice that we know is dear to Gestalt therapists as well as to us—we would like to dwell on the myth of the Chinese princess Turandot, which inspired Puccini's famous opera. Turandot is a very beautiful princess—of regal appearance, frosty, and desperately wicked. Her frostiness and wickedness are due to the fact that one of her ancestors suffered a rape, which Turandot sets out to avenge by killing her suitors. In order for these killings to be "lawful," however, Turandot tells her suitors that they will be spared, and that she will accept their marriage proposal, if they solve the three riddles she will present. Some elements of Turandot seem to appear in Anna directly: for example, the frosty and desperate regality. The iciness and indifference instead seem to appear in reverse, as if rather than killing her suitors Anna continues to kill herself through a "sexual ritual" in which her own body becomes the place where the family field of unacknowledged and therefore dissociated abuse is manifested. If we recall the unsettling fact of the mother's confusing freedom and abusive sexual promiscuity, we can better understand the intensity of the pain inflicted on Anna's body and the psychological drama that goes with it.

The theme of the riddle seems to us very much in keeping with this case if we also refer to the extraordinary work on myths by Claude Lévi-Strauss (1983). In an ingenious comparison between the myth of Oedipus and that of Parsifal, which the author claims is the same myth in reverse, Lévi-Strauss argues that the riddle—as in Oedipus—is ultimately a "question waiting for an answer," while its reverse—as in Parsifal—is "an answer waiting for a question." In the myth of Parsifal, in fact, the sick king has an answer in store—"You are now the king"—for the first person who will ask him "How are you feeling?" The situation of the riddle in which royalty is attained by means of a mortal danger that is cognitively overcome is contrasted with its reverse: a situation in which royalty is granted without any risk as a reward for empathy to the first person who will ask the right emotional question. Anna, taking upon herself an entire family field in which abuse is dissociated, presents the therapist with a riddle: "Why do I do this?" Over time, the therapist's empathic listening will construct the reverse situation of the right question in relation to the trauma: "How are you feeling?"

Let us now comment on the third stage of the trajectory presented by Paola Zarini. Anna is pregnant, but she decides to leave her partner because he becomes violent as a result of substance abuse. Paradoxically, Anna is carrying her pregnancy in a situation quite similar to the one her mother experienced when she was born: The plight of a young pregnant woman who cannot share the journey of becoming a mother with the father of her unborn child. She presents herself as a beautiful goddess-mother in a perturbing contrast to the emotional shambles that characterizes her life. The partner was the only one with whom Anna "felt" anything; in fact, at first the relationship with him seemed like the fulfillment of a dream, a heaven that later became a hell of violence. Anna declares that she continues to "feel nothing" and it is only a sense of rational responsibility for the baby girl who is to be born that makes her decide to leave her abusive partner. This time she asks for help to "distinguish what is right from what is wrong." As we know, it is affections that serve as our compass in our choices regarding the underlying values and meaning of our experiences. Anna continues to perceive this severe lack of an affective compass; with her request for help, she puts the therapist in a position to provide her with the fundamental function of guidance and secure base that she has lacked in the past. Unlike her mother, Anna relies on the therapist who engages in holding together and creating bridges between seemingly irreconcilable dissociated self states. Can what is good for the mother be good for the daughter? Is it possible to have multiple meaningful emotional ties without falling back into the polarization between fusionality and indifference?

The disconnected crying that "vibrates" between patient and therapist returns, but now the therapist's subjective experience is different because of the presence of the baby that is growing inside of Anna. She writes: "It is as if her womb does not carry life, nor death; it is as if she is suspended in another dimension, a dimension of 'not-being'." What the therapist feels in the therapeutic field is similar to a "numbness" warmed by Anna's beauty, then concern for the child suspended between birth and the absence of vitality—movements that the therapist feels are not reconcilable. She tends to confuse Anna with the baby girl, holding them together in her own vital horizon is really very difficult.

We could say that the therapist is able to tolerate the strain of "standing in the spaces" (Bromberg, 1998) of the dissociated states, thus managing to provide a holding function for the dialectic between the baby's "being-being born" and Anna's "not-being." But to tolerate and sustain this difficult process, the therapist needs to broaden the therapeutic field, to feel other adult people beside her, even to the point of fantasizing a co-parenting of sorts in the request for help that she brings to us and to the larger reflection group of the conference.

Paola Zarini has managed to carry us inside the intersubjective field of therapy with Anna in an enlightening way, and by sharing her co-parenting fantasy she has expanded the field itself; perhaps we can hope that a broader field may facilitate the birth to affective vitality not only of the baby girl but ultimately of Anna herself. We would like to quote Bromberg's words again: "The analyst is not simply a guide accompanying his patient on a journey down the royal road; he is a participant in the road's construction and, we hope, in the paving of its potholes" (Bromberg, 2006, p. 44).

Reflecting on this case has confirmed an intuition we had at the outset: the feeling that the exchange between the Gestalt approach—in the meaning shown by Paola—and the relational approach can be enriching for both in deepening attention to the implicit and bodily dimensions of the therapeutic relationship and in introducing a reflection on the multiplicity and complexity of the relational field in which a meaningful transformative process emerges and evolves for the benefit of the patient and the therapist. And to end with the image we have proposed, it pleases us to recall here that in the myth of Turandot, the final resolution is the discovery that the solution to the riddle lies beyond the cognitive sphere. In fact, the name of the prince so frantically sought by Turandot is not a name but a sentiment: *love*.

References

Beebe, B., & Lachmann, F. M. (2002). *Infant research and adult treatment: Co-constructing interactions*. The Analytic Press.
Benjamin, J. (1995). *Like subjects, love objects*. Yale University Press.
Bromberg, P. (2006). *Awaking the dreamer*. The Analytic Press.
Bromberg, P. M. (1998). *Standing in the spaces*. The Analytic Press.
Kohut, H. (1984). *How does analysis cure?* The University of Chicago Press.
Kuchuck, S. (2021). *The relational revolution in psychoanalysis and psychotherapy*. Confer Books.
Lévi-Strauss, C. (1983). *Le regard éloigné*. Plon.
Mahler, M.S., Pine, F., & Bergman, A. (1975). *The psychological birth of the human infant: Symbiosis and individuation*. Basic Books.
Mitchell, S. A. (1988). *Relational concepts in psychoanalysis: An integration*. Harvard University Press.
Nebbiosi, G., & Federici S. (2022). Miming and clinical psychoanalysis: Enhancing our intersubjective sensibility. *Psychoanalytic Inquiry*, 42(4), 266–277.
Sander, L. (2007). *Living systems, evolving consciousness, and the emerging person: A selection of papers from the life work of Louis Sander*. Routledge.
Solomon, J., & George, C. (Eds.). (1999). *Attachment disorganization*. Guilford Press.

Stern, D. N. (1985). *The interpersonal world of the infant: A view from psychoanalysis and developmental psychology*. Basic Books.

Stolorow, R., & Atwood, G. (1992). *Contexts of being: The intersubjective foundations of psychological life*. The Analytic Press.

Sullivan, H. S. (1953). *The interpersonal theory of psychiatry* (H. S. Perry, & M. L. Gawel, Eds.). W.W. Norton & Company

Van der Kolk, B. (2014). *The body keeps the score: Brain, mind and body in the healing of trauma*. Viking.

Chapter 10

Anna KO

Fabio Rivara

In this chapter I will present the case of Anna. The hypotheses are developed according to an approach based on Post-Bionian Psychoanalytic Field Theory (PFT), and the material from Paola Zarini's case presentation will be, mainly, examined in a way similar to the one usually applied to the initial psychological sessions.

In a Post-Bionian Field Theory perspective, in the consultation phase (i.e., in the sessions preceding the possible agreement for psychotherapeutic treatment) all the narratives coming from the patient—but also from any other source (e.g., parents, mental health professionals, teachers, etc.)—are considered as a "revealing dream" concerning the patient's psychological processes. On the other hand, during the psychotherapeutic treatment, all the narratives coming from the patient (in each session) are considered as "revealing dreams" of the way the patient perceives the "therapeutic field."

As one can easily imagine, the title "Anna KO" is inspired by Sigmund Freud's case of Anna O., which, like the present study, has several aspects that recall incontinence and hypercontinence patterns. The attribution of "KO" is intended to syncretize, on the one hand, Anna's condition of suffering, caused by being "Knocked Out" by intense and impetuous emotions, and which induces her to undertake psychotherapeutic treatment; and, on the other, the wish of pursuing psychotherapeutic work will promote the individuation of O (which for Bion represents all that is ignored by the patient, concerning his/her psychic reality) through K (Knowledge processes). KO would therefore represent the understanding of Anna's emotional truth (O) through (K) developments.

DOI: 10.4324/9781003597308-11

The aim of this contribution is twofold:

- To summarize the foundations of a psychotherapeutic approach based on Post-Bionian Psychoanalytic Field Theory (PFT);
- To outline some considerations regarding Anna's case, on the basis of this approach.

10.1 The psychotherapeutic approach based on Post-Bionian PFT

The peculiar nature of the first psychological sessions is usually considered as a situation that calls for the collection of data and information about the patient's history, and the type of psychic suffering she/he experiences in order both to formulate a diagnosis and to identify whether there are indications for psychotherapeutic treatment. The type of approach to initial interviews that is here suggested aims, conversely, to formulate some hypotheses concerning the patient's "internal field" and to identify whether they wish, and feel able, to undertake psychological treatment.

In such a mental setting, the diagnostic aims are, therefore, focused on outlining the configuration of the patient's "internal field" rather than tracing a symptomatological configuration, perhaps even of psychoanalytic leanings, which refers to diagnostic categories, or to personality structure, or to levels of functioning. It is, therefore, very important to keep in mind that this type of approach to initial psychological interviews can leave the patient totally free regarding the information they want to give to the therapist. That means that they can talk about whatever they like, without necessarily having to provide anamnestic data. And, even if they bring information concerning their own life, their interpersonal relationships, and their symptoms, such data should in any case be used according to the following directions:

1. Consider everything the patient says as if it were a dream. A "revealing dream" in which the narratives brought by the patient are transformed into "representations" that allow the formulation of hypotheses concerning the configuration of the patient's "internal field";

2. Trace, in the material emerging during the consultation, the elements that outline the patient's degree of motivation for psychological treatment;
3. Use the *reverie* capacity to interpret the material of the first interviews in order to formulate hypotheses concerning the eventual treatment plan.

It is therefore necessary, even during the initial interviews, to plunge the external reality into darkness (Ferruta, 2003), just as during psychotherapy based on PFT, in order to imagine how the material brought by the patient may reflect his/her problems, but also to monitor (secondly) the emotional climate of the interview.

The psychotherapist needs to activate a kind of "dream-like listening" that treats the material of the first interviews, not as a raising of the patient's anamnestic data, but as "revealing communications" aimed at synthesizing: 1) their problems, related to the management of their emotions; 2) how motivated they might be to undertake psychotherapeutic treatment; and 3) what kind of relational and interpretative style (on the part of the therapist) might be most appropriate for them.

Therefore, whatever kind of material the patient brings during the initial interviews—really any (including if they want to talk about the shopping they did at the supermarket or a film they had seen the evening before)—the therapist, through the capacity for *reverie*, can attempt to answer the following three questions:

1. What could be the patient's problem?
2. How motivated does the patient appear to be to begin possible psychological treatment?
3. (If the patient can be considered sufficiently motivated to undertake psychotherapy) What kind of "setting" should be proposed (e.g., number of weekly sessions; couch or *vis-à-vis*; in presence or online) and what kind of relational and interpretative style should be adopted at the beginning of the psychotherapeutic treatment?

According to this kind of approach to initial interviews, the therapist should try to transform the material brought by the patient into "representations" that allow the formulation of hypotheses that answer, in some way, the above-mentioned three questions.

This can only be made possible by a "totally dreamlike" listening. "Dreaming" the initial psychological interviews through one's *reverie* abilities facilitates "unison" with the patient in the understanding of the patient's possible problem, and of the most appropriate therapeutic proposal.

In the course of psychotherapy based on PFT, everything the patient says is considered an indicator, more or less easily clear, of how the patient is perceiving (at that particular moment) the relationship with the therapist and the climate that characterizes the "therapeutic field." In the course of the initial psychological interviews, conversely, dual listening is required of the therapist:

- A main (or primary) listening, which tries to identify which of the patient's narratives may be a convincing metaphor, or a puzzle to be decoded, to answer the above-mentioned three questions;
- A secondary listening, attentive to any patient narrative that reflects how he/she is perceiving the therapist, and the therapist's interventions, during the initial interviews. In fact, although during the consultation phase it is important to focus on primary listening, what the patient says after a therapist's remark should also be listened to as a possible indicator of how that remark was experienced.

If, nowadays, psychoanalysis is increasingly oriented towards making the patient aware of what they are feeling, concentrating, therefore, more on the exploration of the patient's "moods" than on their defense mechanisms and unconscious functioning, one can consider that the main objectives of psychoanalytic psychotherapy, mainly based on the Post-Bionian PFT, are, broadly, the following:

- Keeping constantly in mind that all the material that emerges in the sessions reflects, in a more or less decipherable way, how the patient is experiencing the psychotherapeutic relationship and the atmosphere that is characterizing the "therapeutic field";
- Being able to offer the patient a kind of understanding that is purely focused on helping them recognize their own inner states and emotions, describing them in the most appropriate way for the patient;
- Facilitating, therefore, the therapist's comprehension (always through the patient's narratives) of which could be the best way to talk to the patient about their inner states and feelings, also in order not to exasperate persecutory experiences;

- Supporting a plain legitimation of any kind of emotion (or feeling) that one finds oneself talking to the patient about, to achieve a "citizenship status" for any kind of "feeling." The attempt to promote the acceptance or (better still) the appreciation of a "multi-ethnic" affectivity can help reduce the suffering linked to "states of clandestineness" and, above all, to those sufferings generated by feelings of "racial hatred" towards certain types of "emotional ethnicity" and, thus, also towards possible "clandestine infiltrators";
- Creating a basic welcoming and benevolent attitude, on the part of the therapist towards the patient, which makes it possible to reduce the expulsive aspects that are likely to be generated by an accentuated "neutral" behavior;
- Concentrating on the patient's "internal reality" and not on the external one, as the main purpose is to "visit" with the patient their "states of mind" during the sessions and towards the therapist. The external reality is, therefore, taken into consideration just to identify which factors may describe what is happening in the "therapeutic field";
- Keeping to a type of approach in which the therapist's thoughts can be linked more to listening to the patient's narratives than to one's own theoretical model of reference.

A psychoanalytic perspective more inclined to focus on external reality may tend to be concerned (and worried) also with the patient's behavior in daily life. The Post-Bionian PFT perspective, on the other hand, aims to explore with the patient the "emotional states" that emerge through the material that they bring in the course of the sessions, simply in order to imagine how they could, in some way, talk about the "therapeutic field." This type of mental set-up can help to fortify another important goal: that of helping the patient to become themself as much as possible, and trying to do so in the most appropriate, and individualized, ways for each patient. In this perspective it will be the patient who will guide the therapist in finding the most suitable approach for them, in the constant effort to help the patient be and become themself.

10.2 The case of Anna

The considerations concerning Anna's case, presented by Paola Zarini in three phases, will be reported using the information contained in the

First and *Second Phases* to outline a "revealing dream" that will help to answer the above-mentioned three questions (concerning the initial psychological interviews). The information from the *Third Phase* will be used to "dream" what happened in the "psychotherapeutic field" at the beginning of Anna's psychotherapy, and what seems to be happening with the restart of psychotherapy after a two-year period of interruption.

10.2.1 First and Second Phases

The information contained in the *First* and *Second Phases* will hereafter be used not as facts that happened in the patient's real life, but as "symbolic revelations" of the problems that make Anna suffer. There is no doubt that those real events may have intensified Anna's problems, but more importance is given to identifying the type of problem she is experiencing, rather than the factors that caused it. This is a bit like the orthopedist who, for example, when faced with a torn ligament, is not at all interested in knowing whether the patient has injured it themself, or whether the rupture was caused by someone else, but is interested in identifying, first of all, the type of problem that has occurred at the physiological level, and subsequently the type of surgery to be performed. All this, regardless of the factors that created that problem for the patient. In fact, the type of surgical intervention that will be performed will always be the same, whether the injury was caused by the patient or by others. Therefore, even with psychotherapeutic treatment, whether the violent emotions perceived are mainly caused by exogenous events, or are determined by purely endogenous factors, the type of "emotional damage" is the same and it should, then, be faced with the same psychotherapeutic tools.

Turning back to Anna's case, the contents that might make up the above-mentioned "revelatory dream" will be examined below to try to answer the above-mentioned three questions.

10.2.1.1 What is Anna's main problem?

The rape she suffered at the age of 15 and the rape inflicted by three boys, under the influence of drugs (when she was 18), could reflect the presence of violent and abusive emotions that, besides being uncontrollable and overwhelming, might be perceived as determined by exogenous factors ("caused by drug use") and not as her own emotional experiences she might feel responsible for. On the other hand, the information about her not having wanted to report the crime could represent her "not revealing" to herself the "emotional rapes" she experiences. This difficulty in recognizing that she is being "abused by violent emotions" might also be associated with her feeling ashamed of her psychic situation.

10.2.1.1.1 HOW DOES ANNA DEAL WITH THIS PROBLEM?

The various references to detachment, distance, opacity, remoteness, closure, coldness, and emotional impassivity outline a personality organization to some extent autistic. Such organization could highlight the use of avoidance strategies to deal with one's problems, and the attempt to manage the problem of emotional incontinence through hypercontinence.

10.2.1.1.2 WHAT ARE THESE "VIOLENT EMOTIONS"?

In the case presentation, there are many references to depressive experiences: separations, abandonments, and deaths.

- The early separation of the family unit.
- The distance and abandonment of the father (whom Anna abandons in turn).
- The death of the grandmothers.
- The rupture of the mother–daughter symbiotic bond.

In a Post-Bionian PFT perspective, symbiotic relations can be seen as a ♀♀ type of mind-relation (Ferro, 2006a).[1] The representation ♀♀ (introduced by Antonino Ferro as a possible declination of the sign ♀♂ used by Bion as representative of the container-contained relation and, therefore, also of projective identification) points out a "fusional" interaction between minds that implies a state of "pacification" and "psychic alexithymia," which also has the function of "keeping out" ♂ emotional contents, or ♂ emotional hyper-contents, which are very threatening or violent. It would, therefore, be a type of interaction between minds that falls under avoidance strategies and, in this case, can be graphically represented with the following figure, ♂/♀♀, or with this other figure, ♂/♀♀. Both represent an emotional content (or emotional hyper-content) that is kept "outside" to determine a state of "emotional calmness."

10.2.1.1.3 WHAT ELSE IS THERE TO THINK ABOUT THE THREATENING AND VIOLENT
          HYPER-CONTENTS?

The three "rapist" boys (alias violent emotions) under the influence of drugs (alias antidepressant > manic results) could recall the use of antidepressant > manic strategies; and Anna's sexual compulsion could also be imagined as an indicator of an antidepressant > manic device. Anna's anguish when she is alone could, in fact, recall the depressive aspect which risks activating the manic defenses.

One can, therefore, think of depression as another possible threatening emotional hyper-content, which is no longer able to lay on ♀♀ "fusional patterns" because of the loss of the "mother–daughter" symbiosis (which was once provided to keep back the threatening and violent hyper-contents ♂/♀♀). Such loss is presumably seeking out antidepressive strategies (which could take on possible manic connotations) and could generate emotional hyper-content that is even more threatening and violent than depression.

This combination of depression and a manic state can be depicted in the following way.

Depression > HYPO-ACTIVATED BEHAVIOR > antidepressant strategies > HYPER-ACTIVATED BEHAVIOR

♂ ♂♂♂

Emotional hyper-content/violent emotional hyper-content

10.2.1.1.4 SOME FINAL COGITATIONS CONCERNING ANNA'S PROBLEMS

Emotional hyper-content is also a consequence of a deficiency of the *container*. If the container has little (or very little) capacity, the content turns out, automatically, to be excessive. An important aim of psychotherapeutic work with Anna is therefore to expand her containing capacity. Her poor containment capacities raise her levels of incontinence, which may also lead to hypercontinence patterns and to the other defensive mechanisms outlined above.

The need for mothering and parenting support, reported in Paola Zarini's clinical study, could mirror the perception of a deficiency in the container (♀ = mother = parenting) that needs help (support), perhaps also expanded and strengthened support.

Another element that emerges from the information concerning Anna's sexuality is the incidence of presumable significant splitting mechanisms. In fact, a considerable splitting process could be pointed out by comparing Anna's mother's narrative (which attributes healthy and vital characteristics to her daughter's sexuality) with the distressing way in which Anna seems to experience her own sexuality. Also in this case, these sexual behaviors are not considered as facts concerning Anna's external reality, but as an indicator of probable significant splitting mechanisms that characterize Anna's psychological functioning.

10.2.1.2 Is Anna motivated for psychological work? And to what extent?

The mother's asking for help for Anna could be imagined as a part of Anna asking for help. Here we have a "split" Anna, who, on the one hand, seeks help and, on the other, fears being "abused" ($\male$ $\female$) by psychotherapy, instead of being able to find a capacious container for her hyper-contents ($\male$ $\female$).

The idea that there is a need for "mothering support" and "parenting support" would suggest that Anna may need "support" not only for the depressive aspects, but even for the development of the container ($\female > \female$). Such a process could also occur through her therapist's containing abilities.

10.2.1.3 How would it be, initially, more appropriate to work with Anna?

According to the considerations outlined in response to questions 1 and 2, one can think of answering this third question by outlining the following initial guidelines:

- Adopt a restrained and restraining approach ($\female$).
- Avoid "penetrating" interpretations altogether ($\male$), such as, for example, transference interpretations, interpretations relating to Anna's functioning and her defense mechanisms, or remarks that can make her feel "observed" and/or "photographed."
- Use as much as possible a way of talking to her based on a very linear type of "unison" (e.g., "it must have been terrible to be in such a situation"; "it is really awful to be in such a situation"; "it would be nice if the person who behaves in this way could realize the suffering they create," etc.).

- Bear in mind that being in unison with Anna, as much as possible, is one of the main factors that can promote the development of the container ($♀ > ♀$).
- Try to make Anna feel a presence that is perceptible to her—but neither too close, nor too far away.
- If Anna interrupts psychotherapy again (due to her relevant avoidance strategies towards emotional contents $♂$ perceived as threatening), it might not be so inappropriate to make some attempts to ask her to come back to therapy in welcoming ($♀$) ways and as little intrusively ($♂$) as possible.

From a Post-Bionian PFT perspective, even when interpretations based on a very linear type of "unison" are adopted, it will still be necessary to suppose how Anna's narrations reflect the climate she perceives within the psychotherapeutic relationship and/or how she perceives the "therapeutic field." That means that even when paying attention to Anna's transferential movements, it is necessary to keep in mind that transference interpretations should be avoided, at least for a while. It would, therefore, be very important that any transference interpretation should be clearly formulated in the therapist's mind without, however, making it explicit to Anna. The avoidance of transference interpretations leads the therapist to formulate, preferably, only unsaturated interpretations (Bezoari & Ferro, 1992). The unsaturated interpretation usually involves types of formulations that highlight to the patient the emotional implications of the patient's narrative, remaining within an interpretative range that may refer to a certain range of emotional aspects (from more or less simple, to more or less complex) without, however, making any parallels with the psychotherapeutic relationship.[2]

10.2.2 Third Phase

The details contained in the section concerning the *Third Phase* of Anna's clinical case will hereafter be considered as inherent to her psychotherapeutic treatment with Paola Zarini and will, therefore, imply the attempt to think of some hypotheses concerning the psychotherapeutic relationship with Anna and the indications that she, unconsciously, gives to her therapist to make their work together sufficiently bearable.

Particular relevance will be given to the following events:

a. Anna interrupting her therapy because of the pandemic.
b. Anna's decision to live abroad.
c. Anna's pregnancy.
d. Anna's jealous partner who becomes violent under the influence of crack.
e. Anna's decision to return home.
f. Anna's desire to distinguish right from wrong.
g. Anna's beauty hypnotizing her therapist.

As pointed out above, in a Post-Bionian PFT perspective, the "real facts" must be converted into "dreams." When listening to the patient's narratives, Antonino Ferro suggests applying automatically what he calls a "magic filter" (Ferro, 2009). That "magic filter" consists in treating (by default) each patient's tale as if it were premised "I dreamed that…" Treating everything the patient tells the therapist as if it were a dream makes it possible to focus more on the emotional aspects. In addition, it helps to imagine in what way each "dream-tale" is, to some extent, recalling the climate that the patient experiences within the "therapeutic field."

a. *"Dreams" about Anna interrupting her therapy because of the pandemic*
     One can "dream" of the pandemic as a very threatening hyper-content (δ) that forces Anna to interrupt her psychotherapy. From a Post-Bionian Field Theory perspective, even the pandemic (however strongly anchored to a fact of reality) should still be imagined as a "character of the field." According to the hypotheses formulated above, based on the data from the *First* and *Second Phases*, it seems likely that Anna could be frightened by the hyper-contents (pandemic) threatening the "therapeutic field" and chooses to interrupt (temporarily) psychotherapy as a strategy to "avoid" the potential dangers, and potential violence, that could infect the "therapeutic field."
     It is, therefore, a hypothesis that seems to fit well with what has been outlined by the attempt to answer the above-mentioned three questions, and it may be important to bear in mind that, while not doubting that Anna may also be frightened by the real situation inherent in the pandemic, she is also very frightened by the presence of emotional hyper-contents that, by infecting the field, could put her in great danger. The pandemic could represent a sort of

dangerous "Alien" that, as in Ridley Scott's 1979 film, circulates within the "field" and can release terrible and devastating attacks.

b. *"Dreams" about Anna's decision to live abroad*

Anna's going abroad may recall Anna's need for emotional distance (her "never having felt anything") and her intention to stay away from psychotherapy (again because of the fears of an "Alien" threatening the "field").

c. *"Dreams" about Anna's pregnancy*

Anna's pregnancy, however real it may be, can represent the "psychotherapeutic pregnancy" following Anna's mental coupling with her psychotherapist before she had to run away because of the "Alien's" threatening presence in the "field."

When Anna says that her daughter's father is the only person, in her entire existence, for whom she has ever felt something, it could also mean that her therapist is the only person with whom she has begun to feel something, and this something may have supported the psychotherapeutic pregnancy. However, considering the effective pregnancy without neglecting the transference mechanisms, one could assume that Anna's ability to feel, for the first time, something for someone (that is, for the father of her daughter) could be a result of the psychotherapeutic work carried out until that moment.

In a Post-Bionian PFT perspective, it would be preferable to stick to the "magic filter" and transform the sentence into: "I dreamt that my daughter's father was the only person, in my entire existence, for whom I have ever felt something." Such a "transformation in dream" (Ferro, 2009) makes it easier to imagine that narrative as an indicator of the progress of the psychotherapeutic relationship between Anna and her therapist Paola Zarini.

d. *"Dreams" about Anna's jealous partner who becomes violent under the influence of crack*

If we suppose that Anna, for the first time in her life, felt something for her therapist, and it is their mental coupling that caused a "psychotherapeutic pregnancy," it would not be so unlikely that her splitting mechanisms led to a defensive configuration in which "one part" of Anna went away in order to ward off the threats of the "Alien," but another part of her is furious at being pulled away from the psychotherapeutic work that was beginning to bring her to life. The intense and violent emotions assaulting her because of this experience of "exclusion from psychotherapy" move her to deal with her depressive feelings (of loss and exclusion) by means of the aforementioned antidepressant-manic strategies, which, instead of reducing the violence of the emotions, strengthens it even more. The crack (also "dreamed" as the tear that implies splitting), although used as an antidepressant remedy, exposes not only the risk of a psychic "crack", but also an affective "crack" that "breaks the heart" and triggers jealousy.

e. *"Dreams" about Anna's decision to return home*

Anna's intention to "return home" may represent her intention to resume psychotherapy with Paola Zarini again, as the danger of the internal hyper-contents (enhanced by the violent emotions of the part of herself that has missed psychotherapy) may be stronger than the hypothetical "Alien" hyper-contents that threaten to invade the "field." The latter, in fact, could be managed together with her therapist (in case they show up) instead of Anna having to be alone in dealing with those hyper-contents that are already abusing her.

f. *"Dreams" about Anna's desire to distinguish right from wrong*

This kind of request, which Anna somehow seems to set as the goal of psychotherapy, would quite plausibly represent her desire to recognize emotions: from feeling nothing to being able to distinguish emotions and, finally, to understanding what she feels. This intention of Anna's is quite important, also because it would point to a degree of motivation for psychotherapeutic treatment that is probably greater than before.

g. *"Dreams" about Anna's beauty hypnotizing her therapist*

The question concerning Anna's beauty strongly evoked to me the beauty of Helen of Sparta.

Helen of Sparta or Helen of Troy? Helen of Menelaus or Helen of Paris?

Even this *reverie*, triggered by Anna's statuesque beauty, refers to her hypothetical splitting mechanisms which can dazzle the therapist (just like her beauty), hypnotizing and emotionally involving her also through a relevant incidence of projective identification mechanisms.

10.3 Some prognostic considerations

The thoughts and the emotions that the therapist outlines in the final part of Anna's case presentation highlight very well her *reverie* abilities, her confidence in the psychotherapeutic method she has adopted, her trust in the "field," and the idea that it can contribute to the development of the container ($\female$). Her expressing the "need for an experience of co-parenting" and feeling it as a legitimate and realizable desire underlines her trust in the method used to carry out psychotherapeutic work (together = co-parenting).

These elements are of great importance for a favorable prognosis as they are factors that could not only encourage Anna to continue her psychotherapy, without necessarily having to fall back on further interruptions, but might also be important potential "healing" factors for Anna. Such factors could enhance her capacity to deal with her emotions and to counterbalance her depression with genuine vitality.

The above-mentioned reference to "trusting the method" should be considered a very important element in psychotherapeutic practice. A therapist who underestimates the importance of the method he or she adopts risks being somewhat like a parent who underestimates the importance of the other parent role and, thus, the importance of "co-parenting." Such an underestimation of the role of the other parent interferes to a great extent with the family atmosphere; in several cases, it spoils the good growth of children. It is, therefore, not so unlikely that such an underestimation of the role and work of a psychotherapist interferes both at the level of the "field" atmosphere and with the course of psychotherapy.

Notes

1 The figure $\female\male$ represents, conversely, a type of relationship between minds that allows them to interpenetrate, in an emotional sense, and in which there is room for growth and change for both sides. Such growth and change are also possible thanks to the fact that each mind can, possibly, alternate in performing the $\female$ or $\male$ function. The depiction $\male\male$ (Ferro, 2006b) outlines a type of mental interaction that implies competition; a clash between minds in which both minds search for a $\female$ container that is, however, not available. A type of interaction in which minds cannot interpenetrate and which, therefore, generates frustration, conflict, and suffering.

2 In order to further emphasize the type of approach outlined above—which leads us to use the material of the initial interviews as a "revealing dream" inherent to the patient's psychological configuration—I report some elements relating to the case of Anna O (mentioned at the beginning of this contribution). Anna O's symptoms, which can be used as "revelatory" of incontinence, are aggressive and uncontrolled behavior, paradoxical dysphasia, strong motor arousal, severe anxiety, recurrent somnambulism, and also the feeling of walls falling on her body. While "suggestive" elements of hypercontinence may be paralysis of muscles, contracture of the arms and of legs, memory lapses, muteness, afternoon torpor, and even headaches, which could be imagined as an "internal head pressure" due to mental hypercontinence.

References

Bezoari, M., & Ferro, A. (1992). A journey through the bipersonal field of analysis: From roleplaying to transformations in the couple. *Rivista di Psicoanalisi*, *37*(1), 4–47.

Ferro, A. (2006a). *Psychoanalysis as literature and therapy*. Routledge. (Original work published 1999).

Ferro, A. (2006b). *Tecnica e creatività*. Raffaello Cortina.

Ferro, A. (2009). *Tormenti di anime. Passioni, sintomi, sogni*. Raffaello Cortina. (English translation, *Torments of the soul*, Routledge, 2015).

Ferruta, A. (2003). Trattare l'ambiente in termini di transfert. Il concetto di interpretazione negli scritti di Winnicott. In P. Fabozzi (Ed.), *Forme dell'interpretare*. FrancoAngeli.

Chapter 11

"We wish you a good life, Anna!"

A field-theory-informed view
of Gestalt therapy

Jan Roubal

Thank you, Paola, for sharing your work with Anna so that we can learn from it as we explore together. Thank you, Anna, for being with us this way.

If I want to look at Anna's case and think about it, I first need to clarify my own position in relation to the case. Where am I placed? Because what I see and what I can do as a therapist depends on the point of view I take up. There are three perspectives we can take in Gestalt therapy: a monopersonal perspective, a bipersonal perspective, and the field theory perspective. Each of them provides us with a specific kind of understanding and offers us different guidelines. Historically, all three perspectives were developed in Gestalt therapy from the beginning. Nowadays, the use of the field theory perspective in clinical situations appears to have become one of the growing edges in contemporary Gestalt therapy.

Here I will focus on field theory and explore Anna's case from this perspective. I would like to introduce what new and specific insights the field theory perspective brings to my work. To do so, it will be helpful to contrast field theory with the monopersonal and bipersonal perspectives. As such, I will also briefly mention them in the context of Anna's case, before discussing the field theory point of view.

I would also like to mention how I would eventually like to handle the results of my exploration (if I imagine myself in the place of a therapist working with Anna). In exploring the case of Anna, I have followed the three basic steps of case formulation (Eells, 2007)—*observation* (provided here by the therapist's description), *conceptualization*, and *guidelines*—and applied them in a way that is inherent in Gestalt therapy (Šromová & Roubal, 2022). The observed phenomena are conceptualized into a type of meaningful picture. This is only partly accomplished

DOI: 10.4324/9781003597308-12

through intentional thinking about the client and therapy and is often perceived by the therapist largely in a holistic way. It appears by observing the client and the therapy process from a distance, letting the details blur to enable the main figure to emerge.

Such a holistic picture offers us specific guidelines. In my understanding, the guidelines that emerge from the meaningful organization of observed phenomena are meant to make therapists more sensitive to specific aspects of their contact with clients. The guidelines are not meant as prescribed ways of working. Rather, once the guidelines become explicit, the therapist then "forgets" them and lets them fade into the background, to return to the ever-evolving here-and-now of the flow of contact with the client. However, the therapist is now supported by the background sensitivity developed by the case formulation guidelines.

11.1 Monopersonal perspective[1]

From the monopersonal perspective, we observe the process of change in clients in different aspects of their life. We appraise their habitual ways of functioning, which ways have helped the person survive in difficult conditions, and which still help the person feel safe. At the same time, we support clients in discovering new possibilities and in awakening their potential for growth.

Psychopathological symptoms are seen as original, creative adjustments of the organism for coping with difficult conditions, drawing on the resources available to it. Symptoms are not seen as something dysfunctional to be repaired, but rather as what was originally a useful coping strategy, but which later in life has become a limitation on the organism, because of its rigidity, and does not allow the organism to adjust creatively to new conditions. In general, therapy aims to enhance the client's ability to adjust creatively to changing life conditions.

How can therapists support such change? By helping clients become aware of how they function in life. When clients are aware of their fixed patterns, they can live their lives more freely and more responsibly by choosing to either use those patterns mindfully or change them. As therapists, we help them to find new ways of creatively adjusting, so they have a broader spectrum of choices. The change is enabled by the therapist through awareness-raising interventions that specifically balance supportive and challenging contact. This means that we support the person and challenge the fixed patterns at the same time (Roubal, 2019). The change is mainly observed on the level of the *ego-function* (Perls et al., 1951/1994; Spagnuolo Lobb, 2005): in what clients learn to *choose and do* differently with our support. The therapeutic approach is also based mainly on the level of the ego-function: on *what the therapist does* in active interventions towards the client.

The position of the therapist who approaches the client from the monopersonal perspective can be captured by a metaphor. Imagine the client as a tree with its unique shape, a shape that reflects past creative solutions (in the specific ground and weather conditions) and builds a basis for future growth. As a gardener, the therapist waters it with just enough support. Without aiming to change what already is, the therapist stays with the uniqueness of the growth.

Approaching Anna's case from this perspective, we would honor her creative way of adapting to relationships as the best possible creative adjustment to unreliable and dangerous relational conditions. On the one hand, she protected herself from further hurt by armoring herself and refusing all feeling. On the other hand, however, she did not give up. She followed her desire for contact and her vitality (expressed in sexuality and now physically visible in her pregnancy).

At the same time, though, we would help her to become aware of the limitations that her way of contacting the world inevitably brings. In therapy, she could learn to distinguish between what is safe and what is not, what is right and what is wrong, what she likes and what she does not. She could learn to use her senses (How does this food taste? How does this music sound?) to restore the sense of a border between herself and the world, where mutually respectful and nourishing contact can happen.

11.2 Bipersonal perspective

From the bipersonal perspective, we focus on the here-and-now relational dynamics co-created by both the client and the therapist. In the therapeutic relationship, repeating relational patterns come to life, and so they become available for phenomenological exploration. The patterns are co-created by both the client and the therapist, so both of them can explore their contributions to the pattern as it appears. This enables them to become more aware of their fixed relational patterns both in and outside therapy. We also use the therapeutic relationship to offer our clients a new relational experience, which supports a change in the way they experience themselves. They can then bring the new relational experience as a form of self-support to their other relationships.

From this perspective, psychopathological symptoms appear in the here-and-now of the relationship in the therapy setting, revealing the lack of a specific kind of support. They are seen as an individual expression of a specific relational experience. The therapist is the other who is present with the client in the moment and, at the same time, is representing the general experience of the other in the client's life. The therapist is part of the psychopathological dynamic that is actualized in the present relationship. Psychopathology is then seen as co-created by the therapist and the client here-and-now. In the case of depression, for example, we can say that the client and therapist are depressing together (Roubal, 2007).

This bipersonal perspective offers a direct possibility for change. Both the therapist and the client can become aware of how they contribute to the co-creation of the current experience, helping them to step out from the fixed relational pattern and offering the possibility of a new relational experience. Working from the bipersonal perspective, the therapist stops treating symptoms and meets the person instead. The change happens on the relational level between the client and the therapist, where a new, healing relational experience is co-created, in which the longing for the missing kind of support is recognized, and the symptoms may no longer be needed. Clients feel accepted as they are and can learn to accept themselves as they are. This opens a space for the actualization of their human potential, in which clients change by becoming more of who they are.

How can therapists support such change? Basically by being open to engagement in the dialogue as a person, as a human being in contact with another human being. This requires therapists to show an ability to switch between two ways of functioning: being immersed in the meeting with the other and being able to observe the quality of the relationship in order to adjust their own part in it. Clients have a chance to be themselves more truly with us when we are truly ourselves with them. By engaging in the relationship with the client in a genuine, honest, and open way, we offer the opportunity for new ways of contacting to be co-created. *What we do* as therapists (*ego-function*) is less important than *who we are for each other* (*personality-function* comes to the foreground).

This can be seen as a relational dance between the client and therapist—a metaphor often used in recent Gestalt therapy writings (Jacobs, 2018; Philippson, 2019). The metaphor helps us to refrain from pushing for some specific kind of change, and to wait instead for the change that appears through live and genuine engagement. We can then see the fixed relational pattern in the therapeutic relationship as the "old dance" the client (and the therapist, too) is accustomed to dancing, and we can discover what "new steps" might appear in the genuine here-and-now of contact.

In our case study, we would focus on who the therapist is with Anna and who Anna is with the therapist. It might be difficult, for example, to see the Anna behind the facade of beauty and trauma, which could easily lead the therapist to slip into a position of a fascinated observer. Anna would become a beautiful and wounded, pregnant object—an object of observation, an object of treatment, adoration, or pity. This is not far off Anna's usual experience in her life of being mistreated and abused as an object. When the therapist becomes aware of her part in co-creating the relationship, she can step out of it. The therapist can try to bring herself in as a living person during the therapy session, expressing her own points of view and showing her own emotions. In this meeting of two women, a new relational experience might emerge. The experience of two women who respect each other and care for each other.

11.3 Field theory perspective

Field theory shifts the perspective onto perceiving the ongoing and ever-changing process through which the field becomes organized in the current situation. Change is now understood as an emergent process with its own dynamics, which goes above and beyond the individuals interacting in the therapy setting. Here, change appears in the way the field dynamics are freed and reorganized to allow every now to flow naturally into the next. The change is happening and it "uses" the people involved in order to happen (Roubal, 2019).

From this perspective, not only the traditional monopersonal approach, but also the bipersonal concept of the co-creation of change still seem too anthropocentric (you and I are making the change). The field theory paradigm overcomes this and humbly acknowledges that change can happen differently than intended and expected. It can even happen without any intention or understanding on the part of the therapist or the client. The field theory perspective accentuates humility, as healing processes are seen as forces of the field that are greater than the therapeutic relationship. Change is then supported by a humble acknowledgement of the therapeutic situation as it is.

There is something new that appears in a meeting of people that transcends the individuals involved and even the relationship that they co-create. The situation as a whole is more than the sum of the people who meet each other (Wollants, 2008). Moreover, the situation is forever changing from one moment to the next. This constant change, the flow of the situation, follows its own dynamics and the people involved are constantly transformed by it, since they are functions of the situation in every here-and-now moment. Both the client and the therapist are seized by the field's forces.

The healthy situation is grounded in the here-and-now and follows a natural flow to the next moment. This enables the intrinsic tending of the situation, its intentionalities, to be expressed and developed. The intentionalities give power to the flow. They channel it and give it a direction, which enables the situation to move naturally and smoothly to the next here-and-now. As functions of the field's dynamics, the individuals involved can then be seen by each other, express themselves to each other, receive responses from each other, and be transformed by the experience of the live flow of contact.

In psychopathological situations, the natural flow of the situation is distorted in a specific way, and both the client and the therapist are functions of it. Such psychopathological dynamics actualize them into rigid patterns, squeezing them into rigidly formed processes, like running water flowing into a deeply eroded riverbed. In this way, the client cannot satisfyingly experience contact, and this suffering becomes embodied in observable psychopathological symptoms. The therapist also experiences the devitalizing dynamics because they also emerge as a function of the field's psychopathological organization.

How can the therapist support change? Adopting the field perspective, we assume that change transcends the individuals involved, emerging as a process with its own dynamics, which "uses" the people involved. Here, the therapeutic approach is based on therapists' aesthetic experience (Bloom, 2003; Francesetti, 2012) of their embodied presence in the flow of the situation. Therapists lend their flesh to embody the forces of the field. They let themselves be formed by the intentionalities of the field, the intrinsic tensions pushing towards the kind of contact where the potentialities of the field can be developed, where the situation's dynamics can be transformed (Francesetti & Roubal, 2020; Roubal & Francesetti, 2022). Therapists are often alarmed by this experience, seeing it as something inappropriate, or inadequate. Such an experience that a therapist would rather not see can appear like a "stranger at the door" (Francesetti, 2019; Francesetti & Roubal, 2020), which we might imagine here to be the field knocking on the door of change. It is crucial to acknowledge this part of the therapist's experience as belonging to the situation. Accepting it, inviting it in, and exploring it with curiosity can transform the therapist's way of being in the situation, presenting an opportunity to allow what is striving to emerge to come into existence. "We perceive no Thou, but nonetheless we feel we are addressed and we answer [...] with our being" (Buber, 1937, p. 6).

In a field theory perspective on psychotherapy work, the metaphor of a river can be useful. The client and the therapist find themselves together in a river driven by forces beyond all human power, where they are carried along by a flow that is complex and more or less turbulent. The river may flow rapidly or spiral into whirlpools, or may remain placid and still, and with it both the client and the therapist, whose movements are thus part of the phenomenology of the situation. This is something therapists need to accept and respect in their responses.

Here, change happens mainly on the level of the *id-function* of the situation, where the embodied but undifferentiated intentionalities do not belong to the single individuals, but are a function of the flow of the situation. What is important is not so much what therapists do, but how they are present. Their intervention grows from how they are present. Transforming the *therapist's embodied presence* in the situation would therefore appear to be crucial for working from a field theory perspective. Whatever we actively do as an intervention is important primarily for us to remain calm and stay quiet enough to listen to the tacit call of the potential, natural, fluent flow of the situation, which is longing to be released from the prison of the psychopathological organization of the field. By changing our way of being with the client, a transformation process is unlocked, redirecting the fixed dynamics of the field's processes and opening an opportunity to free the natural flow of the situation. At this point, our main task is not to stand in the way of this newly developing movement, allowing it instead to find its own way in the unique conditions of the situation here-and-now.

11.4 The Anna-and-I of the field

In looking at Anna's case from the field theory perspective, I imagine myself in the position of her therapist. I want to feel myself bodily present with Anna, and then curiously explore my experience. To do so, I keep two key points in mind.

First, my attention should not be deliberately focused. It needs to be dispersed so as to capture phenomena on the periphery of my perception. I wait for phenomena to come to me, rather than seeking them out actively. This way, I hope to perceive all of what is present in the situation as a whole. I also hope to perceive what is missing, what needs to happen but does not have enough support to emerge. These "absences" will show me the way.

Second, I have to be convinced that what I do as a therapist is not so important. What is important is how I am present when making any kind of intervention. The quality of the therapist's embodied presence in the therapy situation is crucial. So, I first need to work on myself, before I work with the client.

Doing so, three pictures come to me. I want to share them with you now.

11.4.1 Picture one: Acknowledgement

Anna strikes me as a woman warrior on the battlefield, dressed in shining armor but bleeding under it. Her shining armor (*the statuesque beauty*)[2] hides a living female body, protecting it from being seen, met, and touched (*indifference, but also warmth, at some far-off level*). Blood seeps through from unhealed wounds under the armor, occasionally falling in drops (*episodes of anxiety; sudden and inexplicable bursting into tears*).

What does this picture tell me about my task as the therapist? What does it need from me? I think my task is to acknowledge (or even adopt) the reality of the situation as it is. I need to welcome both the blood (coming from Anna's repeated traumatization) and the armor (Anna's creative adjustment). I need to acknowledge both of them without focusing on them, without being fascinated by Anna's suffering and beauty. I need to engage with the phenomena, so expressive and powerful in their way, while holding onto my own freedom at the same time.

Accepting the other means accepting everything that happens to me in her presence. I need to welcome all my experiences, including those that are jarring—especially those that are jarring. Those strange experiences that I would rather not see, from which I would rather turn my head away, are precious because they inform me about what is missing. What is it then? What do I see when I do not turn my head away?

I feel ashamed at seeing Anna in all her female nakedness. The touch of her skin on the cold iron of the armor brings excitement mixed with disgust at the smell of blood. Shame, excitement, disgust. Welcome, my experiences, you are mine, here-and-now. This is what it needs. In welcoming the "stranger at the door," I need to create a space of acceptance in myself for everything that comes with Anna, for everything I feel in encountering her armor, her bleeding, the naked human being underneath the armor. Meeting the other also means "risking ourselves" (Rogers, in Anderson, 1997, p. 85). How can I risk myself? How can I be with Anna in a "naked" way so that we can meet as two naked human beings? In a spa, perhaps? Yes. Relief comes with the image of a spa, where a naked human body is being taken care of gently. That is what was missing; that is what is needed now. I need to feel this in myself, in my body, when meeting Anna. I need to work on myself in this way, transforming my way of being embodied in the therapy setting. All this would strictly be my own inner work, not to be shared explicitly with the client. Such inner work would enable me to set up a new position of quality from which to make my interventions (whatever they might be).

11.4.2 Picture two: Compassion

A weird picture comes to me. I see a land where mutants are born, mutilated and wounded. A land where mothers give birth to their children too early, before they can recover and regenerate from their wounds and mutilations. So, their children are also born wounded and mutilated. Anna, abused and raped, is going to bring a child into the world. Anna's mother was also very young when she gave birth to her. We can only guess what happened when hearing about her *blind spot in sexuality* and *dissociation in relation to sexual abuse.*

I feel like a foreigner in this land of mutants. I need to learn the language of the locals. To do so, I need to find my inner mutant. I need to get in contact with the mutilated creature in me who can naturally live in such a land and interact with others there. As a therapist, I need to get in touch with what remains mutilated and wounded in me. What comes to my mind is my father, and how he died so prematurely, when I was just 18. I could not learn from him, learn how to become an old man (which I am becoming now anyway). This is a wound I carry with me. This is my mutilation.

I guess I need to take the risk of feeling the pain connected with it and bring my mutilation to the session with Anna. Not explicitly, of course. I would not speak about it out loud. But I would sit with it in front of her. I would feel this mutilation is part of me, part of my embodied experience here-and-now with Anna. Allowing myself to be present in this mutant way would hopefully allow us—Anna and me—to feel each other's presence on the planet of mutants.

Taking such a personally risky step of being a mutant with her, feeling the pain of the mutant's way of living, would be a crucial chance for a transformation to open up right here, in the middle of all the suffering. I imagine mutants taking a long warm bath, giving their bodies enough time to regenerate. The bath can take as long as they need, so it is clear that there is no urgent need to strive for survival. No urgent need to have a new baby mutant before it is too late. No, there would be enough time for everything that life brings. The bath can last as long as it takes to feel life with all its pain and with all its joy.

Sitting with Anna, I would give my inner mutant such a bath, but I would say none of that to Anna. I would discuss with Anna the issues she wants to bring to therapy. I would work in my usual way, doing what I can do. But at the same time, I would work with myself in this mutant way, transforming my way of being present with her. I believe her embodied presence would resonate with mine. As if the transformation were happening underground, in the undifferentiated mycelium of our fore-contact, for which words and concepts are too big and clumsy.

Throughout all of this, I would stay open to any issue that Anna wishes to share with me in therapy. Open with curiosity. What mushroom might grow from the transformed mycelium? How will she talk about her life in such an atmosphere? I am curious.

11.4.3 Picture three: Dignity

I spend one whole day with Anna. Working in the garden, I let myself meet Anna and anything that emerges in me. In the morning that day, I had finished reading the book *More Than I Love My Life* by David Grossman (2021). It describes the lives of women like Anna—women raped in wars, like the current war in Ukraine. Women abused behind the closed doors of their homes. Women who survive, despite all that life throws at them, bringing to life new generations of human beings through themselves. My body felt a kind of painful gratitude to those women. I was filled with respect and humility before the dignity of this sisterhood of life.

11.5 Conclusions

Acknowledgement, compassion, and dignity—that is what came to me in these three pictures. I understand that what the situation would need from me is to make space for acknowledgement, compassion, and dignity in myself when meeting Anna. To transform in this way my embodied presence in the here-and-now with her. Through me, I believe, a door could be opened for these three key elements to emerge in the therapy situation, so that they might emerge for Anna too. I wish you a good life, Anna!

One individual (the therapist), however, is not enough. Such suffering comes to us through generations of people. The warmth and care (the shared bath in a spa) of many people is needed. And that is what we are doing here, right? What is needed is actually happening—first during the conference and now in this book! So many people are devoting their precious time to Anna. So many people are opening their minds and hearts to her with acknowledgement, compassion, and dignity. It is amazing how the field works. We all can be at the service of the field's forces now. We wish you a good life, Anna!

Notes

1 I have explored the concept of these three perspectives in past writings (Roubal, 2012, 2019). The way it is presented here is an abridged and simplified version of the concept as developed jointly by Gianni Francesetti and myself. For greater depth of detail, see our original papers on field theory (Francesetti & Roubal, 2020; Roubal & Francesetti, 2022).

2 In italics I quote from the case description provided by Anna's therapist (see the chapter by Paola Zarini).

References

Anderson, H. (1997). *Conversation, language, and possibilities: A postmodern approach to therapy*. Basic Books.

Bloom, D. (2003). Tiger! Tiger! Burning bright. Aesthetic values as clinical values in gestalt therapy. In M. Spagnuolo Lobb, & N. Amendt-Lyon (Eds.), *Creative license: The art of Gestalt therapy* (pp. 63–78). Springer.

Buber, M. (1937). *I and Thou*. T. & T. Clark.

Eells, T. (2007). *Handbook of psychotherapy case formulation*. Guilford Press.

Francesetti, G. (2012). Pain and beauty. From psychopathology to the aesthetics of contact. *British Gestalt Journal, 21*(2), 4–18.

Francesetti, G. (2019). A clinical exploration of atmospheres. Towards a field-based clinical practice. In G. Francesetti, & T. Griffero (Eds.), *Psychopathology and atmospheres. Neither inside nor outside* (pp. 35–68). Cambridge Scholars Publishing.

Francesetti, G., & Roubal, J. (2020). Field theory in contemporary Gestalt therapy. Part one: Modulating the therapist's presence in clinical practice. *Gestalt Review, 24*(2), 113–136. https://doi.org/10.5325/gestaltreview.24.2.0113.

Grossman, D. (2021). *More than I love my life*. Knopf Publishing Group.

Jacobs, L. (2018). Comment. In M. Spagnuolo Lobb, D. Bloom, J. Roubal, J. Zeleskov Djoric, M. Cannavò, R. La Rosa, S. Tosi, & V. Pinna (Eds.), *The aesthetic of otherness: Meeting at the boundary in a desensitized world. Proceedings* (pp. 37–40). Istituto di Gestalt HCC Italy.

Perls, F. S., Hefferline, R. F., & Goodman, P. (1994). *Gestalt therapy: Excitement and growth in the human personality*. Gestalt Journal Press. (Original work published 1951).

Philippson, P. (2019). *Paper 4: We can be together, but you and me can meet* (Topics in Gestalt therapy: Occasional Kindle papers by Peter Philippson). E-book. https://www.amazon.co.uk/Together-Meet-Topics-Gestalt-Therapy-ebook/dp/B06Y1D2X14/ref=sr_1_12?keywords=philippson&qid=1557160100&s=digital-text&sr=1-12 (last accessed March 1, 2024).

Roubal, J. (2007). Depression. A Gestalt theoretical perspective. *British Gestalt Journal, 16*(1), 35–43.

Roubal, J. (2012). The three perspectives diagnostic model: How can diagnostics be used in the Gestalt approach and in psychiatry without an unproductive competition. *Gestalt Journal of Australia & New Zealand, 8*(2), 21–53.

Roubal, J. (2019). Theory of change. In G. Francesetti, C. Vázquez Bandín, & E. Reed. (Eds.). *Obsessive-compulsive experiences: A Gestalt therapy perspective* (pp. 9–20). Los Libros del CTP.

Roubal, J., & Francesetti, G. (2022). Field theory in contemporary gestalt therapy. Part two: Paradoxical theory of change reconsidered. *Gestalt Review, 26*(1), 1–33. https://doi.org/10.5325/gestaltreview.26.1.0001

Spagnuolo Lobb, M. (2005). Classical Gestalt therapy theory. In A. L. Woldt, & S. M. Toman (Eds.), *Gestalt therapy: History, theory, and practice* (pp. 21–37). Sage Publications.

Šromová, V., & Roubal, J. (2022). Case formulation in Gestalt therapy. *Gestalt Review, 26*(1), 63–83. https://doi.org/10.5325/gestaltreview.26.1.0063

Wollants, G. (2008). *Gestalt therapy: Therapy of the situation*. Sage.

Chapter 12

What we see and do depends on the point from where we look

Beatrix Wimmer

My starting point in this conference is that I find myself comfortably in a mutually friendly, appreciative community, where each of the speakers and commentators is genuinely interested in, and inquisitive towards, the other, the others' concepts, and understandings of terms.

The topic of the conference is described in the invitation: "The conference will explore the way in which field perspective changes therapeutic interventions, the conceptualization of the clinical relationship, and how these changes re-create the theories and practices of the various approaches."

The concept of field theory is explored by representatives from three different psychotherapy approaches: Post-Bionian Psychoanalysis, Relational Psychoanalysis, and the Phenomenological Approach of Gestalt therapy. In a good Gestalt therapy tradition, the conference concept is based on dialogue between speakers and their commentators.

Far from agreeing and being confluent, broadly speaking, the speakers describe their concepts and understanding regarding field theory and the commentators contribute their ideas and understanding of the concept.

Representatives of three different psychotherapy approaches meet and share their understanding, knowledge, and differences of, about, and in psychotherapy and, in particular, the concept of field theory, seen through their different approaches. Much has been said from all three of the approaches on the first day of the conference and it seems that it has been put into practice, when Paola Zarini's delicate case description was discussed by the three colleagues on the supervision panel.

DOI: 10.4324/9781003597308-13

12.1 Co-parenting with the therapist

I would like to start at the end of the discussion of Anna's case, with Jan Roubal's contribution to the therapeutic process of Paola and Anna.

The conclusion he arrived at was acceptance, compassion, and dignity. With these words he describes something beautiful that applies not only to the case of Anna, but also to what happened at the conference. Being interested in, and curious about, what others have to say, my spontaneous idea is that "the other" in my profession is not only the client I am working with in my therapy room, but also the wider field, in this case the other modalities presenting their concepts. It is an ethical as well as a professional duty for me to accept them, to try to understand them, to get into a dialogue with them, and to appreciate what they are contributing to the community of psychotherapy. This is what I became aware of when I followed the panel discussion this morning and the way the conference was rolled out from the beginning. It is a new experience for modalities to look at each other with respect and appreciation. This was not always the case and is still sometimes not universally common.

Paola Zarini has been laying out her supervision case with impressive subtlety. I was very touched and moved by reading her description of Anna's case, feeling tears welling up and sensing goosebumps on my skin.

That happened again when Paola spoke about Anna. The center of what was discussed in the theoretical part of the conference as well as in the panel discussion between the different modalities is the focus on the experience of the therapist.

It is the centerpiece of our work; we are trained for years in getting to know about, and refining, our sensorium of awareness. I clearly remember when Gianni Francesetti once mentioned, at some point somewhere, "therapy is happening when the therapist is aware of what is going on with him or herself." This is exactly what the key point was in the panel discussion.

All contributors referred to their own experience, fantasies impulses etc., everything that was emerging when they related to the supervision case. But what does that say about the similarities and differences of the understanding of field theory perspective in those three different approaches?

Fabio Rivara was elaborating on "Revelatory Dreaming" in Post-Bionian Psychoanalysis, something which was a new concept to me. This image speaks to me, the image of the revelatory dream. It speaks to me in such a way that the therapist lets everything come to her/himself in the experience with the client. It is a different language as we use different terms to give meaning to what we experience with each other. Still, when Jan Roubal speaks of "the embodied presence" of the therapist, how s/he is dispersing the attention and becomes as fully aware as possible of the situation and the phenomena of the periphery, it is something that might also be occurring in the revelatory dreaming. A field theoretical perspective as an attitude is not intentionally focused but is the starting point for becoming aware of all the phenomena emerging in the situation and ideally understanding what is happening.

A very important question regarding the topic of the conference and our tradition of Gestalt therapy still remains in the definition of what is a field, because we can see the field from different perspectives. I refer here to Jean Marie Robine's understanding of the field concept that is based on Perls et al. (1951). Robine clarifies his understanding in his comment at the conference: "A field is specified by an organism/environment-field. It is not a quantitative entity but a singular experience of a subject. We are *of the field* which indicates an inseparable belonging between individual and environment" (my italics). In his book *Social Change Begins with Two*, Robine refers to the foundational text of Gestalt therapy: "The field discussed by Perls and Goodman is not an entity; it is neither the environment nor the context" and he continues "I am the creator of the situation in which I find myself and I am created by this situation" (Robine, 2015, p. 50). He suggests using the word "situation" rather than field, because "this process is exactly what is described in our conception of the field" (p. 50).

It is my experience that not only between the modalities, but also here in our modality, the terms are discussed time and again; there is no fixed Gestalt in these terms.

In this regard my second comment is on Dan Bloom's remark on Donnel Stern's understanding of "the field," as a representative of Relational Psychoanalysis. Dan Bloom mentioned that we speak the same language but use different dialects. But even when we are speaking the same language the dialects are often not even understandable for each other in the same country, let alone different countries. Let me give an example: I come from the German-speaking country Austria. There are also other German-speaking countries, like, for example, Switzerland. But when a Swiss person speaks to me in Swiss German, I barely understand a word of what they say, unless we explore together what is really the meaning of the word or what the person is trying to say.

Following the discussion, I see this as a very promising start as experts in our modalities to clarify a lot more of what is really meant by the way we are working or how we are relating to the client and what kind of concepts we are relying on in that work. What is different, what is common.

In the discussion I get the impression that we share many similarities which seem to be supporting the therapeutic encounter. But if we are talking about the theories that are underlying the practice, we must be very precise. Fabio Rivara also mentioned the word "*unisono*," which I would translate as "attunement" and would support from a Gestalt Therapy perspective. Pursuing this position, we are going into the direction of acceptance of, support for, and compassion with our clients.

In Anna's case, the hypnotizing aspect is for me transformed into a resonance. The hypnotizing aspect is experienced when I feel "taken" by what is happening. Making this realization is a first step to focusing on my awareness when being with the client. In a reflecting process, I find words for that experience, not necessarily expressing my personal process to the client but developing clarity for myself of what is going on with me. This enables me to eventually find meaning for my resonance when being with the client.

As an example, there is an instrument making a sound. I resonate with the sound, but I am not the instrument. To mention this difference between therapist and client is important to me because there was a remark on the first day that it would not matter if the emergent property comes from the client or from the therapist. I am not sure about this, because I am not the instrument that is making the sound. I am resonating with the instrument; I can move and sing with the sounds of the instrument and by doing this I bring my background to the situation.

From my personal and professional experience, the relational psychoanalytic approach is very close to Gestalt therapy. We also saw it with Donna Orange's comment from an angle of intersubjective psychoanalysis on Gianni Francesetti's and Michela Gecele's contributions to the phenomenological Gestalt therapy understanding of the field concept.

Gianni Nebbiosi and Susanna Federici as representatives of relational psychoanalysis point out the "desperate attempt to feel" that is carried out by Anna and that is carried with her and into the therapeutic situation with Paola, who was speaking, again very subtly, about "her tears that are coming up, but only just." This seems to have similarities with terms used in Gestalt therapy, the understanding of suffering and psychopathology, and the way in which this is addressed. Like a desperate attempt to feel and to feel with somebody, and to attend to the phenomenology of the person.

Jan Roubal's wording of "sisterhood for life" describes something that is probably in the female background as females are walking in this world on a different ground, describing a field perspective from another angle. An angle that refers to the political aspect of the field perspective that derives from Gestalt therapy and is imported into psychotherapy. It underlines the definition of the field concept from Jean Marie Robine (see above) that indicates an inseparable belonging of individual and environment and the process of creating and being created by the situation.

In his comment to Fabio Rivara, Jean Marie Robine pointed out that we are "of the field" and that we are carrying this with us. If we are able to make ourselves aware of what this environment contains, we are also agents of change in this environment. It seems that "the field perspective as an attitude" is very important for all our approaches, but that many differences remain.

12.2 How many parents does it take to raise a child?

Susanna Frederici and Gianni Nebbiosi start with their approach of Relational Psychoanalysis. Federici points out that the relational approach is a large umbrella for different variations and asks the question of compatibility in contemporary psychotherapy. Relation can be the foundation of reality and it seems quite close to Fritz Perls's "contact is the first reality." Federici describes the "Me–You relation" as a field and distinguishes a society and individual relationship dimension. She asks for context to be given to the words we are using, e.g., "attunement," as it is a mutual creative adjustment in a therapist and client relationship, like a kind of tuning in to one another.

Having additionally a systemic approach in the background, she points at the absence of the father as a third party in the family. For her, mother and daughter are perceived as a couple. She recommends going "beyond in my contribution, to explore what do I as therapist, love of my female beauty, what is part of the presence of the therapist and is going deeper into the subjectivity of the therapist, the reality of the therapist."

Gianni Nebbiosi follows with his contribution of "What I can see depends on my stance" and describes the field as a field of "you and me plus a social dimension, which is fluid and shifting." Nebbiosi puts Anna's process into a wider domain and spreads out the ground of the situation further as to the actual moment of meeting of client and therapist. His remark of "co-parenting and becoming aware of a sense of warmth" refers to the emerging phenomena in the therapist, and his pointing out "the girl's pregnancy is similar to the mother's experience, who says Anna is like her" refers to the wider field, generational aspects, and also perhaps unfinished business for the mother. In any case, the attitude of the field theoretical perspective is clearly there.

According to the Post-Bionian analytical field theory, Fabio Rivara defines two distinct moments. He speaks of an "internal field of the patient" and the beginning of psychotherapy with a "revelatory dream," which begins with material delivered by the patient. It is an instrument for defining what might be the problem for the person seeking help with a psychotherapist and the therapist's way of relating to them. Rivara speaks of "what happens in our internal field" and this seems to me different to a Gestalt therapy understanding of the term field, as we do not speak about an internal field but about a field that we are of, which shapes the individual, and is shaped by the individual. In this way he refers to the individualistic aspect, which is also present in all our approaches.

Later Rivara says the "internal field is statuesque." What might be described in a phenomenological way as the client's expression of her experience and the therapist's making meaning of it is for Rivara an internal field, where a revelatory dream of the therapist is our information. In relating to the client, the therapist "dreams for the patient." What seems like a difference can also be understood as developing a kind of attitude towards the psychotherapeutic process, where all occurring phenomena are welcomed as information about awareness in the here and now.

Rivara also speaks of an empathic response as *"unisono,"* a moment where therapist and client seem to resonate with each other. At this point once more, "tuning into one another," or "attunement," is mentioned. In Gestalt therapy we often refer to the process of creatively adjusting to one another. And it is this creative adjusting to one another that is the ground where phenomena emerge to be explored for the therapist as well as for the client.

In his contribution, Jan Roubal starts exactly the way Gianni Nebbiosi did, with a statement that "what we see and do depends on the point from where we look." He lays out three perspectives that we can choose from and use in different moments in the therapeutic process, in a session as well as in the longer process.

A "monopersonal" perspective focuses on the client and the nature of her suffering; the therapist's role is to explore what s/he can do to support her. In a bipersonal perspective, by contrast, the focus shifts onto the relational space. The relationship towards each other is explored and the therapist turns his/her awareness to "who the therapist is with her/his client." This relational perspective in the therapeutic situation has been furthered and discussed a lot in the last decades.

Now a third, even more complex perspective comes into play. The perspective of field theory is well known and discussed in Gestalt therapy. The novelty seems to be the developing of an attitude towards the psychotherapeutic process, where our attention is dispersed to perceive the whole. The therapist acts as a hypersensitive sensor and explores how s/he is present in this situation and with that attitude explores his/her embodied presence. In cultivating this attitude, the attention is not intentionally focused. The therapist is aware of phenomena at the periphery as they come to us and everything that emerges in our awareness. S/he is with the question, "What is missing, what wants to happen?"

In my understanding this seems to bear some intentionality because it is supported by both an aesthetic, thus embodied awareness of something that is missing and an impulse within the situation of "what wants to happen." In this way, concentrating on a field theory perspective in a therapeutic encounter is "not a method, but an attitude supporting the therapist to be as present as possible," as Donna Orange puts it in her commentary on Gianni Francesetti's and Michela Gecele's contributions on the field theory of Gestalt therapy.

12.3 Of warriors and sisters

12.3.1 Conclusion

In this panel discussion we heard of revelatory dreaming, being hypnotized by statuesque beauty, of female warriors, and sisterhood for life. All these words describe phenomena that emerged for the supervisors when they explored their resonances to the case description of the therapist.

What becomes very clear is that this attitude of a field theoretical perspective is inherent in all three of the represented psychotherapy approaches. It seems to describe a quality that emerges when we creatively adjust to the client and allow ourselves to become aware of all phenomena emerging in the situation. Even those that might be embarrassing, shocking, unpleasant, or irritating. By allowing all these sensations, feelings, and thoughts into the present moment, it enables supporting the process of awareness towards a moment of wholeness.

In my personal experience, it seems to me that a theoretical concept is put into the practice of psychotherapy and at the same time finely dissected and re-discovered in the way we practice psychotherapy. It might be recommendable to have a lot more discussion of the definition and understandings of terms both between modalities and within modalities, as it is necessary to look at the different theoretical concepts very carefully and appreciate similarities and differences with curiosity.

References

Perls, F. S., Hefferline, R., & Goodman, P. (1951). *Gestalt therapy. Excitement and growth in the human personality*. Julian Press.

Robine, J.-M. (2015). *Social change begins with two*. Istituto di Gestalt HCC Italy.

Chapter 13

Field and psychotherapy

Attempting a new paradigm

Annibale Bertola

Perhaps among the seeds hidden in the fertile soil of psychotherapy, from the Freudian experience onwards, there is a spring perpetually waiting to manifest itself. It tries to do that, or at least to come to light, sometimes timidly and sometimes in a more confident way. Accepting it would mean reconciling the subversive potential of the psychotherapeutic experience with the evolutionary seeds hidden in it, sometimes suffocated by the social conventions of collective "common sense." It is an experience perceptible in all the great innovative ideas that have marked the history of human inventions and discoveries. And it is so also regarding psychoanalysis and the various forms of psychotherapy that derive from it; even if it is true that in the face of this epiphany one of the main obstacles consists precisely of that "common sense" which, as my analyst, the late Laura Telmon, used to say, "is not always 'good' sense."

These feed on shared concepts, which, due to their generality, are often mistaken for "true" or "valid," even when they are properly the reflection of individual prejudices and generalizations. Sometimes it is due to the prevalence of mental laziness, or to the omnipotence of the various psychotherapeutic models which go beyond individual creativity. So the spirit of research deriving from a healthy comparison between paradigms, models, and the personal experiences of therapists is not practiced as a natural ground for expanding the space of research and allowing the progress of practice and knowledge (Kernberg, 1996).

Universal realities—at least at the level of the phantasmal/cultural production that has characterized a society, and to a various extent conditioned the individual experience of each of us (see Greek mythology, with its myths of Oedipus, Narcissus, etc.)—also clash with the moral ("moralistic"?) prejudices of every era. Currently, they are overwhelmed

DOI: 10.4324/9781003597308-14

by the liquidity of today's world and find it difficult to establish themselves in a context where ideas, social representations, stereotypes, and opinions rapidly appear and often disappear even before they can be articulated as defined models, built with usage rules that account for their effectiveness and their internal consistency.

It is interesting to note that Freud, in his writings on technique, felt the need to invite colleagues to communicate their experiences, to pool them, and to make comparisons that contributed to the mutual enrichment and progress of psychoanalytic practice. This is also one of the reasons why psychotherapeutic models of all kinds proliferate. It therefore makes sense that, in addition to the legitimate curiosity to explore its foundations and validity, the desire arises to undergo field testing and comparison with other models, in the long-standing search for a "common ground" of many models and, at the same time, a sufficiently shared definition of the specificity of each of them (Zerbetto, 2007).

In this text, thanks to the availability, competence, and dedication of three great colleagues, Gianni Francesetti, Michela Gecele, and Paolo Migone, we are about to undertake an exercise that goes in this direction: to investigate the differences and identities of three models, each with its specificities and shared theoretical constructs. It stems from a meeting where the concept of "field" has been explored from the point of view of Gestalt therapy and two psychoanalytic approaches.

This comparison concerns models that are not only consolidated but also provided with a remarkable theoretical background, which possess an exceptional epistemological and heuristic potential: the models of Gestalt therapy, of Post-Bionian analysis, and of Interpersonal/ Relational Psychoanalysis (IRP in the styling of one of its leading representatives, Donnel B. Stern).

13.1 The clinical case: Discussion between three points of view

This comparison reached a "high" point when there was a comparative reflection on a clinical case, in which each of the participants brought the gift of their competence and the theoretical interpretation keys of their differentiated models.

In the shared space of our meeting, we entered an area that was as constructive as it was demanding. Accepting that mutual knowledge helps us better define our own reference model, so that, as Migone underlined, by knowing more models, our knowledge of the clinical situation is as complete as possible, we can understand and know more about the patient. Perhaps the Post-Bionian friends who took part in our meeting would talk in terms of "saturating" the patient's needs, feelings, and requests as best as possible.

An important difference that I detected in the three proposed models was the theoretical definition of "field" itself—the place determined by the dynamics of projective identification, for the Post-Bionians; the joint action of the experiences of psychologist and patient when they agree to transform "unformulated experiences" into communicative acts (Stern, 2015); the interpersonal situation full of tensions, pushes, and counterthrusts that is created in the encounter between therapist and client for Gestaltists with a "field perspective."

One construct that seems important to me to underline is the universally known formula *hic et nunc*, "here and now." This was not born from the iconoclastic fury of overcoming a certain psychoanalytic approach which saw the present only as an infinite reformulation of the subject's past, understood as an irrepressible matrix of the patient's repetitiveness and complexity, but as a formula which re-evaluates their singularity as a person, transforming "need" into "feeling" (Solms, 2022) and building a request for help on this (Carli & Paniccia, 2003). The space of time in which this process is built includes the therapeutic situation and takes place in a given moment and in a given space. While the "here and now" sanctions the conclusion of a diachrony, it is certainly not a mechanical diachrony, made up of physical time. It is the subjective time that counts and that embraces—when the request for help has been accepted—the figure of the therapist.

13.2 When is the "field" born?

The similarities and differences expressed in the contributions of the authors participating in the meeting present different nuances. In the Neo-Bionian approach, the patient's subjectivity is charged with the previous temporal dimension that accompanied him/her and contributed to building the question first and then the relationship with the therapist. In the IRP approach, diachrony must always give way to synchrony, to that particular moment in which the therapist's unconscious derivations act in the relationship, transforming it into a therapeutic field (Stern, see his chapter in this book). In the specific Gestalt therapy approach presented, we follow "a movement that will take us onto an epistemological terrain that is different from that of an individualistic perspective (...) this field is also different from a two-person paradigm in which the relationship is co-created by two individuals who meet and which together produce a change" (Francesetti & Griffero, 2022, p. 41). According to the latter perspective, both are agents constituted by a "field," which acts in and through them right from the premises for the establishment of the psychotherapeutic relationship.

Referral, first contact, and mutual exploration by the participants in the psychotherapeutic encounter are the first manifestation of a common participation in the same experience—an experience that is delimited by their presences, but also by the outcomes external to the field they build, which inevitably modulate their relationship, being the agent that moves and motivates them. Is this an extreme meaning of this important "field perspective"? Pragmatically, observing and listening to colleagues who have illustrated their point of view (and the reciprocal observation points from which they look at this perspective), I would quietly say that from a heuristic point of view it is very promising. It allows us to explain many phenomena that would seem paranormal, or that might be hastily classified in the category of "perceptions without stimulus" (Kilpatrick, 1961).

I remember a patient's dream made up of sheep, angry dogs, and a small country chapel, which ended with supernatural intervention, with the Madonna saving a shepherd in danger. The mention of the Sanctuary of Divine Love by the therapist would lead to an immediate sense of relief and the closure of a gestalt built on the verge of a mortal danger, finally defined, and avoided precisely by common recognition. Both patient, in the first place, and then therapist are not only safe, but thanks to one of the forces acting in the field, symbolized by the Madonna, they will be able to continue their journey unscathed.

I used to do aikido. Nothing in my office, nor in my communications referred to this sphere of my private life, yet as many as three patients, almost at the same time, told me that they had started on the discipline, relating it to me with the attitude of someone who is sure to find a shared interest in the other party. But if everything is a "field," if it pre-exists even to the patient–psychotherapist encounter itself, do we not risk being accused of wanting to "field" the world, an accusation directed at Antonino Ferro (2017), a scholar of the Neo-Bionian approach?

It is hard to give a single answer. Certainly, we cannot remain silent about the perspective advocated by Gianni Francesetti, as the "field" perspective can be seen as a paradigm shift in psychology and psychotherapy, in the sense identified by Kuhn (1962). And it would be a desirable shift, because it does not refer to the specific components of one model rather than another but embraces the technical peculiarities, even the automated ones, of each model in order to open up new spaces for comparisons between the models themselves, bypassing the inevitable one-sidedness that each of them entails.

At this point of the discussion, it seems to me we can say that the dialectic, of which this text is an example, is fruitful precisely because it not only allows comparisons between psychotherapeutic models but pushes each of us to rethink the relationship with the patient and to grasp elements that we had not valued enough.

I would also like to mention the experience recounted by Jan Roubal in relation to the "case of Anna." He relates how he spent a whole day of work with her in the garden, accompanying the tasks of his hobby with the knots of the case presented by Paola Zarini.

One of my teachers suggested an interesting method for dissolving blockages, or stalls during therapeutic interventions, which was to "take a walk with your patient." In other words, when the therapist finds that the therapeutic path is not proceeding, when she/he has difficulty connecting the "*hic et nunc*" of a session with the achievement of a better overall well-being of the patient, or feels helpless or burdened by an overwhelming and sudden feeling of incompetence, it can be useful to enjoy a solitary moment, protected from external disturbances, in which to fantasize freely about the relationship with the patient, relying on the imagination to search for a scenario that goes beyond the routine of the session and on the emergence of sensations, images, and thoughts that circumvent the stalemate by providing new material for the therapeutic alliance. What does this patient arouse in me? What would I do with them? A hike in the mountains, a visit to a museum, attend a conference together? What would I hate in his/her presence? And so, through the "active imagination" (Jaffé, 1961), arrive in this way at a re-reading of one's own counter-transference, to discover the resonances that the co-created field offers and the suggestions useful for overcoming the blocking situation.

It seems to me that this suggestion resonates with what Roubal related to us. Perhaps we similarly need to experiment with the "field" perspective as a new paradigm, listening to each other, imagining that not only does one's own world enter our office with the patient but that we, thanks to them, have access to everything that they mean in their humanity and that they themself need to touch it, enlivened by a different personal perspective, that of the therapist.

Perhaps it is also a good way of escaping an antinomy which has held back our science and our therapeutic art for a long time. An antimony that leaves us caught between the Dodo's disappointing verdict that "everyone has won," regarding the capacity of the psychotherapeutic model to be more effective than others, almost as if a form of treatment could disregard the qualities or limits of the therapists who implement it as a therapy (De Felice et al., 2019), and the "autocratic" celebration of the superiority of each reference model (Carli, 1987).

In addressing this, I intend to start from a reflection I have dwelt on at length, confronted—for several years now, I could say since the beginning of my career—with the plurality of psychotherapeutic models.

13.3 Towards a new perspective

I have always been interested in identifying the differential criteria used when a person is referred to a psychotherapist. It would be best if in every clinical situation the most effective treatment could be identified for the case as it presents itself, considering the needs of the patient and the competence of the therapist to whom they should be referred. However, if precedence is given only to this second criterion (the competence of the therapist), where I refer a patient to a therapist because they work with the model I know and myself practice, then the criterion becomes that of respecting the orthodoxy of one's model. So, if I am versed in psychoanalysis, I will choose a capable psychoanalyst; if I practice hypnosis, I will choose a hypnologist, and so on.

Proceeding in this way, I apparently obey a clear-cut, correct methodology. In reality, I put into practice a cognitive paradox whereby, when I take care of a patient in the light of a judgment of the viability of my model, I implicitly exclude other possibilities, forcing myself (and forcing the patient) to make a choice without considering the actual clinical conditions of the patient and the model's application. In other words, I neglect the person of the patient, whose characteristics and

potential I postpone to my pre-judgments and the biases that my specific training has—unknowingly and inevitably—inculcated in me (Carli
& Paniccia, 2003).[1]

As care professionals, how can we avoid the lethal risk of neglecting
the first criterion, i.e., serving the needs of those who turn to us for
help? I believe we need to reflect fundamentally on the institution of
psychotherapy itself and to investigate its roots in psychology, science,
and clinical practice, which implies identifying the points of contact
between the different perspectives present in psychotherapeutic models.

Referring a person to a colleague in this way exemplifies a concept
that we could define as "the concept of elective therapy" in the identification of the best treatment for the type of suffering, the cognitive style,
and the personal reality of the patient (Grasso et al., 1988, p. 122). How
can we stop ourselves from making this methodological error, considering that, as care professionals, it expresses a lack of respect for the person who turns to us in a moment of difficulty?

I think that the problem can only be solved by considering the very
special status that psychology has in the panorama of science. It seems
to me that a useful clue can be found in a work edited by Hofstaetter. It
is dated now, but it seems to me valuable for its capacity of having predicted the development of general psychology, and clinical psychology
in particular, over the half-century that has elapsed since its publication.
The key I am referring to is "Buhler's triangle" (Figure 13.1).

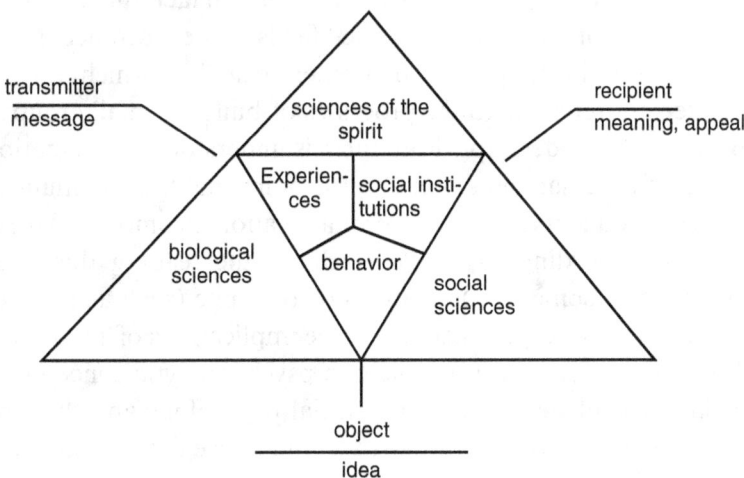

Figure 13.1 Buhler's Triangle.

According to this approach, psychology simultaneously intersects with the social sciences, the sciences of the spirit, and the biological sciences. Thus, Buhler (1927) sees our science as embracing experiences, behavior, and social institutions (e.g., language, works of art, and human constructs).

The task of the researcher, therefore, is to affirm the continuity and interdependence between the three areas. In this way, psychology's (and psychotherapy's) claim to scientific status is supported by recognizing that each of its constructions, arising from the fundamental value of pursuing the well-being of the person, consider both their psychophysical condition and the dimension of their "social being" (Hofstaetter, 1957, p. 10)

Buhler's scheme summarizes the interdependence between the application fields of psychology and the methods that are employed. It expresses the ambiguity, but also its potential within the realm of the sciences, as it claims, to capture all the complexity of human nature in its maximum individualization, that of the person. People are the embodiment of a biological substratum, a sphere of values, and a compass of behaviors that are not merely dictated by instincts and automated processes built up over the centuries by human biological history—people are "political animals," social beings *par excellence*, builders of a sociality that is, similarly, free from any pre-established instinctual schemes (Bertola & Casadei, 2018).

Hofstaetter views this scheme as an information theorist would, reading in it the source of many misunderstandings that weigh down the dialogue between psychologists. It happens, in fact, that a statement referring to one of the three semantic "fields" is decoded according to the postulates and rules proper to another "field," for which, for example, a statement referring to the processes of building small groups and the formation of leadership within them is understood as a dictation of values and vice versa, and so on—to the point that the communicative potential of the agents makes the communication incomplete. An example of this—according to Renzo Carli—is the reading that Franco Fornari gives of some of the realities of our time (such as the atomic situation, or the conceptualization of the implications of modern society (Fornari, 1975)), resorting solely to psychoanalytic concepts without making use of derivatives from social psychology and thus losing sight of interesting points of view that could have corroborated a perspective that instead turned out to be excessively sectorial.

The meeting from which this text was born (Field Perspectives and Psychotherapeutic Practice. Three Models Compared) follows a completely different logic. A perspective (that of the "field") is assumed and, in addition to analyzing it by displaying its significance, it makes it a privileged point for comparison and encounter between three different psychotherapeutic perspectives.

Let me examine what emerged from this comparison as stimulating and promising for further insights and developments and the suggestions I found for fruitful "cross-pollination." A promising premise for the future development of our psychotherapeutic path, built on an analysis of the beneficial effects that come from an enriching comparison of models of the same origin (Lolli, 2012).

It is true that many mental health professionals have always found in the comparison of different models an opportunity to rethink the characteristics of their own practice. In that comparison they have found stimulus and fertile soil for sowing seeds that would later blossom as an evolutionary moment of their work. But with regard to these comparative ideas, it is an area that is perhaps still under-explored.

Let me try and explain. Thanks to the case presentation of Anna and the discussions concerning her, I have the feeling that this way of comparing models revives and integrates a practice that, while welcoming the specifics of each model, knows how to see the common points of the models (taking us back to the idea of a common ground) and draws the stimulus and inspiration to revisit the metamodels and paradigms that underpin them.

Two very clear images come to me as to the differences between the consolidated mode and the way in which we have viewed this seminar. Almost always, until now, comparison was a matter of exploring the theoretical/practical "field" of others, almost with the spirit of the zoo visitor who, standing outside the primate cage, questions the differences between chimpanzees, gorillas, and humans. In this way we see how a cognitivist would behave in the face of this situation, how, and how much, a gestalt therapist would allow the past to interfere in the interpretation I am about to provide, and so on. In the shared space of this meeting, we entered a much more constructive, and demanding, area. Accepting that mutual knowledge helps us to better define our own reference model, so that, as Migone (2023) pointed out, by knowing more models, our knowledge of the clinical situation is as complete as possible, we can understand and know more about the patient, or as our post-Bionian friends attending our meeting would, perhaps, say, "saturate" the patient's needs, feelings, and demands best.

The concept of "field" seems to be one of the key concepts on which to continue to reflect and deepen each psychotherapeutic model. Or going further, to focus consideration on the "field" within the field that unites the various psychotherapeutic models can be an intriguing prelude to paradigm change in the conceptualization itself of psychotherapy. In other words, every model can be enriched by the comparison with other models, through the rethinking of its foundations, making comparison a key for consolidating the scientific positioning of the psychotherapeutic art.

13.4 A historical note

Speaking of comparisons, I would like to cite what seems to me a precedent, at least regarding the Italian situation.

The comparison between models has now become part of the history and, I would say, the daily practice of Italian psychologists, with the establishment of the FIAP (the Italian Federation of Psychotherapy Associations). This association arose from a prehistory that saw Riccardo Zerbetto become President of the European Association for Psychotherapy (EAP) in 1997. As EAP President, he organized the first-ever EAP Conference in Italy in June of the same year in Rome—an event connected to the VII EAP Conference, dedicated to "Common Foundations and Diversity of Approaches in Psychotherapy," attended by representatives from the national associations of 26 European countries. Thus, right from the start, the task of the EAP—and the FIAP with it—was to research the common sources and shared ground underlying the different psychotherapeutic approaches, while emphasizing the specific peculiarities of each model.

The FIAP was established under the umbrella of the EAP, but it immediately established its own autonomy. In an equally clear way, the FIAP also plays a linking role between the various psychotherapeutic models by operating in the training field, building on its experience of the organization of psychotherapy in the country and the delicate task of training psychotherapists. The FIAP has therefore become in Italy a leading promoter of comparisons, mutual influences, and enrichments that have allowed associations, and their psychotherapy training schools, to reap the benefits of cross-pollination, without detracting from the original discipline and model represented by each association. Instead, it provides a space in which the various "modus operandi" can enrich themselves and "pollinate themselves."

Note

1 Renzo Carli distinguishes between the various psychotherapeutic models: ideological models (such as psychoanalysis); autarkic models (such as some forms of group psychotherapy); and tautological models (behavioral therapy). The identification of a "methodological" meta-model, oriented towards a solution to the problems and an answer to the questions of the patient, is the task of researchers in clinical psychology and psychotherapy.

References

Bertola, A., & Casadei, A. (Eds.). (2018). *Psicoanalisi e spiritualità*. FrancoAngeli.

Buhler, K. (1927). *Die Krise der Psychologie*. Velbrueck. Discussed in A. Bertola. (2010). Introduzione. In A. Musco (Ed.), *Narcisismo e mentalizzazzione*. Alpes.

Carli, R. (1987). *Psicologia clinica: Introduzione alla teoria e al metodo*. Utet.

Carli, R., & Paniccia, R. M. (2003). *Analisi della domanda. Teoria e intervento in psicologia clinica*. Il Mulino.

De Felice, G., Giuliani, A., Halfon, S., Andreassi, S., Paoloni, G., & Orsucci, F. F. (2019). The misleading Dodo Bird verdict. How much of the outcome variance is explained by common and specific factors? *New Ideas in Psychology, 54*, 50–55.

Ferro, A. (2017). *Pensieri di uno psicoanalista irriverente*. Raffaello Cortina Editore.

Fornari, F. (1975). *Psicoanalisi della Guerra*. Feltrinelli.

Francesetti, G., & Griffero, T. (Eds.). (2022). *Psicopatologia e atmosfere: Prima del soggetto e del mondo*. Fioriti Editore.

Grasso, M., Lombardo, G. P., & Pinkus, L. (1988). *Psicologia clinica. Teorie, metodi e applicazioni della psicodinamica*. NIS.

Hofstaetter, P.R. (1957). *Psychologie*. Fischer Bucherei KG.

Jaffé, A. (1961). *Memories, dreams, reflections of Carl Gustav Jung*. Random House.

Kernberg, O. F. (1996). Structural derivatives of object relationships. In P. Buckley (Ed.), *Essential papers on object relations* (pp. 350–384). New York University Press. (Reprinted from the *International Journal of Psycho-Analysis 47*, 236–253, 1966).

Kilpatrick, F. P. (Ed.). (1961). *Explorations in transactional psychology*. The Institute for International Social Research.

Kuhn, T. (1962). *The structure of scientific revolutions*. University of Chicago.

Lolli, F. (2012). *È più forte di me. Il concetto di ripetizione in psicoanalisi*. Poiesis.

Migone, P. (2023) Come gestire la pluralità dei modelli in psicoterapia. *Psicoterapia e Scienze Umane, 57*(3), 479–500.

Solms, M. (2022). Una revisione della teoria delle pulsioni. *Psicoterapia e Scienze Umane, 56*(3), 363–422.

Stern, D. B. (2015). *Relational freedom: Emergent properties of the interpersonal field*. Routledge.

Zerbetto, R. (Ed.). (2007). *Fondamenti comuni e diversità di approccio in psicoterapia*. FrancoAngeli.

Chapter 14

Historical remarks on the relationship between Gestalt therapy and psychoanalysis

Bernd Bocian

As a kind of motto, I would like to begin this chapter with a quote from the lecture given by Friedrich Salomon (Fritz) Perls, psychoanalyst and central founder of Gestalt therapy, in April 1947 at the White Institute in New York, the home of interpersonal psychoanalysis:

> The safeguard against such a danger (of a one-sided approach or eclecticism) is the concept and experience of the human personality as being an indivisible whole and as always embedded in and related to an environmental, personal, and social field.
>
> (Perls, 2012, p. 38)

I will now briefly trace, with special reference to the psychoanalytic readership, how Gestalt therapy developed against the background of psychoanalysis and how it did so out of a specific current and tradition of the psychoanalytic movement. It was a tradition whose evolution was interrupted when the National Socialists took power in 1933, but which was preserved, kept up, and further developed in Gestalt therapy. In this context, I am also concerned with remembrance work, drawing attention to forerunners and pioneers of relational and field-oriented psychoanalysis, of whom many interpersonal/relational psychoanalysts seem to have little or no memory, although it is part of their own history. The same can be said for many Gestalt therapists, who are barely aware of their own past.

Paolo Migone is right when he writes in his foreword to the book by Gestalt therapist Margherita Spagnuolo Lobb:

> Listening to these theorizations of Gestalt therapy, how can we fail to think of the developments of relational psychoanalysis, for example by someone like Mitchell, or of the intersubjective

DOI: 10.4324/9781003597308-15

perspective (explicitly phenomenological and "holistic") of Stolorow and others? There is an evident close similarity, but with the difference that certain positions had been taken by the Gestalt therapists several decades previously.

(Migone, 2013, p. 17)

Accordingly, I am writing my "historical remarks" for a book which appears to document an interest in, and openness to, attempting dialogue between approaches that represent avant-garde developments within their respective schools. The schools represented in this book, including Gestalt therapy, emerged from the psychoanalytic tradition and movement. Referring to Donnel Stern and his contribution, I would like to recall that the early protagonists of Gestalt therapy and the "interpersonal tradition" (see Hirsch, 2015) had already met in the past and their paths crossed more than once. Here I am concerned with the memory of two professional networks in which initial attempts were made to integrate different theoretical traditions and clinical approaches. Those efforts broke off for the psychoanalytic mainstream when Hitler came to power in 1933, but arrived in the U.S.A., in New York, via two paths. One was through Erich Fromm, who brought it to the White Institute with Frieda Fromm-Reichmann; the other was through Fritz Perls, who, after initially cooperating with the early White Institute in 1947, founded his own approach, Gestalt Therapy (1951), with his wife Lore Perls and another collaborator, Paul Goodman. The attempts at integration we are dealing with here were initiated, on the one hand, by the analysts who founded the first Frankfurt Psychoanalytic Institute in 1929, and, on the other, by the group of character analysts and left-wing Freudians at the Berlin Institute, before they all emigrated. It was within these groups that Fritz and Lore Perls, as well as Erich Fromm, were all trained during this period.

With reference to the subject of this book, the generally accepted opinion is that it was H.S. Sullivan who first introduced the idea of field theory to psychoanalysis. This is not entirely correct. By the end of the 1920s, contact and discussion between psychoanalysis, Gestalt psychology, and field theory was already happening at the Frankfurt and Berlin Institutes. Fritz Perls, who was trained as a psychoanalyst in Frankfurt, Vienna, and especially Berlin, and his wife Lore Perls, a psychoanalytically-trained Gestalt psychologist, introduced field theory concepts into their revision of psychoanalysis as early as the end of the 1930s. They did this apparently in parallel with Sullivan, outlining their approaches in this regard in their first book published in 1942 in Johannesburg, South Africa, where they had fled and would live until the end of the Second World War. In that book, entitled *Ego, Hunger, and Aggression. A Revision of Freud's Theory and Method* (Perls, 1942/1992a), we find what would become one of the basic concepts of Gestalt therapy (1951): "In reality there is never such a thing as an individual or an environment. They both form an inseparable unit in which, for instance, stimulus and readiness or ability to be stimulated cannot be separated" (Perls, 1942/1992a, p. 242). In therapy, change "occurs dialectically and simultaneously [...] involving the aspects of the environmental–intra-organismic field" (p. 291). Together with the conviction brought primarily by Lore Perls, that healing comes through the relationship, the interpersonal dialogue, the meeting between I and Thou, which she inherited from her Frankfurt teacher Martin Buber at the end of the 1920s, the field orientation has remained one of the basic concepts of Gestalt therapy. Perls says in a 1957 lecture, and we can find similar passages through to his last publications in the late 1960s:

> Now we come to the basis of our approach. Namely, we consider ourselves, as I consider myself right now, a part of the field. If I am with the field and experience myself and my reactions as part of the field, then I use myself as a tool of therapy. I get involved. I can get involved with the total field situation, which we call "sympathy."
>
> (Perls, 2012, p. 145)

Basing myself on Fritz and Lore Perls's psychoanalytic training and experience, I will now attempt to trace the development of this early relationship- and field-oriented attitude, which was preserved and developed in Gestalt therapy.

14.1 A brief historical overview

The majority of the revisions to orthodox analytic positions that Gestalt therapy proposed can be traced back to the dissidents of Freud's school (see Bocian, 2010; Bocian & Staemmler, 2013). And since psychoanalysis is "a research project," as Perls once said (Perls, 1977, p. 142), and "as a science of the human being cannot be monopolized" (Cremerius,

1992, p. 24), in my view Gestalt therapy remains a figure against the background of psychoanalytic history, theory, and practice. The development of Gestalt therapy remains part of the emigration history of German-speaking psychoanalysts beginning in 1933. It can particularly be characterized by the preservation and perpetuation of radical elements in Freud's approach (see Bocian, 2013, pp. 46ff.).

Before Hitler's rise to power and the beginning of the great emigration in 1933, Berlin and Frankfurt, where Fritz and Lore Perls were both trained, were the "think tanks" where progressive psychoanalysts became involved with Marxist social scientists, Gestalt psychologists, and field theorists, entering into dialogue with them. The importance of Frankfurt and Berlin for the development of Gestalt therapy lies in the interdisciplinary and integrative climate at the University of Frankfurt, marked by a strong contingent of holistic theorists (the Gestalt psychologists, Kurt Goldstein, etc.) and the early socio-critical Frankfurt School, of whom Horkheimer was a central figure (Bocian, 2010, pp. 160ff.), while in Berlin, Fritz and Lore Perls assimilated active character analysis and the contextual, field-theoretical approach of left-wing Freudians (Bocian, 2010, pp. 204ff. and pp. 231ff.).

One of Perls and Goodman's main concerns in the founding text of 1951 was to conceptualize as complementary polarities different currents of psychoanalysis (some of which had been pushed into dissidence) that focused on certain parts of human reality and differentiated themselves from each other, integrating the insights which they considered valuable. Among the approaches mentioned by Perls and Goodman that focus on the "structure of the present situation" (Perls et al., 1951/1996, p. 236), we find Freud's concept of transference, Ferenczi's "active method," Reich's character analysis, Sullivan's interpersonal approach, and Otto Rank's emphasis on the creative act.

Deepening and expanding the discourse of *Ego, Hunger, and Aggression* (1942/1992a), the book *Gestalt Therapy* (1951) marked the beginning of a paradigm shift that for many leading representatives of the "relational turn" in psychoanalysis seems to have begun much later. Aron and Harris, for example, write that starting from the White Institute, especially through Mitchell, a paradigm shift took place in the 1980s and the "myth of the isolated self" (Altmeyer & Thomä, 2006, p. 108) was called into question. At its core is the issue of relatedness and the restoration of the "connection between the inner world and the outer world that had been lost in ego psychology" (Altmeyer & Thomä, 2006, p. 12). Altmeyer points out that, in his work, Mitchell attempted the integration of various traditions that had gone "their own ways" and had long since been marginalized, or had left voluntarily "because they did not want to accept the identity-creating shibboleth demands of the founding era or submit to corresponding confessional pressures" (Altmeyer & Thomä, 2006, p. 12). Perls and Goodman tried to do just that, but much earlier.

14.2 The ineffectiveness of "passive technique"

In the middle of the 1920s, when Perls began his training at the Berlin Psychoanalytic Institute, psychoanalytic treatment characteristically consisted of lying on a couch, making associations, and being interpretated by the analyst. In his memoirs, Wilhelm Reich, then training analyst at the Vienna Institute, described the dominant opinion at that time, saying:

> that the "passive technique" was the only correct one. Among themselves, colleagues joked about the temptation to sleep during analytic hours: if a patient failed to produce associations, they had to smoke a lot to keep awake. Some analysts even derived high-sounding theories from this.
>
> (Reich, 1942, p. 64)

What Reich describes here is exactly what Erich Fromm and Fritz Perls experienced on the couch in Berlin—Fromm with Hans Sachs, and Perls with Eugene Harnik. For both men, it was a very personal motivation for them to change their way of working as therapists and to continue Ferenczi's and Reich's development of an active technique. The "passive technique" involved extensive concentration on verbal content and, in particular, on the reconstruction of the patient's childhood, the result of which was a collection of intellectual insights that, in Reich's words, produced "the typical hopeless picture of an analysis rich in interpretations and poor in results" (Reich, 1942, p. 63).

In *Gestalt Therapy* (1951), Perls and Goodman acknowledge that free association can disrupt the "frozen relation of figure and ground"

(Perls et al., 1951/1996, p. 329) and let unfinished and unconscious material, such as "hidden impulses (the charged background)" (p. 60), become foreground. The analyst guesses and concludes something that the patient is not aware of and interprets the relation between figure and ground, thereby suggesting a closing of the Gestalt.

The "orthodox" setting put the patient in too passive a position—"the problem is that in the activity that *he* was engaged in, he had been ver-balizing a stream of meaningless words" (Perls et al., 1951/1996, p. 328). It is "the therapist who is concentrating on the stream and creating whole figures in it (finding and making them)" (p. 327). The therapist is "the grown-up, knows everything; and oneself can never know the secret unless told" (p. 330). Instead, rather than just "introjecting the wisdom of an authority" (p. 328), the patient can also be involved as "an active experimental partner" (p. 248), who

> learns that something, not known as his, comes from his darkness and yet is meaningful; thereby perhaps *he* is encouraged to explore, to regard his unawareness as *terra incognita* but not chaos. From this point of view, he must of course be made a partner in the interpreting.
>
> (pp. 329ff.)

I will return to the importance of this radical dialogical stance (related to interpretation as a definition or explanation of someone, their behav-ior, or the common situation) later, when I briefly address some critical points of the field approach towards the end of the chapter.

As early as 1924, Ferenczi and Rank made the lack of therapeutic results of analytic practice, as described by Reich, the starting point for their efforts to develop analysis and make it more effective, in the book *The Development of Psycho-Analysis*. Following on from the early cathartic technique of Freud and Breuer, they especially stressed the great importance of actual remembering, of experiencing and living through affects in the presence of what happens in the current situation between patient and analyst, instead of a merely theoretical under-standing of the past, advocating for active interventions. From that moment on, the step from the method of free association to the focus on the relationship in the here-and-now was, in principle, possible, a development through which various traditions have emerged.

The predominant direction that development would take involved increasingly relating the patient's experience to the person of the therapist—a direction already embedded in Ferenczi and Rank's work. On the one hand, this led to attempts at investigating the relation between transference and counter-transference more thoroughly; on the other, it resulted in practices that relate any impulse of the patient to the analyst, in what at times could lead to a sense of persecution for patients. In "orthodox" analysis, for instance, a client's memories and fantasies regularly acquire their meanings in the context of unconscious transferences. The "drama" takes place in the psyche and its unconscious relational fantasies, which are projected onto the neutral analyst and need only be uncovered by the analyst through interpretation. As is the case in any exclusive relationship between two people, the only two persons present have to represent everything for each other. This can swamp both of them, and the analyst or therapist as a positive other can become lost. This is, I believe, called transference neurosis.

Another, alternative line of development leads from Ferenczi's active experiments in the 1920s (not his later work on trauma) to the group at the Frankfurt Psychoanalytic Institute and to the character analysts around Wilhelm Reich in Berlin, and from there, through their student Fritz Perls, to Gestalt therapy.

14.3 Pre-Nazi "think tanks"

14.3.1 Frankfurt and the Gestalt concept—thinking in terms of context and relationships

After several months of training therapy with Karen Horney, and on Horney's advice, Perls went to Frankfurt in September 1926 where he remained until September 1927. Frankfurt University had developed into a center for the social sciences in Germany. Just like in Berlin, there was also a Psychological Institute, where Gestalt psychology played an important role (see Plänkers et al., 1996). Lore Perls studied and received her doctorate here. The professorial staff included Max Wertheimer, Ademar Gelb, Wolfgang Köhler, and Friedrich Schumann. Gelb collaborated closely with neurologist Kurt Goldstein, a holistic-organismic thinker. At the time, Goldstein directed the Neurological Institute and the university clinic's Institute for Research on the Consequences of Brain Injury, which had developed out of his work with soldiers suffering from brain injuries. Perls was a member of Goldstein's group of assistants for about a year. In Goldstein's circle, Perls also came into contact with field theorist Kurt Lewin's early works written in Berlin (see Perls, 1977, p. 62). The grand holistic world concept developed by Jan Smuts, considered a recommended read for the insiders among Goldstein's assistants, only became an important source after Perls emigrated to South Africa.

Goldstein's holistic-systemic approach viewed the individual neuron as a node in a network where neurons are constantly interacting with each another. Accordingly, he proceeded under the assumption that people who have been injured—for example, cases involving perceptual disturbances caused by localized brain lesions—always react as a unit, and the organism forms a system that functions as a whole. During those years, Goldstein was one of the physicians trying to return the focus of medicine to "the whole human being." He strove for a "multidisciplinary, psychosomatic vision of human distress" (Harrington, 1996, p. 160) and did not differentiate mechanically between physical and emotional disturbances, instead viewing the "problem of the whole organism in relationship to its milieu" (p. 161). Goldstein criticized both somatic medicine and psychoanalysis for failing to recognize that categories such as mind and body or ego and id were mere symbols or abstractions of a single, holistic, organismic reality. This would influence the field-theoretical "theory of self" that Perls and Goodman developed in New York in 1951, as distinct from the ego/self theories of Freud, Anna Freud, and Paul Federn (see Bocian, 2013, pp. 56ff.; Perls et al., 1951/1996, pp. 385ff.). Perls' holistic perspective of the relationship between mind and body was built on Goldstein's "organismic theory," as well as on Reich's ideas on organismic self-regulation.

Let us look at a brief example of the influence that Gestalt psychological thinking had on Perls's psychoanalytic thinking. Fritz Perls met his wife Lore Posner towards the end of October 1926 at a seminar held by Goldstein and Gestalt psychologist Ademar Gelb entitled "On Consciousness and the So-Called Unconscious" (see Sreckovic, 1999, p. 34). What Perls and Goodman in 1951 referred to as the "basic principle of the context" (Perls et al., 1951/1996, p. 398) is also described as the process of figure-background formation in Gestalt psychology. Figure and background only form a totality, a Gestalt, when taken together, and they are related to one another through a process. Therefore, the relationship between *the conscious and the unconscious* is not viewed as an ultimately irreconcilable division within the personality, but rather as a dynamic and fluid process that includes to a considerable degree the opportunity to expand consciousness into areas that have not been previously perceived. Freud—the "usher," as Perls called him—constructed a space, the unconscious, from which impulses and spontaneous thinking seem to emerge (Perls et al., 1951/1996, pp. 384, 440). For Perls, as a disciple of Goldstein's, this perspective objectified a living, holistic process:

> Freud said (this is not his formulation, but my understanding of what he meant) that in a neurosis a part of our personality or our potential is not available. But he said this in an odd way; he said, "it is *in* the unconscious," as if there were such a thing as *the* unconscious rather than simply behavior or emotions that are unknown or not available. Freud also saw the basis of the Gestalt formation in what he called the "preconscious." We call it the "background" out of which the figure emerges.
>
> (Perls, 1970, p. 16)

Perls always kept his sights set on "rebuilding the personality," in the sense intended by Kurt Goldstein. That means attempting to combine analysis with the reorganization of behavior, which includes *concrete* experimenting with new ways of behaving in interpersonal contact. Perls and Goodman's concept of "therapy as Gestalt analysis" (Perls et al., 1951/1996, p. 232) has roots in Goldstein's understanding of "holistic analysis." In holistic analysis, the researcher or therapist seeks to reconstruct "the whole organism itself in its Umwelt" by oscillating between the figure and its background in a "dialectic movement" (Harrington, 1996, p. 153).

Goldstein's influence on the early Interpersonal Approach and Gestalt therapy was important. His thinking on the relativity of the concept of health and his idea of "blocked self-realization," or inhibited personality growth, had theoretical and practical relevance for Perls as well as for Goldstein's former collaborator Frieda Fromm-Reichmann and for Karen Horney. All three left the "orthodox" path and had the courage to go their own way.

14.3.1.1 An integrative atmosphere

A fertile interdisciplinary exchange of ideas developed at Frankfurt University in the 1920s. A key player in the process was the Institute for Social Research (IfS), from which the *Frankfurt School* (the "Critical Theory" of Horkheimer, Adorno, Marcuse, etc.) would later emerge. Max Horkheimer was employed by the IfS while also holding the position of private lecturer at the university. Within the IfS, there was a "Kränzchen" (circle or discussion group) bringing together various scientists. In addition to the Marxist sociologists, Gestalt psychologist Ademar Gelb, Kurt Goldstein, and social philosopher and theologian Paul Tillich also participated. All three were important teachers for Lore Perls and their influence also extended to Fritz Perls.

In October 1926, the Southwest German Working Group for Psychoanalysis was founded. Key members included Karl Landauer, Erich Fromm, Frieda Fromm-Reichmann, Karl Meng, and Clara Happel. The group remained in close contact with Georg Groddeck in Baden-Baden, who also hosted meetings with Karen Horney and Sandor Ferenczi. Perls and Lore Posner-Perls attended some of the meetings with Groddeck. While working as an assistant for Goldstein, Fritz Perls was undergoing training analysis with Clara Happel, and Lore, inspired by Fritz, likewise started analysis with Happel in 1927. When Happel moved to Hamburg, Lore switched to Karl Landauer for roughly two-and-a-half years.

Though he is largely unknown today, due to his early death from starvation in 1945 at the Bergen-Belsen concentration camp, Frankfurt psychoanalyst Karl Landauer was an important analyst at that time (see Rothe, 1987, 1996; Bocian, 2015). He had been in analysis with Sigmund Freud and was Horkheimer's analyst and, later, close friend, publishing also in the Frankfurt School's *Journal for Social Research*. Lore Perls said about Landauer:

> I learned a lot in Frankfurt, especially through my own analysis which was a comparatively free one. Landauer was a friend of Ferenczi and Groddeck, both of whom were already among the more avant-garde people at the time.
>
> (Perls, L., 1982, p. 8)

Fritz Perls became well acquainted with Landauer as a supervising analyst, but only after he had emigrated to Amsterdam, and likewise thought very highly of him.

Landauer was an independent and creative thinker. Some themes of his work anticipated aspects of contemporary psychoanalysis and influenced Gestalt therapy (see Landauer, 1991), such as his thoughtful and careful use of active psychoanalysis, his emphasis on thinking and feeling in an independent way, his close attention to affects and body language (in a way that resembles later developments in infant research), and his growing interest in social factors. In his last article, in which he approvingly quoted Perls's lecture on "oral resistance" at the Marienbad Congress in 1936, he writes: "To be sure, the centre of interest has now shifted from the sexual zone and aim involved to the factor of social demands and the reactions to these" (Landauer, 1939, p. 425).

On February 16th, 1929, the Frankfurt Psychoanalytic Institute (FPI) was founded. Once again, the founding members included Landauer as director, Fromm, Fromm-Reichmann, and Meng. The FPI was housed as a guest organization on premises provided at the Institute for Social Research. Erich Fromm was an active member of both institutes and played an important part in gaining consideration for psychoanalytic perspectives within the interdisciplinary social analytical approach taken by emergent critical theory. Beginning in 1930, Siegmund Heinrich Fuchs became another member of the institute. Fuchs worked together with Perls as an assistant to Goldstein in Frankfurt in 1926. After emigrating as S. H. Foulkes, he became a pioneer of analytical group therapy, using concepts from Gestalt psychology and field theory, which were particularly relevant to his ideas on the "group-matrix" (see Foulkes, 2019). Fritz Perls shuttled back and forth between Frankfurt and Berlin and participated together with Lore in lectures and seminars at the Institute. Lore Perls, for example, took part in Fromm-Reichmann's theoretical seminars on the "Theory of Drives," which Perls also occasionally attended.

14.3.1.2 Buber and the forgotten relational and field-oriented tradition

In the context of the emergence of Gestalt therapy, the development towards an increasingly relational orientation was possible from the beginning, through European, especially German, dialogical philosophy. A tradition that was represented by Lore Perls, having studied under Martin Buber at the "Free Jewish Teaching House" (which Fromm also frequented), and under Paul Tillich at the university. Writing about them, she says, "I learned more from meeting them than from their writings. I was deeply impressed by their way of being, their presence, and their respect for others. They influenced me more than any psychologist" (Perls, L., 1989, p. 178). What Buber called *Begegnung* (meeting/encounter), we call "contact," that is, "the perception of and engagement with the other as the other" (Perls, L., 1989, p. 179).

Interestingly, for some time now, American relational and intersubjective analysts have been "rediscovering" Martin Buber, phenomenology, Gadamer's hermeneutics, and Hegel's dialectic. In this context, Bohrleber has pointed to a "tradition of forgetting" (Altmeyer & Thomä, 2006, p. 213) within psychoanalysis in the German-speaking world, which has been in the process of importing "new" theories from the United States. In doing so, it seems to have been forgotten that in the 1950s and 1960s, intersubjectivist theories were already having their heyday in Germany. Drawing on Buber's philosophy of dialogue from the 1920s, the concept of "meeting" was introduced into the therapeutic discussion at that time, especially by Ludwig Binswanger and Victor von Weizsäcker. For the psychoanalyst Felix Schottlaender, for example, "meeting" was something that went beyond the transference/countertransference dynamic (Altmeyer & Thomä, 2006, p. 211).

That tradition remained alive in Gestalt therapy, as it drew directly from sources in Frankfurt from the 1920s. An example of how this tradition was preserved until the 1950s is given by Wolfgang Hochheimer, who, like Lore Perls, studied Gestalt psychology in Frankfurt from 1928 to 1931 and did his doctorate with Goldstein and Gelb. And like Lore Perls at this time, he was a student at both the university's (Gestalt) Psychological Institute and the Frankfurt Psychoanalytic Institute. In 1954, Hochheimer published *On the Analysis of the Therapeutic Field*, in which he considered analytical therapy practice in terms of field theory and, in a language reminiscent of Buber, describes the meeting between therapist and client and the overlapping of their respective "life fields" as healing factors that cannot be rationally planned and understood. For him, the therapist's contribution to the field is not sufficiently taken into account by Freud's abstinent couch arrangement, through which the therapist tries to take himself out of the field. Hochheimer instead worked with concepts such as "interpersonal field," "atmosphere of life," and, referring to Lewin, he discusses the differences between the "analytic situation," the "therapeutic field," and the "life field" (Hochheimer, 1986, pp. 244ff.).

14.3.1.3 Intermezzo at the Vienna Institute

Perls went to the Vienna Psychoanalytic Institute for his supervision, on Clara Happel's advice. Perls lived in Vienna from September 1927 to March 1928. At the Vienna neurological clinic, Perls worked as a staff physician under Professors Wagner von Jauregg and Paul Schilder, participating in Schilder's Saturday "psychoanalytic case demonstrations." Perls also enrolled in the entire theoretical training program of the Viennese training institute and additionally attended the Vienna Psychoanalytic Association's bi-weekly lecture evenings, staying on a number of times to take part in the discussions that ensued afterwards (see Bocian, 2010, pp. 169ff.). Importantly for Perls, it was in Vienna that he first met Wilhelm Reich. From 1924 to 1930, Reich was director of the "Seminar on Therapeutic Technique" and at the same time he was also deputy director of the outpatient clinic. Perls attended Reich's lecture series about "Psychoanalytic Character Theory and Character Analysis" and presented cases at Reich's "technical seminars," which were held in the form of group case discussions. Beyond that, he had personal supervision with Helene Deutsch and Eduard Hitschmann. Paul Federn also left a lasting impression on Perls with his groundbreaking work on psychosis (see Federn, 1952) and his concepts of the "ego boundary" and the "ego feeling," which anticipated certain aspects of Kohut's self-concept. In September 1927, Perls attended the Psychoanalytical Congress in Innsbruck, where lectures by Ferenczi, Fenichel, and Reich were certainly important for him.

14.3.2 Berlin: Active technique, the whole field, and the resonating unconscious

Back in Berlin, Perls spent eighteen months in training analysis with Harnik, where he lay down on the couch five times a week "without being analyzed" (Perls, 1977, p. 48). The "catatonic" (pp. 41, 107, 130) sessions with Harnik were supplemented by supervision with Otto

Fenichel, to whom Lore Perls also went for supervision. Both appreciated Fenichel as a theorist, but found the supervisions relatively useless. Perls attended the Institute's lectures and gainfully took part in the character-analytic-oriented case discussion group held by Karen Horney. After breaking off analysis with Harnik, Perls continued his training (on Horney's advice) on Reich's couch and took part in the political and anti-fascist activities of the group of analysts around Reich (see Bocian, 2010, pp. 204ff.).

14.3.2.1 Character analysis as the moment of transmission and re-integrating the splits

A hallmark of Gestalt therapy is its integration and further development of the active and experimental analytic tradition (Perls and Goodman agreed on this; see Perls et al., 1951/1996, p. 236), which gradually expanded the involvement of the analyst, with character analysis appearing as a transitional phenomenon at the end of the 1920s. Ferenczi and Rank's (1924/1986) early criticism of an often-ineffective analytical practice was intended to vitalize and emotionalize the processes between therapist and patient in the therapy room by means of an "active psychoanalysis" and to promote holistic experience. Starting from Breuer's and Freud's early attempts to use psychodramatic and cathartic techniques, Sandór Ferenczi played a prominent role in these efforts with his active "stimulation therapy" (*Reiztherapie*) as early as 1919–1926 (see Bocian, 2009).

Contact with Reich's character analysis, from 1927 until both escaped Germany in 1933, was the moment when this tradition was passed on to Perls. Perls's training analysis with Reich was characterized by an entirely different dynamic than the "catatonic" months spent on Harnik's couch. Reich followed up on Ferenczi's active technique with the inclusion of body language and experiments with "forced fantasies" (1923/1994), which Perls also pursued (see Bocian, 2009), and the "neo-cathartic method" (Ferenczi, 1930).

The kind of analysis Perls experienced with Harnick was interested in words and fantasies, but neglected "all the subtler expressions of the body language, the importance of which has been pointed out by W. Reich and G. Groddeck" (Perls, 1992, p. 82). In Berlin, Reich continued to be interested in "negative transference." He had no fear of negative reactions from his analysands and, in some cases, actually sought to elicit them through provocation, because it often provided a way of reintroducing movement into a stagnated therapeutic process. A person like Fritz Perls certainly experienced that as a relief.

Perhaps because of the problems associated with the exclusion of the inconvenient communist and anti-fascist Reich from all psychoanalytic organizations in 1933/34 (see Nitzschke, 2003), this character analytic phase is, in my opinion, still not sufficiently appreciated and understood in all its potential, both by so-called orthodox and by more relational contemporary analysts. At that time, character analysis, which Perls studied for many years, had little to do with Reich's later theory of muscular blocks and resistances, with which it is frequently confused by Gestalt therapists today; instead, it was a current within the development of psychoanalytic ego psychology. It is relevant for the history of psychoanalysis and Gestalt therapy that, at that time, the first attempts were made to reintegrate the *splits* that psychoanalytic practice had established, in particular those between psyche and body and between individual and society—or, ultimately, between inside and outside.

Reich was concerned with *extending* interest in the past to the present situation, from the symptom to the whole person, from the verbalized and fantasized content to the experienced and observed phenomena. The emphasis on "how" the patient speaks, how he is silent, how he moves and so on, led to a general focus on nonverbal bodily and emotional processes in the here-and-now, in particular on dissociated and ego-syntonic body-signals and emotions and on preconscious perceptions. In other words, these analysts[1] began to look at what today Daniel Stern (2004) calls "implicit relational knowledge." They were no longer mere listeners but increasingly began to observe and perceive more. The analyst "morphed" from being a more or less invisible and speechless listener to being an increasingly present "embodied analyst" (see Sletvold, 2014), who also sees and uses all his/her resonating senses.

Laura Perls gives a good example of Gestalt therapy's origin in character analysis:

> Description prevails over explanation, experience and experiment over interpretation. Working strictly from the surface, e.g., from the actual awareness at any given moment, we avoid the mistake of

contacting depth material prematurely, that in the first place was and had to be 'repressed' because at a certain point in the patient's history it was unsupportable.

(Perls, L., 1992, pp. 95ff.)

14.3.2.2 The embodied analyst and the horizontal unconscious

For some time now, there has been debate about the "phenomenological foundation of psychoanalysis" (see Lohmar & Brudzinska, 2012), in which the topic of embodiment is central. The interesting thing is that there seems to be little memory of how these avant-garde approaches already existed and were practiced within what I call the active psychoanalytic tradition. What has been newly introduced—by analysts (Buchholz, 2012) or in the work of phenomenological psychotherapist Thomas Fuchs, "Body Memory and the Unconscious" (Fuchs, 2012)—as not repressed but implicit, as resonating, as horizontal unconscious, can already be found in the concrete therapy work of the psychoanalyst Wilhelm Reich and, thanks to his student Fritz Perls, has been part of Gestalt therapy theory and practice for over seventy years. This unconscious is not somewhere in the "depths," but shows up in the relationship, in actual behavior; it is a "style of existence" (Merleau-Ponty). For Fuchs, the unconscious of body memory is "characterized by corporeal and intercorporeal presence in the lived space and in the day-to-day life of a person" (Fuchs, 2012, p. 69). It is about a holistic, embodied view of internalized "object relations" or, rather, "schemes of being-with" (D.N. Stern, 2004), early "me–you patterns" (Sullivan, 1953), or unaware "organizing principles of a person's subjective world" (Atwood & Stolorow, 2014, p. 30).

In the words of Wilhelm Reich from 1933:

How is the infantile, historical experience preserved *in the present* ? [...] it did not rest as a kind of deposit in the unconscious but was absorbed into the character and expressed essentially as formal modes of behavior.

(Reich, 1988, p. 303)

Accordingly, in *Psychopathology of Awareness*, Perls makes it clear that he is interested in "what of the past is still in the present" (Perls, 2019,

p. 20). What is generally understood today as countertransference, i.e., personal resonance, or *"reverie,"* as the post-Bionian analysts call it, was already characteristic of Reich's analytic work at that time. In a letter written in 1935, Reich refers to his "ability to sense other's emotions before they have manifested themselves; that is what made me a character analyst" (Reich in Sletvold, 2014, p. 24).

At the beginning of an analysis, Reich mirrored the patient's mostly unconscious nonverbal behavior by pointing it out to the patient or sometimes imitating it in order to bring it into the patient's self-awareness. The following short example shows the extent to which what we think is typical of and unique in Gestalt therapy has ultimately been inherited from character analysis. Otto Fenichel, discussing this character analytic technique, which was sometimes perceived by the patient as too confrontational, proposed a more "cautious" intervention in 1934: "Pay attention to what your legs are doing now and how it relates to what we have been talking about now or what we discussed yesterday" (Fenichel, 1998, p. 204).

In this context, it is important to note that during those years in Berlin, Fenichel and Reich received decisive impulses from women with regard to the concrete integration of body awareness in their work. The Berlin gymnastics teacher Elsa Gindler is considered a pioneer of body therapy. In 1917, she began researching the interplay between external movement and breath. In doing so, she discovered the importance and connection of alert awareness, organismic self-regulation, and human growth. Fenichel's wife, Clara Fenichel, had been trained by Else Gindler, and Reich's Berlin girlfriend, dancer Elsa Lindberg, later also worked as a Gindler teacher in Oslo (see Sharaf, 1983, p. 330). Under the influence of these two women, Reich and Fenichel also participated in Gindler's seminars. Lore Perls, who already had many years of experience with various methods of expressive dance and holistic gymnastics, in parallel with her psychoanalysis training in Frankfurt, also attended Gindler's courses in Berlin. Fritz Perls studied the Gindler method intensively for a while, after his arrival in New York, with Charlotte Selver (as did Erich Fromm). Selver was a Gindler student and called her approach "Sensory-Awareness."

Gestalt Therapy is an embodied therapy, and Gindler's work with breathing and body awareness was concretely integrated into training and clinical practice from the beginning (Gregory, 2001), forming the basis for the bodily sensitivity, resonance, and cognition that are particularly important in relational and field theory approaches.

14.3.2.3 *Wilhelm Reich, the subjectivity of the analyst and the talking dummy*

At about this time, Reich was already discussing critical aspects of psychoanalysis that were taken up by psychoanalysts with a Freudian background only generations later. Then, as today, it was a question of interpretation as an exercise of power and of the "psychoanalyst as a talking dummy" (Moser, 1987). For Reich, the analyst's subjectivity and influence on the therapy process was never in question. In 1933 he wrote in the chapter on counter-transference:

> It is easy to understand that the temperament of any given analyst constitutes a decisive factor in the treatment of every case. [...] The analyst has the tasks of using his own unconscious as a kind of receiving apparatus to "tune" the unconscious of the analysand and of dealing with each individual patient in keeping with the patient's temperament.
>
> (Reich, 1988, p. 145)

He criticizes the "setting of sensory and interactive deprivation" (Moser, 1987, p. 113) that Perls and Fromm experienced in their training analyses with Harnik and Sachs, referring also to the personal and uncontrolled sadism of the analyst that easily lapses into "the well-known analytic silence" (Reich, 1988, p. 149). When he writes, "It is a mistake to interpret the general analytic rule (the analyst must be a 'blank sheet of paper' on which the patient writes his transference) to mean that one must always [...] adopt a 'mummy-like attitude'" (p. 149) which prevents many analysands from "coming out of their shell," he anticipates relational views. For Reich it is also clear "that the analyst changes his attitude toward one and the same patient depending upon the situation" (p. 149).

Here is an example of how Reich began relationship-oriented analytical work. Spurgeon-English, an American training candidate, was once annoyed that Reich wanted to reschedule an analytical session but reacted strongly when Spurgeon-English refused because he had an important private appointment of his own. When the candidate complained to Reich in the next session that he himself had kept all of his appointments until then and that it was Reich who was overscheduled, Reich quietly listened to him and then responded, "You're perfectly right" (in Sharaf, 1983, p. 176). Here, the training analyst used neither silence nor interpretation as an instrument of power or defense. Spurgeon-English recalled: "I had the first and perhaps greatest lesson in my life of the fact that a human being may be self-assertive and be given the right to an opinion and not be criticised for it or have acknowledgment given grudgingly" (in Sharaf, 1983, p. 176).

During this time, the Berlin Institute served as a development ground both for the abstinent standard technique, which Perls later encountered in American ego psychology as the "normative ideal technique" (Mertens, 1990, p. 199), and for the active or interactive tradition, which is about a holistic perspective in understanding the "inner world" in its inseparable connection with the body, concrete behavior, and the interpersonal, social, political, and ecological world.

14.3.2.4 Political Freudians and the whole field

During their Berlin years, Fritz and Lore Perls were trained in the left-wing Freudian circle.[2] The political Freudians had launched an attempt to address the integration and analysis of the whole life field—in which biology, psychology, and sociology were to be kept together—which was also the declared intent of Perls and Goodman. As Marxists, they were among the first to flee the country in 1933, and their social network increasingly fell apart. Their efforts to combine Marxist sociology and Freudian psychology make them pioneers of a contextual perspective. With their attempt to describe the reciprocal interpenetration of the individual and society, they laid the foundation for a psychoanalytical social psychology (see Brunner et al., 2013). It was Reich, Fenichel (1928/1987), and Gerö, in particular, who also increasingly incorporated body awareness into their thinking and work.

A kind of love for the early Freud and his culturally critical writings was typical for them. On the question of social and cultural change, Freud must be viewed essentially as a pessimist. The most radical position he took against the sickening, culturally prevalent sexual morality can be found in his 1908 monograph "'Civilized' Sexual Morality and

Modern Nervousness" (Freud, 1959a). The paper became a cult text for left-wing analysts, as in it Freud describes personal suffering as caused by external, social circumstances, and not by inner-psychic conflicts. Young analysts like Reich and Fenichel read this as a call for radical sexual reforms and revolutionary social change.

The fact that Perls was trained in this analytical context later interested Paul Goodman when collaborating with him. Among New York's postwar left-wing intellectuals, Goodman, a "communitarian and anarchist, was a pioneering figure in the rediscovery of Freud's radical potentialities" (Zaretsky, 2004, p. 302). Freud was one of his heroes,[3] and he held in high esteem the early character-analytical and politically active Reich of the Berlin years (Goodman, 1945/1977).

14.3.2.5 Siegfried Bernfeld, Lewin, and the "social place"

Siegfried Bernfeld had already begun to take a serious interest in Gestalt psychology and Lewin's Field Theory before emigrating to become one of the founding members of the San Francisco Psychoanalytical Institute. In 1934, he published a lengthy article on "Gestalt Theory" which hinted at areas where psychoanalysis and Gestalt theory might overlap or complement each another (see Bernfeld, 1934).

In Berlin, where Lewin taught at the university, there was concrete cooperation in a "Working Group of Psychoanalysts and Gestalt Psychologists" from March to June 1932 (see Bernfeld, 2020, pp. 725ff.). In addition to Lewin, Karl Dunker, and other Gestalt psychologists, the psychoanalytic participants were Bernfeld, Georg Gerö (like Perls, Reich's analysand and later a teaching analyst at the "official" New York IPA Institute), Rene Spitz, Hans Sachs, Gustav Bally, Eva Rosenfeld (later analysand of Melanie Klein in London), and Felix Schottlaender.

Bernfeld was a leftist Freudian. Accordingly, his 1929 article "Social Place and its Importance for Neurosis, Neglect, and Pedagogy" was an attempt to underline again the importance of the client's social reality for psychoanalytic thinking, which was becoming increasingly medically-oriented, limiting the context more and more to the intrapsychic world. He emphasizes that the concrete reality of a milieu shapes the emotional processes, and it is, above all, an individual's social place that determines what he or she will suffer from. An individual's way of thinking and feeling will depend on the person's respective place in society, for example, the middle class or the blue-collar milieu, and it will also determine his or her chances for the future. Referring to Bernfeld and his knowledge of Lewin's work, Lore Perls remarked: "His social place is unequivocally a field concept" (in Sreckovic, 1999, p. 54; see also Bernfeld, 2020, p. 882).

Psychoanalyst Ernst Federn, son of Viennese psychoanalyst Paul Federn, wrote the following to me in a letter addressing the development of Gestalt therapy out of psychoanalysis: "Perls and Goodman write, 'The definition of an animal involves its environment.' Much earlier, Bernfeld stated that the 'social place' is part of the individual. The difference lies only in words."[4]

The approaches that the two Perlses had brought with them, and then combined with Goodman's position, flowed into an integrative concept when Gestalt therapy was developed in New York. In their concept of "creative adjustment" based on "organismic self-regulation," life is understood as growth that is realized in a specific environmental field and encompasses mutual adaptation *as well as conflict and de-structuring aggression*. Herein lies the difference with the conservative and "conflict-free" view and practice of adaptation in American ego psychology at that time.

14.3.2.6 Flight and problems with the IPA

After Hitler's rise to power, Fritz and Lore Perls fled to Amsterdam. Fritz Perls was supervised by Karl Landauer (who had also fled) and became a member of a new, second Dutch analytical association, founded by German emigrants and recognized by the International Psychoanalytical Association (IPA). At the end of 1933, with the help of Ernst Jones, the two Perlses emigrated again, this time to Johannesburg, South Africa, where they remained until the end of the war. In 1936, Perls gave a lecture on "Oral Resistance" at the International Congress in Marienbad. Although the lecture was not well received and the rejection of his requests to see Freud in Vienna was a great blow to him, Perls nevertheless became a full member of the IPA. Perls was regarded as a disciple of Reich, and therefore a representative of a politically-involved current of psychoanalysis. After Reich was silently struck off the IPA membership list for political reasons in 1933, this, in addition to his "difficult" character, was a source of trouble for Perls, as we can see from the correspondence between the members of the IPA's Central Executive Committee. On May 29th, 1933, Max Eitingon wrote to Johan van Ophuijsen:

> Perls was in Berlin, Frankfurt and Vienna. Wherever he was he gave the impression of being a problematic, impulsive person. Quite intelligent, probably also gifted for therapy, but also endangered by his enormous impulsivity. *He doesn't seem to have been tamed or disciplined* by any of the people he was in analysis with and he saw several of them.
>
> (in Bocian, 2019, p. 126, my italics)

By 1937, it had become clear that Perls would not be granted teaching status and the training institute that the two Perlses had founded in 1934 was not recognized. He retired from organized psychoanalysis and began working with his wife on his first book.

14.4 Perls at The White Institute 1947: Field and challenging directness

In 1946, Fritz Perls arrived in New York and found a completely changed situation compared to prewar Europe. After the exodus of psychoanalysts from Germany and Austria, analytical ego psychology developed increasingly after 1945 into a medically-oriented, rigid, and abstinent treatment procedure. Makari writes that the Viennese and Berlin "'I' psychology, with its connection to lived experience, mutated into an abstract, impersonal ego psychology" (Makari, 2008, p. 483). With the help of numerous Berlin and Viennese immigrants, a "new Freudian orthodoxy" (p. 483) developed that hardly resembled "the pluralistic field of the inter-war years" (p. 484). It can be said that so-called "classical analysis" is actually a post-Second World War invention (see Wachtel, 2008, p. 5). The hegemony of this version of ego psychology, which increasingly spread internationally, led "psychoanalysis" to be defined by high-frequency hours, the absence of the analyst as a subject, and interpretation as the only real "classical" intervention.

In contrast, after they emigrated, Perls and Fromm preserved and further developed the more radical and avant-garde political and clinical developments that had begun especially in Berlin and Frankfurt, in their respective ways. It is not surprising that Perls briefly toyed with the idea of becoming a member of the White Institute. He already knew Fromm and Fromm-Reichmann. As late as 1968, Perls still remembered Fromm-Reichman as "an excellent therapist who came from the same Frankfurt School as me" (Perls, 1980, p. 172), and Lore Perls called her "my first teacher" (Perls, 1980, p. 141). Moreover, he saw enormous parallels with his own ideas, referring to the two "defining characteristics" (Stern, 2017, p. 19) of interpersonal psychoanalysis—Sullivan's Interpersonal Field Theory (which had been influenced by Lewin's work)[5] and Erich Fromm's existential humanistic approach, with its often-extreme emphasis on authenticity and a challenging directness of the therapist (see Stern, 2017, pp. 14ff.)

Lore Perls remembers the first contact with the White Institute and Clara Thompson in particular:

> He [Fritz] went to New York and he saw Erich Fromm. And Fromm said: "I guarantee within three months you have a practice in New York." So he came to New York. Within three weeks he had a practice. He took over a practice from Dr. Saperstein. He took on four or five patients from him, and then he made friends with *Clara Thompson* and she sent a lot. They wanted him actually as a training analyst in the White Institute at the time, but they had wanted him to take his medical degree here again, and that would have meant going to school. At that point, Fritz was already in his fifties and he said: "If I go to school, then I go as a teacher and not as a student." But still they sent patients, and mostly they sent people they had given up on, people who wanted to become members, but they didn't feel they had gotten through with their analysis.
>
> (In Amendt Lyon, 2016, p. 177)

The good professional, and apparently personal, relationship between Fritz Perls and Clara Thompson can possibly also be related to Thompson's interest in Reich's character analysis, with its active defense analysis, focus on nonverbal communication or behavior, and strong attention to negative transference. Around 1934, she was running a "Reich Study group" in which Reich's character analysis was translated and read (see Meigs, 2017; Levenson, 2018).[6] In Perls she met someone who had already taken Reich's seminar in Vienna in 1927 and who had been in training analysis with Reich from around 1930 until both emigrated in 1933, and who also had belonged to Reich's circle and taken part in his political and anti-fascist activities. Perls was a trained character analyst in theory and practice (see Bocian, 2010, pp. 208ff.).

In early April 1947, Perls held a conference at the Institute "before a dozen people, the inner circle of the group" (Perls in Sreckovic, 1999, p. 113). We can hear his hope for a new belonging in this touching passage:

> Then a miracle happened to me. A few months ago I met some members of your group, and I was deeply moved as I had been seldom in my life. After all, there were people on this globe who saw the world as I saw it, who spoke a language similar to mine. It was like a dream, nearly too good to be true. I felt like a sailor who knew he was steering the right course, but became weary that he would never see land again, and suddenly, unexpectedly, there it was.
>
> (Perls, 2012, p. 39)

In his lecture, he talked about concepts that would remain central to him throughout his life. For example, he stressed how some patients "require the prolonged spadework of intense character analysis before one can attempt the phenomenological analysis" (Perls, 2012, p. 33). The "basic rule" of Perls's *phenomenological analysis* was "the concept of the now" (p. 28). Perls would ask "the patient to start every sentence with the word 'now' or even with the words 'here and now'" (p. 26). Ultimately, it is about broadening the patient's "horizons of awareness" (Atwood & Stolorow, 2014),[7] of what he or she feels, fantasizes, and does in the interpersonal contact in and beyond the analytical situation. Or, "the neurotic (and I shall confine myself to him) is a split and dissociated personality and the cure has to be effected by a reintegration of the personality and its intrapersonal relations" (Perls, 2012, p. 18). And of course there is the view, of particular importance here, that the safeguard against the problems that could be created by a one-sided approach or eclecticism "is the concept and experience of the human personality as being an indivisible whole and as always embedded in and related to an environmental, personal, and social field" (p. 38).

His lecture was apparently not given the importance he had expected or hoped for (see Sreckovic, 1999, p. 115). Moreover, he was not willing to adapt and meet the requirements for his license to practice in the U.S.A. In the end, Fritz and Lore decided to take a path independent of all analytic schools; there was also no longer any contact with Reich, so that we were once again on our own. Then, when I lived in New York for a while, we worked with Paul Goodman on our own approach.

(Perls, L., 2016, p. 190)

On March 3rd, 1947, still with hope, Fritz wrote to Lore: "He [Fromm] is very interested in our special approach. I have the feeling that one day he and we will form the newest group" (in Sreckovic, 1999, p. 114). What makes Perls's and Fromm's approaches similar (which I cannot go into here due to a lack of space) is their common psychoanalytic and political socialization in Frankfurt and Berlin, as well as their experience as *émigré* German Jews. Both were interested, for example, in focusing on emotional experiencing in the here-and-now, attending to body language and expanding awareness, integrating Buddhist and Taoist approaches, and there was a focus on the personal and social fields and the influence of Martin Buber.

Perls and Fromm believed that if therapists attend too much to the "regressive" or "infantile" aspects of their patients, they "might communicate to them that they were not responsible for difficult life choices and possibly interfere with their progressive goals of separation and autonomy" (Hirsch, 2015, p. 144). In contrast to the British "Middle Group" (especially Balint and Winnicott), the early interpersonal approach—and I include Perls here—was adult-centric and "firmly prods patients toward the future" (Hirsch, 2015, p. 131). Hirsch gives a concise summary of a problem inherent in the practice of active analysis, which ranged from Reich's Berlin techniques of character analysis to the approach of the first Interpersonal Analysts, to Perls's personal style of Gestalt therapy, taking Fromm as an example: "Analysts of Fromm's heritage could be [...] too certain about observation, excessively present and confrontational" (Hirsch, 2015, p. 144). The confronting way in which Perls would sometimes work in his demonstration sessions is directly descended from Ferenczi's "active technique" and "*Reiztherapie*" (stimulation therapy). Similar approaches can be found in the work of Reich, Gerö, Horney, and Fromm. For instance, Fromm would still respond forcefully, in 1974, if a patient turned "free association [...] into free chatter" (Fromm, 1994, p. 117); he held that then it is in my opinion the task of the analyst to cut him off and to say, 'Now, all you're telling me is only to fill out the time, and it has no purpose; I'm too bored, I'm not going to listen to this'.

(Fromm, 1994, p. 117)

If I had not indicated here that it was Erich Fromm ("the apostle of love") who said that, it could also be an example of the often-criticized way in which Perls ("the dirty old man") practiced and demonstrated Gestalt therapy. What we have here is simply the character-analytic style practiced sometimes too confrontationally, as Perls had become familiar with it in Berlin, and as developed as an active response to the largely useless passive years they had spent lying on the couch.

Donnel B. Stern writes that the set of Fromm's

existential-humanistic clinical values [...] led a broader group of interpersonalists to work in the here-and-now, to emphasize the patient's agency, and to acknowledge their own personal and unconscious involvement in the clinical process, long before that emphasis was as widely recognized as it is today.

(Stern, D.B., 2017, pp. 19ff.)

It is interesting that in the lecture that he gave at the White Institute in 1947, Perls presented a clinical example of his own personal involvement, which anticipated the more relational and dialogical form of Gestalt therapy that was developed later on:

As I am not in the habit of blaming a patient and making her responsible for her resistance, I had to look for my own deficiency, and I found the following fact: I was personally involved in her case. She had to be a feather in my cap.

(Perls, 2012, p. 30)

In Gestalt therapy, the late 1980s saw the emergence of an explicit dialogical approach, strongly influenced by the revaluation of Buber (reinforced by the influences of the intersubjective theory of Orange et al. (1997)), which largely corrected the problematic aspects of the confrontational approach (see Yontef, 1993; Jacobs & Hycner, 2009; Staemmler, 2011). Here it was also possible to draw on the more cautious and supportive style of Lore Perls, who was directly influenced by Buber. Of course, we should see the confrontation and challenging directness of Perls and the more patient and supportive work of Lore Perls as dialectical complements. This is in the integrative spirit of the Gestalt therapeutic model.

What was introduced in 1951 as Gestalt therapy was an attempt at, and a further step in, the development of an integrative approach in theory and practice which sees the interconnectedness between inside and outside and includes both the body and the environment. It was about "a unitary method" that included all levels as far as possible, to concentrate on "orientation in the environment (analysis of the present situation)" (Perls et al., 1951/1996, p. 99), on "the world of 'objects'—interpersonal relations, fantasy,[8] memory, etc. and on releasing bodily mobility and appetite, and also on the structure of the third thing, the emotion of the self" (p. 409). "Only if the outer and the inner can be harmonized and integrated can the patient ever be discharged as 'cured'" (p. 99). This corresponds with the later attempt at integration by Greenberg & Mitchell (1983), and with Lewis Aron's emphasis that the term "relational" takes into account the dialectical entanglement between real interpersonal relations and their intrapsychic representations or personifications (Aron, 2009, p. 17). The three schools presented in this book are currently trying, based on the existing potential within their respective approaches, to broaden the perspective once again and to explore the field aspect of human experience and behavior more deeply, to make it usable in clinical practice.

14.4.1 Perls, object relations and the "external stage"

Seemingly different from *early* interpersonal psychoanalysis (see Greenberg & Mitchell, 1983, p. 104), right from the start, Perls integrated insights about internalized self–other (object) relations into his thinking and working. Karl Abraham's introduction of an oral sadistic phase with the assumed desire for annihilation in the child and an aggressive and *destructive* intention to bite and hurt (see May, 2018, pp. 117ff.), later taken up and continued by Melanie Klein, was criticized by Perls. Influenced by Lore Perls's experience with her first child (a private "infant research"), he presented an alternative that was rich in consequences (Perls, 1942/1992a, pp. 153ff.). For Perls, it is about the *de-structuring aggression* that is now possible through the teeth, which serves one's own growth. Both physical and "mental food" (Perls, 1942/1992a, pp. 144ff.) can and must be "chewed through" and assimilated independently, made into something truly one's own and not "swallowed" as an introject coming from an external authority. Perls also refers here to psychoanalytic theory and Nazi propaganda (Perls, 1942/1992a). His discussion of Abraham's contribution is based on Freud's paper "Mourning and Melancholia" (1915/1959b) (the beginning of object relational thinking), and his distinction between introjection and assimilation has strong parallels with Fairbairn's thought and coincides almost word for word with Guntrip's views more than twenty years later (Perls, 1942/1992a, pp. 153ff.; Ludwig-Körner, 1992, p. 248; Eagle, 1984, pp. 75ff.; Eagle, 2011, p. 152). Like Fairbairn, Perls saw introjects as internalized "rejecting objects" or "internal saboteurs," and both sometimes used metaphorical terms like demon or *dybbuk*:

> If you are poisonous, that means that [...] you have got a dybbuk, a demon, in you, somebody who poisons you, whom you have swallowed whole. The Freudian idea that we introject the person we love is wrong. You always introject people who are *in control*.
>
> (Perls, 1992b, pp. 163–164)

I do not have the space here to go into this topic in more detail.[9]

When Gestalt therapy became an independent approach, Fritz Perls, the most experienced clinical practitioner of the founding trio, developed his well-known psycho-dramatic and dialogical "two-chair" or "shuttle" technique (Perls, 2019, p. 23), with which the splits and "dichotomies of a personality can be integrated" (p. 23). It must be said that for Perls, "integration" is a process without an end and a unified self is an illusion.[10]

The idea is that the inner representation of the interaction with a parent that had turned into an introject, a negative self state, an "internal I-position" (Staemmler, 2018) can be externalized, transposed from the inner relational world to the therapy room, whereby "the parent" becomes a third person who is virtually present and with whom a dialogue begins, while the protecting therapeutic relationship remains intact. Perls built on the early experiments of Breuer and Freud (1895/1957) in a similar style to the entire tradition of active psychoanalysis. He would dramatize psychic conflicts on an "external stage" and would have the patient emotionally re-live and "act through" (Perls & Clements, 1968) unfinished situations. In this way, a scenic unity of content, action, affect, and language was achieved, as was also characteristic of Freud and Breuer's cathartic method (see Lorenzer, 1993, pp. 168ff.), and as was picked up again later by Ferenczi in his "neocatharsis" and by Wilhelm Reich.

Psychoanalysts such as Tilmann Moser, who have experienced Gestalt therapy themselves, acknowledge the value of this procedure, especially in work with intrapsychic splits. A psychoanalytic setting that focuses only on generating a transference:

> makes it difficult to reintegrate the denied parts that were split off under great danger; the exiled parts of the self [...] show themselves only very shyly, because the ego is afraid of being excommunicated, depreciated, and mutilated once again. This is without any doubt a simplified way of putting it. In any case, only when I experienced and reflected on Gestalt therapy did it occur to me for the first time that there are therapeutic approaches that offer different possibilities of making diagnostically visible and enacting divergent parts of the self. Under the threat of an accumulating negative transference, there [in Gestalt therapy] the therapist does not disappear in the swirl of negative experience, but stays available as an accessible auxiliary ego which can also establish contact with the split-off parts.
>
> (Moser, 1990, p. 11, my translation)

14.4.2 The field approach and the old interpretative power

Finally, there is a critical aspect I would like to address. An aspect that concerns the therapist's power to define what is happening. In the new analytic and Gestalt approaches, it sometimes seems that the therapist is the "expert" who "feels" or "dreams" what is going on in the field, in the "between," and ultimately in the other. As humans, we have a capacity for resonance, and Gestalt therapists and psychoanalysts have certainly refined this capacity through their training. Nevertheless, I find it is a kind of power if the therapist, without clarifying this dialogically with the patient, simply assumes that what he or she is feeling at the moment is what is happening.

Morris Eagle has critically discussed Heinrich Racker's attitude towards countertransference. For Racker, "thoughts and feelings which emerge in [the analyst] will be, precisely, those which did not emerge in the patient" (Racker, quoted in Eagle, 2018, p. 92). We have to be careful that we do not end up adopting the same attitude, just describing it in different words. Some examples from the three schools presented here, which struck me when I read them, include: therapists can seem to "enter" the inner world of the patient and claim to "know" what the patient feels, thinking they are a "part" of the same world as the patient; some seem to decide, unilaterally on their own, the meaning of what the patient answers; and dissociated states of the patient's self can be "known" by therapists through their enactment in the relationship. If I really assume that what is going on in me is also going on in the patient, then we have the same old "the therapist knows what is really going on" attitude, even if it sounds more profound, poetic, or mystic today and less technical than in the past.

Of course, through resonance or *reverie* we can perceive and grasp something that is more than "me." Many of us are good at it too. Nevertheless, it is simply a hypothesis that we can work with, a proposal that is there to be rejected by the patient. What remains is the fundamental Kantian insight, confirmed by Gestalt psychologists among others, that the senses are not neutral receptors. Rather, they are active filters, as are our minds, through which we experience the world and read, see, and evaluate ourselves and others. Our perceptions are interpretations.

I see another critical point that Eagle also makes in his discussion of Mitchell's statement that "the basic unit of study is not the individual as a separate entity (…) but an interactional field" (in Eagle, 2011, pp. 134ff.). Bohleber (2010) sees here the problem that in some intersubjective theories, the subject seems to dissolve in the field: "To take this to an extreme, the subject is reduced to the contingent effect of contexts. […] The self disappears in its independent function as author and active agent" (Bohleber, 2010, p. 9). It is about the subject, the ego or I, which "is dependent on unconscious forces but has nevertheless acquired a certain degree of autonomy" (p. 9). A person is both a "field phenomenon" and an "autonomous subject," living in his "private world" (Perls, 2019, p. 47) with "ego boundaries" that define what is me and what is not me, as an author with personal responsibility. Beyond that, it seems important to me not to promote, with our language, a kind of estrangement or reification of human communication and human pain. Human pain is not the pain of some field, it is individual, "of" a person, and I experience it as my pain.

Günther Bittner (1998), a psychoanalyst from the above-mentioned and largely forgotten southwest German tradition, which is strongly influenced by Buber, puts it well when he writes: "The talk of the 'third' may sound [...] seductive: I just have to be careful that above this third I do not lose the 'first': myself, the analyst subject situated and experiencing the situation with the analysand" (Bittner, 1998, p. 286, my translation). I appreciate that my relational and field-oriented colleagues try not to "lose" exactly this, but Bittner finds the right words for the crux of the matter. He pleads for considering "the analyst's own" as the "*foundation of a bridge of understanding*" (p. 60). Referring to projective identification he writes: "There is no valid criterion for distinguishing whether a mood [...] 'comes from me' or is 'put into me' by the patient" (p. 61)—or, I would add, whether it comes from or is in the "field" or in "the between" (see also Eagle, 2011, pp. 219ff.). To nevertheless assume this and simply assert it on the basis of one's own feeling or mental production is a powerful interpretation that our patients will not always resist, and for me it is something different from the radically dialogical attitude that includes the patient as an "active experimental partner" (Perls et al., 1951/1996, p. 248) that has become central to Gestalt therapy.

Buber's "meeting," which for Lore Perls (1989, p. 179) is synonymous with contact, is a central concept of Gestalt therapy. "Contact is the recognition of 'otherness', the awareness of difference, the boundary experience of 'I and the other'" (Perls, L., 1992, p. 94), "where we touch and at the same time experience separateness" (p. 152). Gestalt therapy is an integrative approach and as such we see the dialectic between the intra-personal and the inter-personal and of course it is useful and important when field-oriented therapists and analysts try to describe further levels of perception and experience and make them clinically practicable. It is about expansion, not replacement. Accordingly, Francesetti, Gecele, and Roubal write that they see "the three paradigms of change (mono-personal, bi-personal, field-theory based) [...] as equally important and in figure in different moments of the therapeutic process" (Francesetti et al., 2022, p. 54).[11]

Both Perlses were representatives of an early field approach and at the same time emphasized the importance of one's own delimited individuality and the personal "ego boundary" (Federn, 1952; Perls, 1942/1992a). This is a theme that brings us into contact with history and the past as part of the field.

14.4.3 Autonomy instead of Auschwitz: The importance of individualism

Perls clearly perceived the reality of the situation in 1933 and fled the murderous field in time. Like many of his fellow émigrés, Perls has left us a legacy that is part of our current field. Against the backdrop of two world wars and his experience of National Socialism and the German tradition of obedience, Fritz Perls's (and maybe Fromm's)[12] sometimes unbalanced inclination toward individuality and autonomy and his fundamentally anti-confluent posture cannot simply be dismissed as a personal problem.

Gestalt therapy has to do with the experience of totalitarianism and the experience with the "great we." Nazi ideology was an ideology of anti-individualism that demanded confluence, submission, and abandonment of the ego boundary. In response, a small group of outsiders, intellectuals, and artists of the Weimar Republic became advocates of the individual and demanded self-responsibility. Gestalt therapy carries within itself experiences that contain a utopia of wholeness as well as traumatic experiences in dealing with uprooting, flight, and threats to identity and life (see Bocian, 2010, pp. 249ff.). As a leftist German Jew, Perls knew the importance of focusing attentively on the boundary between the individual and the environment. He realized that for a person such as himself, merging with a greater whole was not an option, and that a lack of alertness, a failure to abandon "the whole" in a timely fashion, was potentially life-threatening. He knew that confluence can kill and that projections can cost lives. He knew that the ability to "individualize" oneself, to trust in one's own strength and self-support, can save one's life.

There is a historical lesson to be learned from the survival experiences of the "Expressionist generation" to which Fritz and Lore Perls belonged. With reference to Theodor Adorno, I have summarized this stance as "Autonomy instead of Auschwitz" (see Bocian, 2010, pp. 255ff.). I believe that as a therapist, Perls wanted to pass on something precious, a kind of summary of his life experience, of a "survival" experience in the true sense of the word. "Many could have been saved if they would have mobilized their own resources instead of waiting for someone to rescue them" (Perls, 1977, p. 127). Although we fully realize that Gestalt therapy was conceived as a relational and field approach from the outset, keeping these experiences alive is part of our European legacy.

Andrea Castiello d'Antonio writes:

> So when we look at the years of analytic experience that Perls gained as a patient-candidate, we can see that 'the system' of institutionalized psychoanalysis was not able to destroy his creativity (despite its having implemented various of the famous 'thirty methods to destroy the creativity of candidates in psychoanalysis' described by Otto Kernberg). But 'the system' was nevertheless able to exclude an original mind and a free spirit permanently from psychoanalysis.
> (Castiello d'Antonio, 2012, p. 285, my translation)

For some years now, there have been various contacts and dialogues, made possible, perhaps, because we all come from the psychoanalytic "stream"—a stream which has become again very broad and plural. I hope that my contribution can help us all understand this common past and ground and that it may be possible to really meet and perhaps learn from each other, without losing our contours and our specific Gestalt.

Notes

1 In the Berlin years, besides Reich, these analysts were above all Otto Fenichel and George Gerö, who, like Perls, was Reich's student, and later, as a training analyst at the New York IPA Institute, still arranged the analytic setting so that he could see the patient (see Gerö, 1994, p. 228).
2 Which included, among others, Wilhelm Reich, Otto Fenichel, Erich Fromm, Siegfried Bernfeld, Edith Jacobson, Ernst Simmel, and Georg Gerö, as well as Karen Horney, with her early feminist critique of patriarchal culture.
3 Goodman included "'Civilized' Sexual Morality and Modern Nervousness" in a collection of works by Freud, *Freud: On War, Sex, and Neurosis*, published in 1947 by Sander Katz. Paul Goodman, who was already in touch with Perls at that time, wrote a preface for the book and compiled a glossary of psychoanalytic terms (see Stoehr, 1994, pp. 60ff.).
4 Ernst Federn in a letter to the author dated March 13th, 1997.

5 Some passages of *Gestalt Therapy* (1951) that refer to interactions within the mother–infant field (Perls et al., 1951/1996, p. 270) and anticipate the findings of modern infant research are almost identical to what Sullivan, referring also to Lewin, thought and wrote about the "need for contact" (Sullivan, 1953, p. 40) and the dynamic "organism/environment complex" (Perls et al., 1951/1996, p. 78).

6 Edgar Levenson, an important personality in the history of the White Institute, remembers:

> That was about the time that Wilhelm Reich's book *Character Analysis* (1933) was popular and everybody was very stimulated because it was the first move away from Freudian dynamics to something that had to do with character structure. Fromm was very much interested in character structure too (Levenson, 2018, p. 307).

7 Eagle writes: "Similar to Atwood and Stolorow in the context of Gestalt Therapy, a primary marker for psychopathology is restriction of experience and a primary goal of treatment is increasing the range and depth of experience, particularly emotional experience" (Eagle, 2018, p. 48).

8 Goodman was, like Otto Fenichel, Marcuse and Adorno, always very critical of Fromm's and Horney's Freud revisions, and we hear his voice in *Gestalt Therapy* (1951): "It is characteristic for the interpersonal theorists that they have little to say of organic functioning, sexuality and obscure fantasy" (Perls et al., 1951/1996, p. 160).

9 Perls' important contribution to this discussion can only be appreciated with an understanding of the psychoanalytic context of the time. This is made all the more difficult by the fact that Perls hardly ever quotes and only occasionally mentions other authors and apparently assumes that his readership has such knowledge. The parallels with Fairbairn and his student Guntrip are interesting and manifold. To name just one more, Perls, like Fairbairn, sees the parts and figures of a dream as projected parts of the dreamer (Delisle, 2013, pp. 48ff.).

10 It is about getting to know and dealing with different representations of ourselves. His experience of the impossibility of having a single identity as a German Jew and the need for critical outsiders to deal with their multiple identities plays a role here (see Bocian, 2010, p. 262).

11 Bowman and Bowman (2022), for example, give a nice clinical example of how the "classical," more monopersonal style and the contemporary, more relational style intertwine, which corresponds to the integrative and not one-sided approach of Gestalt therapy from the very beginning.

12 In Fromm's *Escape from Freedom* (1941), as in Perls, we find an emphasis on individualism, anti-conformism and spontaneity, in the face of Nazi efforts to eradicate individuality and demand "surrender to authority" (see Kuriloff, 2014, p. 19) and self-sacrifice for the whole.

References

Altmeyer, M., & Thomä, H. (Eds.). (2006). *Die vernetzte Seele. Die intersubjektive Wende in der Psychoanalyse*. Klett-Cotta.

Amendt Lyon, N. (Ed.). (2016). *Timeless experience: Laura Perls's unpublished notebooks and literary texts 1946–1985*. Cambridge Scholars Publishing.

Aron, L. (2009). *A meeting of minds. Mutuality in psychoanalysis*. Routledge.

Atwood, G. E., & Stolorow, R. D. (2014). *Structures of subjectivity. Explorations in psychoanalytic phenomenology and contextualism*. Routledge.

Bernfeld, S. (1934). Die Gestalttheorie. *Imago*, *20*, 32–77.

Bernfeld, S. (2020). *Psychoanalyse—Psychologie—Sozialpsychologie*. Werke, Band 10. Psychosozial Verlag.

Bittner, G. (1998). *Metaphern des Unbewussten. Eine kritische Einführung in die Psychoanalayse*. Kohlhammer.

Bocian, B. (2009). From free association to concentration: About alienation, Ferenczi's "forced fantasies," and "the Third" in Gestalt therapy. *Studies in Gestalt Therapy: Dialogical Bridges*, *2*, 37–58.

Bocian, B. (2010). *Fritz Perls in Berlin 1893–1933: Expressionism, psychoanalysis, Judaism*. EHP–Edition Humanistische Psychologie.

Bocian, B. (2013). Von der Revision der Freud'schen Theorie und Methode zum Entwurf der Gestalttherapie. Grundlegendes zu einem Figur-Hintergrund-Verhältnis. In B. Bocian, & F.-M. Staemmler (Eds.), *Kontakt als erste Wirklichkeit. Zum Verhältnis vo Gestalttherapie und Psychoanalyse*. EHP–Edition Humanistische Psychologie (pp. 35–126).

Bocian, B. (2015). Karl Landauer (1887–1945): A Frankfurt psychoanalyst almost forgotten by psychoanalysis and Gestalt therapy. *Psicoterapia e Scienze Umane*, *XLLX*(1), 37–58.

Bocian, B. (2019). From character analysis to interpersonal psychoanalysis to Gestalt therapy. A historical contextualization of various remarks in Perls's book *Skeleton*. In J.-M. Robine, & C. Bowman (Eds.), *Psychopathology of awareness. An unfinished and unpublished manuscript* (pp. 105–136). L'exprimerie.

Bocian, B., & Staemmler, F.-M. (Eds.) (2013).

Bohleber, W. (2010). *Destructiveness, intersubjectivity, and trauma. The identity crisis of modern psychoanalysis*. Karnac.

Bowman, C., & Bowman, C. A. (2022). A classical beginning and a relational turn. A Gestalt case study. In P. Cole (Ed.), *The relational heart of Gestalt therapy. Contemporary perspectives* (pp. 113–125). Routledge.

Breuer, J., & Freud, S. (1957). *Studies on hysteria*. Basic Books. (Original work published 1895).

Brunner, M. et al. (2013). Critical psychoanalytic social psychology in the German speaking countries. *Annual Review of Critical Psychology*, *10*, 419–468.

Buchholz, M. (2012). Die horizontale Dimension des Unbewussten. *Gruppenpsychotherapie und Gruppendynamik*, *48*, 6–25.

Castiello d'Antonio, A. (2012). Review of Bernd Bocian 'Fritz Perls in Berlin'. *Psicoterapia e Scienze Umane*, *XLVI*(2), 283–285.

Cremerius, J. (1992). Die Psychoanalyse gehört niemandem.—Als Wissenschaft vom Menschen darf sie nicht monopolisiert werden. In J. Wiesse (Ed.), *Chaos und Regel—Die Psychoanalyse in ihren Institutionen* (pp. 34–50). Vandenhoeck & Ruprecht.

Delisle, G. (2013). *Object relations in Gestalt therapy*. Karnac.

Eagle, M. (1984). *Recent developments in psychoanalysis. A critical evaluation*. McGraw-Hill.

Eagle, M. (2011). *From classical to contemporary psychoanalysis. A critique and integration*. Routledge.

Eagle, M. (2018). *Core concepts in classical psychoanalysis. Clinical, research evidence, and conceptual critique*. Routledge.

Federn, P. (1952). *Ego-psychology and the psychoses*. Basic Books.

Fenichel, O. (1987). Organ libidinization accompanying the defense against drives. In *The collected papers of Otto Fenichel* (First series, Vol. 1 (H. Fenichel, & D. Rapaport Eds.), pp. 128–147). W. W. Norton & Company. (Original work published 1928).

Fenichel, O. (1998). *119 Rundbriefe. Vol. 1 Europa 1934–1936* (J. Reichmayer, & E. Mühlleitner Eds.). Stroemfeld Verlag.

Ferenczi, S. (1930). The principle of relaxation and neocatharsis. *The International Journal of Psychoanalysis*, *11*, 428–443.

Ferenczi, S. (1994). On forced phantasies: Activity in the association-technique. In *Further contributions to the theory and technique of psycho-analysis* (compiled by J. Rickman, pp. 68–77). Karnac. (Original work published 1923).

Ferenczi, S., & Rank, O. (1986). *The development of psycho-analysis*. International Universities Press. (Original work published 1924).

Foulkes, S. H. (2019). *Group analytic psychotherapy*. Routledge.

Francesetti, G., Gecele, M., & Roubal, J. (2022). Being present to absence. Field theory in psychopathology and clinical practice. In P. Cole (Ed.). *The relational heart of Gestalt therapy. Contemporary perspectives*. Routledge.

Freud, S. (1959a). "Civilized" Sexual Morality and Modern Nervous Illness. In J. Strachey (Ed.), *The standard edition of the complete psychological works of Sigmund Freud. Vol. IX: Jensen's Gravida and other works (1906–1908)* (pp. 177–204). Hogarth Press. (Original work published 1908).

Freud, S. (1959b). Mourning and melancholia. In J. Strachey (Ed.), *The standard edition of the complete psychological works of Sigmund Freud. Vol. XIV (1914–1916): On the history of the psycho-analytic movement, papers on metapsychology, and other works* (pp. 237–258). Hogarth Press. (Original work published 1915).

Fromm, E. (1941). *Escape from freedom*. Holt, Rinehart, and Winston.

Fromm, E. (1994). *The art of listening*. Continuum.

Fuchs, T. (2012). Body memory and the unconscious. In D. Lohmar, & J. Brudzinska (Eds.), *Founding psychoanalysis phenomenologically. Phenomenological theory of subjectivity and the psychoanalytic experience* (pp. 69–82). Springer.

Gerö, G. (1994). The handwriting on the wall. In L. M. Herrmanns (Ed.). *Psychoanalyse in Selbstdarstellungen* (pp. 199–230). Edition discord.

Goodman, P. (1977). The political meaning of some recent revisions of Freud. In T. Stoehr (Ed.), *Nature heals. Psychological essays of Paul Goodman*. Free Life. (Original work published 1945).

Greenberg, J. R., & Mitchell, S. A. (1983). *Object relations in psychoanalytic theory*. Harvard University Press

Gregory, S. (2001). Elsa Gindler: Lost Gestalt ancestor. *British Gestalt Journal*, *10*(2), 114–117.

Harrington, A. (1996). *Reenchanted science: Holism in German culture from Wilhelm II to Hitler*. Princeton University Press.

Hirsch, I. (2015). *The interpersonal tradition. The origins of psychoanalytic subjectivity*. Routledge.

Hochheimer, W. (1986). *Tiefenpsychologie und Kritische Anthropologie*. Stroemfeld.

Jacobs, L., & Hycner, R. (Eds.). (2009). *Relational approaches in Gestalt therapy*. Routledge.

Kuriloff, E. A. (2014). *Contemporary psychoanalysis and the legacy of the Third Reich. History, memory, tradition*. Routledge.

Landauer, K. (1939). Some remarks on the formation of the anal-erotic character. *International Journal of Psychoanalysis*, *20*(3–4), 418–425.

Landauer, K. (1991). *Theorie der Affekte und andere Schriften zur Ich-Organisation*. Fischer.

Levenson, E. A. (2018). *Interpersonal psychoanalysis and the enigma of consciousness*. Routledge.

Lohmar, D., & Brudzinska, J. (Eds.). (2012). *Founding psychoanalysis phenomenologically: Phenomenological theory of subjectivity and the psychoanalytic experience*. Springer.

Lorenzer, A. (1993). *Intimität und soziales Leid. Archäologie der Psychoanalyse*. Fischer.

Ludwig-Körner, C. (1992). *Der Selbstbegriff in Psychologie und Psychotherapie*. DUV.

Makari, G. (2008). *Revolution in mind. The creation of psychoanalysis*. Harper Collins.

May, U. (2018). *Freud at work. On the history of psychoanalytic theory and practice*. Routledge.

Meigs, K. (2017). The failure of Clara Thompson's Ferenczian (proxy) analysis of Harry Stuck Sullivan. *The American Journal of Psychoanalysis*, *77*(3), 313–331.

Mertens, W. (1990). *Einführung in die psychoanalytische Therapie*. Vol. 1. Kohlhammer.

Migone P. (2013). Preface. In M. Spagnuolo Lobb (Ed.), *The now-for-next in psychotherapy: Gestalt therapy recounted in post-modern society*. Istituto di Gestalt HCC Italy.

Moser, T. (1987). *Der Psychoanalytiker als sprechende Attrappe. Eine Streitschrift*. Suhrkamp.

Moser, T. (1990). *Das zerstrittene Selbst*. Suhrkamp.

Nitzschke, B. (2003). Psychoanalysis and National Socialism. Banned or brought into conformity? Break or continuity? *International Forum of Psychoanalysis*, *12*, 98–108.

Orange, D. M., Atwood, G. E., & Stolorow, R. D. (Eds.). (1997). *Working intersubjectively: Contextualism in psychoanalytic practice*. Analtyic Press.

Perls, F. (1970). Four Lectures. In J. Fagan, & I. L. Shepherd (Eds.), *Gestalt therapy now: Theory, techniques, applications* (pp. 14–38). Science and Behavior Books.

Perls, F. (1977). *In and out the garbage pail*. Real People Press.

Perls, F. (1980). *Gestalt-Wachstum-integration. Aufsätze, Vorträge, Therapiesitzungen* (H. Petzold, Ed.). Junfermann Verlag.

Perls, F. (1992a). *Ego, hunger, and aggression. A revision of Freud's theory and method*. The Gestalt Journal Press. (Original work published 1942).

Perls, F. (1992b). *Gestalt therapy verbatim*. The Gestalt Journal Press.

Perls, F. (2012). *From planned psychotherapy to Gestalt therapy. Essays and lectures 1945–1965*. The Gestalt Journal Press.

Perls, F. (2019). *Psychopathology of awareness* (J.-M. Robine, & C. Bowman, Eds.). L'exprimerie.

Perls, F., & Clements, C. (1968). Acting out vs. acting through. *Voices*, *4*(4), 66–73.

Perls, F., Hefferline, R., & Goodman, P. (1996). *Gestalt therapy. Excitement and growth in the human personality*. Souvenir Press. (Original work published 1951).

Perls, L. (1982). An oral history of Gestalt therapy. A conversation with Lore Perls. *Gestalt Journal*, *I*(2), 7–29.

Perls, L. (1989). Leben an der Grenze – Ein Gespräch mit Milan Sreckovic. In L. Perls (Eds.), *Leben an der Grenze. Essays und Anmerkungen zur Gestalt-Therapie*. EHP.

Perls, L. (1992). *Living at the Boundary*. The Gestalt Journal Press.

Plänkers, T. et al. (Eds.). (1996). *Psychoanalyse in Frankfurt am Main. Zerstörte Anfänge, Wiederannäherung, Entwicklung*. Diskord.

Reich, W. (1942). *The discovery of the orgone. Vol.1: The function of orgasm: Sex-economic problems of biological energy*. Orgone Institute Press.

Reich, W. (1988). *Character analysis* (3rd, enlarged ed.). Orgone Institute Press.

Rothe, H. J. (1987). Zur Erinnerung an Karl Landauer. In *Materialien aus dem Sigmund-Freud-Institut Frankfurt. Number 4*.

Rothe, H. J. (1996). Karl Landauer and the southwest German psychoanalytic study group. *International Forum of Psychoanalysis, 5*(4), 277–288.

Sharaf, M. (1983). *Fury on earth. A biography of Wilhelm Reich*. St. Martins Press/ Marek.

Sletvold, J. (2014). *The embodied analyst. From Freud and Reich to relationality*. Routledge.

Sreckovic, M. (1999). Geschichte und Entwicklung der Gestalttherapie. In R. Fuhr, M. Sreckovic, & M. Gremmler-Fuhr (Eds.). *Handbuch der Gestalttherapie* (pp. 15–180). Hogrefe.

Staemmler, F.-M. (2011). *Empathy in psychotherapy: How therapists and clients understand each other*. Springer.

Staemmler, F.-M. (2018). Gestalt therapy, dialogical self theory, and the "empty chair". In A. Konopka, H. J. M. Hermans, & M. M. Gonçalves (Eds.), *Handbook of dialogical self theory and psychotherapy: Bridging psychotherapeutic and cultural traditions*. Routledge.

Stern, D. B. (2017). Introduction. Interpersonal psychoanalysis: History and current status. In D. B. Stern, & I. Hirsch (Eds.), *The interpersonal perspective in psychoanalysis, 1960s–1990s. Rethinking transference and countertransference* (pp. 1–28). Routledge.

Stern, D. N. (2004). *The present moment in psychotherapy and everyday life*. Norton.

Stoehr, T. (1994). *Here, now, next. Paul Goodman and the origins of Gestalt therapy*. Jossey-Bass.

Sullivan, H. S. (1953). *The interpersonal theory of psychiatry*. W. W. Norton.

Wachtel, P. L. (2008). *Relational theory and practice of psychotherapy*. Guilford.

Yontef, G. (1993). *Awareness, dialogue and process: Essays on Gestalt therapy*. The Gestalt Journal Press.

Zaretsky, E. (2004). *Secrets of the soul. A social and cultural history of psychoanalysis*. A. Knopf.

Index

Pages in *italics* refer to figures and pages followed by "n" refer to notes.

Sullivan, Harry Stack 3, 127, 179–181,
193, 200
supervision 37–40, 74, 82, 96, 99–101,
108, 111, 118, 121–122, 159–160,
190–191
supervisory relationship 41, 101
support 3, 42, 58, 63, 66–67, 71–73, 75,
91, 115–116, 124, 139–140, 148–150,
152, 154, 162, 165, 209; mothering
139–140; parenting 124, 139–140;
self- 150, 209; of the relationship
71–72
supportive: ground 72; relationship 63;
style 204; work 204
sympathy 180
symptom(s) 11, 66, 70–71, 92, 94, 133,
145n2, 148, 150, 152, 192;
psychopathological 94, 148, 150, 152

Tao 102
Taoist approaches 202
Telmon, Laura 167
therapeutic: action 16, 42–43, 46;
alliance 99, 171; approach 95, 149,
152; encounter 56, 88, 162, 165, 170;
field 124–125, 129, 132, 135–136,
141–142, 170, 189–190; intervention
69, 74, 90, 95, 118, 124, 129, 148–149,
153–154, 159, 171, 183, 194, 199;
path 171, 175, 179; process 78, 97, 99,
101–102, 104n17, 160, 165, 192, 208;
relationship 41, 56, 115, 130,
149–152, 205; situation 85, 94, 163,
165, 169, 206; theory 111–112; work
113, 123
Therapeutic Technique, Seminar on 190
therapy 3, 27, 30, 32, 36–38, 42, 62–64,
66, 69, 71–76, 78, 82–83, 92–94, 98,
100–102, 103n14, 104n17, 110, 112,
115–116, 118, 124–126, 130, 141–142,
148–151, 154–157, 160, 172–173, 180,
184, 186, 189, 191, 193–195, 199, 205;
analytic group 188; behavioral 177n1;
body 194; embodied 194; field
perspective in 36–38, 42, 62; here-and-
now of 126; intersubjective field of
130; Kleinian 32; process(es) 27, 82,
100–102, 118, 148, 195; relational turn
in 63; room 116, 122, 125, 160, 191,
205; session 26–27, 94, 115, 151;
setting 73, 76, 92, 118, 150–151, 155;

situation 93, 154, 157; stimulation 191,
202; work 30, 71–72, 193
Thompson, Clara 200
Tillich, Paul 187, 189
Tower of Babel 55
training 23, 96, 99, 102, 104n17, 113, 125,
173, 176–177, 180, 182, 184, 187,
190–191, 194–196, 199–200, 206,
210n1; analyst 182, 196, 200; Bionian
125; Gestalt therapy 104n17;
psychotherapy group 96;
psychoanalysis 194;
psychoanalytic 180
transference 7, 15, 24, 36–37, 56, 59,
140–141, 143, 181–184, 189, 191–196,
199–200, 206–208
transformation 33, 35, 43, 67, 87–88, 90,
92, 95, 98, 102, 143, 153, 156
Transformations (Bion) 34
transformative emergence 26
transgenerational transmission of
trauma 36
transindividual 33
trauma 26, 36–37, 39, 112–113, 126–128,
151, 184; beauty and 151; transference
36; transgenerational transmission
of 113
traumatic: brain injuries 84; experiences
209; memories 39
traumatization 154
treatment 5, 7, 11–12, 48, 113, 132–134,
137, 141, 144, 151, 172–173, 182,
195, 199
truth 17, 19, 36, 43, 47, 49n1, 108, 123;
absolute 47; abstract 47; clinical 123;
emotional 37, 132; expressible 47;
shared 34; truth-dishes 42; truth-
seeking 48
Turandot, 'Princess' 127–128
Turin School of Psychopathology
1, 103n1

unconscious, the 23–27, 34–35, 38, 45,
110, 112, 186, 190, 193, 195
unconscious recognition 38
unformulated experience 169
unison 135, 140–141
unisono 162, 164

Vienna Institute 182, 190
violation 112